Palgrave Studies on Norbert Elias

John Pratt
Institute of Criminology
Victoria University of Wellington
Wellington, New Zealand

Philip Walsh
Department of Sociology
York University
Toronto, ON, Canada

Norman Gabriel
Plymouth Institute of Education
Plymouth University
Plymouth, Devon, UK

Jurandir Malerba
Federal University of Rio Grande do Sul
Porto Alegre, Brazil

Jason Hughes
Department of Sociology
University of Leicester
Leicester, UK

Gina Zabludovsky Kuper
Faculty of Social and Political Sciences
National Autonomous University of Mexico
Mexico City, Mexico

Despite growing, widespread appreciation for Norbert Elias's theoretical approach—often called figurational or processual sociology—there exist only a few, specialized publications on Eliasian social theory, and as of yet, no academic book series.

Palgrave Studies on Norbert Elias will therefore fill a significant gap in the market, appealing to figurationalists across disciplines: Elias's social theory is used not only in Sociology, but also Sports, Psychoanalysis/Psychology and Social Psychology, Education, Criminology, International Relations, History, Humanities (Arts, Music, and Cultural Studies), Political Science, and Public Health. Respecting the multi-disciplinary Eliasian tradition, the series is open to receiving contributions from academics outside of Sociology departments, so long as the research is grounded on Elias's approach. Publications, which shall range from Palgrave Pivots to edited collections, can be expected to explore sports, habits and manners, criminology, violence, group relations, music and musicians, theory and methods, civilizing and decivilizing processes, involvement and detachment in social sciences, formation of the modern state, power relations, and the many dozens of other topics to which Eliasian theory has been applied.

Alon Helled

Israel's National Historiography

Between Generations, Identity and State

Alon Helled
Dipartimento di Culture, Politica e Società
Università degli Studi di Torino
Torino, Italy

ISSN 2662-3102   ISSN 2662-3110   (electronic)
Palgrave Studies on Norbert Elias
ISBN 978-3-031-62794-1   ISBN 978-3-031-62795-8   (eBook)
https://doi.org/10.1007/978-3-031-62795-8

This Palgrave Macmillan imprint is published by the registered company Springer Nature
Switzerland AG.
The registered company address is: Gewerbestrasse 11, 6330 Cham, Switzerland

If disposing of this product, please recycle the paper.

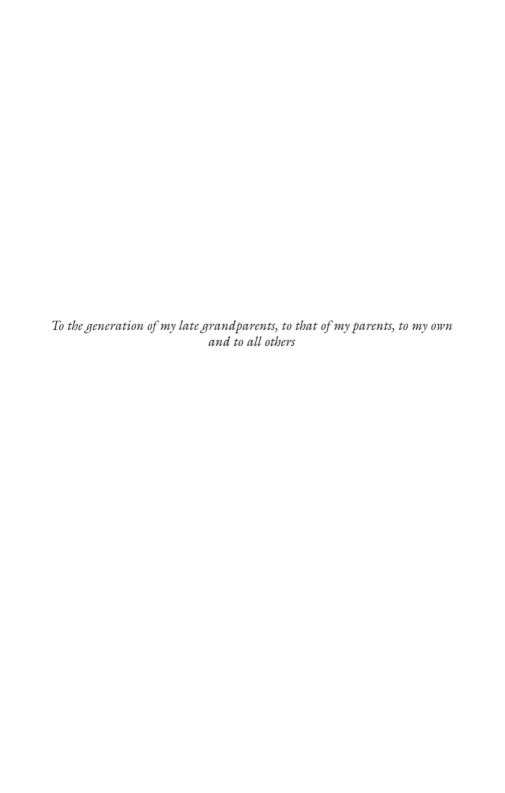

To the generation of my late grandparents, to that of my parents, to my own and to all others

FOREWORD

I am writing this foreword while the Israeli Defence Forces continue their attack on the Gaza Strip, in retaliation for Hamas's murderous raid on southern Israel on 7 October 2023. Rarely can a study in historical sociology or the sociology of knowledge have been as topical as Alon Helled's *Israel's National Historiography: Between Generations, Identity and State*. Nor as potentially relevant to understanding what may prove to be a turning point in world history.

Dr Helled's book is a study of the emergence of a distinct Israeli national identity, and the part that Israeli historians and historiography have played in its development. More exactly, it deals with the development of Israeli *habitus*, a term familiar to sociologists but probably less so to many others. Norbert Elias defined it simply as "second nature". In other words, it refers to everything that we have learned from other people since birth, but which has become so deeply habituated that even to ourselves it feels not learned but innate. All social groups, from families to nations and beyond, may share traits of habitus, many of them unconsciously. These traits include not just aspects of manners and everyday behaviour, but also shared patterns of emotion and personality make-up. Not all of them, of course, are shared by every single member of the group.

So what is distinctive about Israeli habitus or, loosely, "national character"? Dr Helled has been strongly influenced by Elias, who himself wrote about the development of habitus through power struggles in his native Germany but, although himself Jewish, not about Israel. What he always did, however, was to stress the link between fears and dangers, dangers and fears.

In *On the Process of Civilisation* Elias draws a connection between the pacification of habitus and the pacification of territory: "[I]f in this or that region the power of a central authority grows, if over a larger or smaller area the people are forced to live in peace with each other, the moulding of affects and the standards of [emotion management] are very gradually changed as well". Diminished danger, diminished fears. Not that there was ever anything inevitable about this; in all too many parts of the world this potentially benevolent spiral has been spun into reverse by upsurges of violence, invasions and wars. Fears rise with rising danger and, if the dangers persist, the corresponding fears and anger may also become embedded in a group's habitus. Moreover, fearfulness tends to inhibit the capacity for foresight and may foster impulsive aggressiveness.

Which brings us back to modern Israel. Its origins do not quite fit the model of mainly endogenous, relatively steady and gradual, processes observed in the history of Western Europe. Exogenous factors—that is, forces from outside the present national frontiers—came into play. Zionism arose in the nineteenth century in response to the persecution of Jews, especially in Eastern Europe. After the First World War Britain and France carved up the Ottoman empire, and in their own interests made promises which they perhaps never intended to keep, or, more certainly, failed to think through the means of fulfilling them. Then, above all, came the Shoah. The League of Nations' mandate to Britain to rule Palestine (where, ironically, Jews, Christians and Muslims had for centuries lived together largely in peace under the Ottomans) collapsed in 1948 in face of (among other things) Jewish terrorism. The establishment of Israel—but not of a corresponding Palestinian Arab state—was sanctioned by the United Nations, and from the resulting war between it and the Arab states emerged the frontiers now recognized in international law. The war also resulted in the Nakba, the expulsion of hundreds of thousands of Arabs from what was now the land of Israel.

For about its first two decades, Israel—as viewed from Western Europe—appeared a peaceful, idyllic, well-governed social democratic country, "the only democracy in the Middle East". I well remember how fashionable it was for young Europeans of my generation to take themselves off to work on the kibbutzim. Appearances proved deceptive. As Israeli friends have pointed out to me, the 1948 ceasefire boundaries were militarily not easily defensible: at its nearest, the frontier is only 54 kilometres from Tel-Aviv, making the country vulnerable to bisection by a successful military incursion to the sea; there was much to fear even early on. After its victory in the 1967 Six-Day War, the temptation to hold on to its newly occupied territories proved irresistible, in spite of David Ben-Gurion's warning that most of these territories should be returned for the sake of Israel's "inner health". What has followed has included the 1973 Yom Kippur War, violent terrorism, the Israeli invasion of Lebanon in 1982, the First Intifada from 1988 to 1990, the Second Intifada from 2000 to 2005, Hamas taking control of the Gaza Strip in 2007 and the resulting Israeli blockade of the territory, frequent rocket fire and now the appalling conflict in progress as I write. Not to forget, also, the continuing seizure by Israeli settlers of large tracts of the West Bank.

Such cycles of violence, propelled by danger, fear and anger, are not easily or quickly resolved.

History always plays a key part in long-term cycles of violence. The historic cycle of violence closest to home for me is that of the "Troubles" in Northern Ireland from the late 1960s until 1998, which I have often described—only half-jokingly—as the last vestige of the Wars of Religion that beset Europe in the sixteenth and seventeenth centuries. By the late twentieth century the conflict was more about territory, after the partition of Ireland in 1921, than religion as such. But the Catholic, nationalist side traced their grievances back to the "plantation" of Protestants from England and Scotland and their seizure of "Catholic land" in earlier centuries. Meanwhile the Protestant "Unionist" side (unionist meaning defending the union with Great Britain) often harked back to the massacres of their ancestors in the Irish Rebellion of 1641. The Israeli historiography on which Dr Helled focuses is well researched but fulfils a similar function. The history of the Jews in Palestine of course can be traced back thousands of years. But then the history of Islam in the Holy Land is many centuries-long too.

The problem with the use of history in long-running conflicts is that it is a constant backdrop to a social process in which the clock is always in practice set back to zero, to begin again from the latest outrage by the other side. As I write, in the Middle East for the Israelis that means, understandably, the Hamas attacks of 7 October 2023. For the Palestinians it will be, perhaps for decades to come, the Israeli attack on Gaza that followed.

Dr Helled, from a liberal Sabra family in Palestine for generations but himself a resident in Italy since his early adulthood, is exceptionally well placed to examine these issues in a relatively detached way. In drawing attention to "Israeli national historiography", he has done us a valuable service.

University College Dublin   Stephen Mennell
Dublin, Ireland

University of Leicester
Leicester, UK
24 March 2024

PREFACE

I am a strange social scholar. I was born and raised in Tel-Aviv, Israel, in a fully Sabra family committed to the rights and duties of the republican spirit of early Israel; a liberal family whose origins are rooted in Galilee, Jerusalem, and the nascent Tel-Aviv but also in European culture stretched from central Europe to the Mediterranean Sea: a societal merger which embraced Zionism but was not its direct outcome.

It was probably my upbringing that made me attentive to the society that surrounded me. In early adulthood, I moved to Italy, where I completed my higher education, including my doctorate at University of Turin, which offered a joint programme with University of Florence. Although very much European, almost Italianized, I never ceased to study Israel from a different perspective in social sciences. My interest in historical process, theories on nationalism and identity was cultivated throughout my years as a student. The choice to foster my academic ambitions, while applying received knowledge to my own identify, has been somewhat challenging. Almost psychoanalytic self-reflection has become useful and instrumental in order to peel away taken-for-granted dispositions and thus shed some old belief systems whilst examining ingrained ideas.

The volume you are about to read is my attempt to answer to some of my personal questions, namely the relations between Judaism and statehood, the intellectual origins and mental pictures that accompanied, conditioned and chiselled my own socialization. The content is the core part of my PhD dissertation, defended on 28 November 2019, supervised by prof Marco Tarchi (University of Florence) and prof Gisèle Sapiro (École des hautes études en sciences sociales).

The empirical approach and theoretical arguments I present in the book have developed over the years through a fruitful exchange with professors, advisors, colleagues, friends and family I have been blessed to have. I am deeply grateful to Marco Tarchi, my Italian advisor and mentor, not only for guiding me in the labyrinth of doctoral reach but for reading the raw drafts of my research with no intention of denaturalize my in-progress intellectual persona. Alfio Mastropaolo has also been an inspiration during the process of transforming the dissertation into a readable book. His scholarly irony shaped my understanding of the dramas of political life to be dedramatized through work. Laura Gaffuri (University of Turin) turned my attention to the intersections and interactions between religion, identity and history, while Sara Lagi (University of Turin), Arturo Marzano (University of Pisa) and Adele Bianco (University D'Annunzio University of Chieti–Pescara) punctually and amiably kept pushing me to write the book. I express my deepest gratitude to late Maria Grazia Enardu (University of Florence), who was an exceptional mentor and friend.

The intellectual community that surrounded me during my studies between Turin, Florence and Tel-Aviv supplied academic freedom and encouraged me to follow my heart, mind and curiosity and to be interdisciplinary in my research. I thank Paolo Caraffini, my current postdoctoral trainer, for supporting me in the last years of academic disorientation.

Within this community a special place is reserved to the Eliasian friends, who embraced me into their intimate group. The exploration of Elias's sociological teaching would not have been the same without their stimuli. I thank Florence Delmotte and Marta Bucholc, who have given me the floor to present my work in different phases of the research, and, consequently, opened the way for collaboration in the following years. While showing kindness and interest, the Eliasian family became a source of inspiration.

I have presented parts of the research in workshops and conferences over the years and was generously commented by peers in the fields of political sciences, sociology and Israel studies.

I am very thankful to two friends, in particular, Chiara De Bernardi and Carlo Pala, for all the pep talks, useful comments and votes of confidence. The friendship they bring into my life is truly irreplaceable.

My heartfelt gratitude goes to Tatiana Landini and Elizabeth Graber, my editor, who accompanied the manuscript with faith and patience. Thanks to mutual understanding and common grounds, the doctoral research matured into a book, endorsed by the Norbert Elias Series.

In addition, I am greatly obliged to Stephen Mennell, one of the pillars of the Eliasian community, who had read the manuscript prior to its submission, and saw fit to write an insightful and attentive foreword to it, in spite of any personal difficulty and the contextual "minefield" of the book's sensitive topic.

Last but not least, I wish to thank my family. My parents' endless love and valuable teachings are the deepest strata of my intellectual self. I thank my older sisters for having motivated me, both directly and indirectly, to achieve excellence and realize my dreams.

On a personal note, I hope the exploration of the interconnections between state formation and history-writing in Israel, whose finishing line surely exceeds the circumscribed study before you, provides some adequate answers about the country's national identity and the processes that have shaped it. Hopefully, the research will entice other scholars in their own research paths.

The book is divided into three parts and five chapters. Chapter 1 introduces the scope of the research and discusses the literature from which the study took inspiration. It also presents the salience of the enquiry and places it as an interdisciplinary and multi-level analysis (state, academia, generations). Chapter 2 provides an analytical and conceptual overlook that will accompany our enquiry about Israeli historians and their interrelations with the national habitus who they interiorize and experience as individuals but also contribute to shape. The chapter is mostly based upon Eliasian and Bourdieusian theorizations.

After the theoretical premises, in the second part of the book, the reader plunges into three chapters which processually reconstruct the generations in Israeli national historiography in light of the phases of Israel's state-building, as a survival unit, and the development of the country's national habitus. It is the very core of the book. Each generation is contextualized and analysed in a distinctive category linked to Israeli statehood: *Komemyiut*, namely pre-statehood and historiographical enterprising prior to Israel's independence; followed by *Mamlakhtiyut*, that is, the development of the state and academia in the period 1948–1977, while focusing on the weight of the first generation of Israeli historians and the autonomization of their discipline; finally, *Artziyut*: contemporary trends in Israeli historiography and society.

All these end with some conclusions and observations on the case-study and the salience of the generational perspective. The conclusions also invite scholars to further engage in the research of the historiographical,

academic and intellectual fields as lens capable of examining the sociopolitical and sociocultural features of habitus-building in relation to nationalism and collective identities.

Florence, Italy   Alon Helled
March 2024

Praise for *Israel's National Historiography*

"In a historical moment such as the period beginning with 7 October 2023, characterised by dramatic events in the Middle East and a rise in intolerance globally, a work such as Alon Helled's, which aims to scientifically reconstruct, analyse and explain the processes and reasons underlying the formation of the Israeli collective identity, is important and welcome."
—Prof. PhD. Adele Bianco, *Department of Philosophical, Pedagogical and Economic Quantitative Sciences, D'Annunzio University of Chieti–Pescara, Italy*

"Alon Helled not only deciphers the double-binds shaping the Israeli-Palestinian configuration: he offers us a mirror that we urgently need to turn towards all our nationalisms, if we are to develop our means of orientation and emerge from the maelstrom, in Palestine, Europe and elsewhere."
—Florence Delmotte, *Faculty of Economics, Social and Political Sciences and Communication Saint-Louis, Université Catholique de Louvain (UCLouvain), Belgium*

"A book for our troubled times, Alon Helled's intriguing and analytically rigorous investigation of Israeli national identity and historiography is a compelling reading. It brings together detailed research of a very fine grained kind with an outstanding use of an Elias framework."
—Prof Liz Stanley, *Professor Emerita of Sociology, School of Social and Political Science, The University of Edinburgh, UK*

"Rarely does an author find themselves lamenting the relevance of their work, yet for Alon Helled, the heightened international importance of the subject of Israeli national identity is far from a cause for celebration. As we witness the agonizing escalation of conflict between Israelis and Palestinians, there is an urgent demand for a book that unravels the intricate threads of historical narratives that have woven the fabric of Israeli national identity and statehood. Crafted from a blend of scholarly rigor and profound personal insight, this book is firmly embedded in sociological theory while offering a wealth of informative historical detail. An indispensable guide for anyone seeking to navigate the complexities of present-day Israeli identity."
—Marta Bucholc, *Professor of Sociology, University of Warsaw, Poland*

"Alon Helled's 'Israel's National Historiography: Between Generations, Identity and State' provides an original discussion of the interplay between national identity and individual personality structures. By deploying insights from Norbert Elias's process sociology in a highly creative manner, he analyses with unusual depth how successive generations of Israeli historians navigated the complex interdependencies between their identity as citizens of Israel, their conception of the national character of the Israeli state and the wider geopolitical context of that state as their main survival unit. In the process, the author makes a fundamental contribution to a better understanding of not only the Israeli state, its history, contradictions and current predicaments, but also those of the wider region."

—André Saramago, *University of Coimbra, Portugal*

"Alon Helled's balanced account of Israeli state formation and the way historians have shaped Israel's national identity is extremely relevant just now."

—Helmut Kuzmics, *Institut für Soziologie, University of Graz, Austria*

Contents

PART I

Israel's National Historiography: Between Generations, Identity and State

CHAPTER 1

Introduction: Israeli Historiography as a Case-Study Between Nation and Scholarship

What are the interconnections and interrelations between historiography and Israel's national identity? Is the former an element of the latter? Or is it the other way round? Or both ways? Every nation-state possesses a historiographical corpus, that is, a codified elaboration and interpretation of historical facts, which is instrumental in shaping collective identity through channels of education and dissemination, namely, schooling and mass media, as well as erudition, namely academia and specialized expert knowledge. Many debates have concerned the tensions between scholarly work, following the ideal of "scientific objectivity", and the subjective component in science, especially in the so-called sciences of culture that reflect, delineate and explain social phenomena.[1] That is to say that national historiography cannot be about facts alone. Tensions are found not only in scholarly work but also in the surroundings of any intellectual endeavour: inasmuch as each scholar exists, as a social agent, in a specific sociopolitical and cultural context. In recent decades, academic interest has grown in its curiosity to shed further light on the inner and outer dynamics traceable in academic work.

[1] The conceptualization of "*Wertfreiheit*" by Max Weber, one of the fathers of social science, polemicizes over this issue, whilst it juxtaposes judgements of value vis-à-vis judgement of fact. See Weber (1919 [original essay]): "*Science as a Vocation*" in selected papers edited by Eisenstadt (1968): "*Max Weber: On Charisma and Institution Building*", and Sadri (1992): "*Max Weber's Sociology of Intellectuals*".

Properties such as ideology, national sentiment of belonging and individual stories, which combine both particularities and generalities, merge into different contexts and personal and professional trajectories.

In the case of Israeli national historiography, defined as the corpus of Jewish and Zionist historical studies, the abovementioned factors seem to have had a lasting relevance. Since the world of ideas and the world of politics are as multifaceted as they are inclined to continuity and change, any first impression might result erroneous. The Zionist Jewish nation-state, as declared in 1948, may seem perennially at a boiling point; also, in light of the recent political instability, waves of protestation and the dramatic violence which have followed since 7 October 2023; a turning point whose consequences on human lives are of the gravest kind, while showing the short-sightedness of political agents and the tragic weight that will certainly impact today's generation and future ones. The issue of the Israeli-Palestinian relations, absent in the first phases of Israeli historiography, reveals the paradoxical relational figuration in establishing a national sense of belonging, that is, an historical identification between a people and a land, whose natives were considered only a lateral presence. In shaping and codifying a national corpus of historical writing, the Arabs of Palestine, increasingly (self-)identified as Palestinians, became the antagonistic national "other", hence much ignored in Israeli Zionist historiography (and even in the country's flourishing oriental studies until the 1980s). This is to say that the formation of Israeli national identity, as expressed by its historiography, had been based upon a unilateral, one-dimensional, hegemonic direction in building a national history of the Jewish people in ancient times and in centuries-long Diaspora, aimed to bridge the temporal and territorial gap, with very little consideration of what had been the destiny of the biblical "Promised Land" and the chronicles of the population that inhabited it, after the loss of ancient sovereignty (70 CE).

Nonetheless, it is that national history whose inner dynamics consist in structural contradictions eroding the nation-state's capacity to endure as the only Eliasian sociopolitical "survival unit" for the Jewish people to hold onto in times of need (Elias 2000).[2] This capacity is interrelational

[2] The figurational "survival unit" of a specific nation-state not only echoes the need to overcome difficulties from within, namely the traditional antagonistic competition among factions and classes, but it also describes a collective aggregator, whose primary disposition is resilience, given external threats deriving from a risky and hostile environment to cope with (namely, geopolitical conflicts, shifts in the international system, global climate change, pandemics etc.).

by definition, since, as pointed out by Elias, "[A]gain and again, a rising outsider stratum or a rising 'survival unit' as a whole, a tribe or a nation state, attains the functions and characteristics of an establishment in relation to other outsider strata or survival units which, on their part, are pressing from below, from their position as oppressed outsiders, against the current establishment" (Elias 2000: 382). Consequently, one asks whether Israeli historiography has reflected such strata and relations, especially vis-à-vis the otherness of Arab Palestinian Middle Eastern history(ies). The latter may be conceptualized and exemplified by the intrinsic established and outsider relations (Elias and Scotson 1965/2008). However, as much as the Israeli-Palestinian conflict is topical, the analysis presented throughout the book focuses on the Jewish, Zionist, Israeli world of its national historiography. Neither is this a consequence of lack of interest by the author nor is it a result of any subconscious choice. With deep awareness that Palestinian national history exists and deserves full attention and recognition (as we shall see in Chap. 5), the processual generational analysis could only be sufficiently precise, while lingering on the Jewish national "side" of the history of Palestine, as a territory inhabited by different communities, religions and stories. That said, the book aims at providing a structural look at the synergies, correlations and divergences which influenced the passage from Jewish history, produced in Palestine, to Zionist Israeli state-centric historiography and its intellectual dispersion.

All these premises not only open the floor for interrogatives regarding the contribution of historians to Israeli Jewish society, as active social agents, but also necessitate to unpack the modes in which they are shaped by it. A general overview is found in the works published by Israeli historian Shlomo Sand who has affronted the intellectual foundations of Zionist national movement, mainly as a Jewish reaction to anti-Semitism, while situating it in the European ideological and religious context of origin. According to Sand, once the Zionist project became a state, the intellectual *milieu* did not develop an "organic" agency (modelled by Gramscian and Marxist thought). On the contrary, local intelligentsia soon became auxiliary agents of government, and as such avoided overt public critique; a tendency which resulted in diffused elitism, but later on varied and fluctuated between changing political circumstances (Sand 2000, and ibid. 2011). Yet, Sand's somewhat provocative observations do not specifically address the category of historians specialized in Jewish/Zionist/Israeli history (he himself belongs to the so-called general history). Besides, there are still numerous relevant issues to tackle and verify with regard to Israeli historiography, which is a privileged pair of magnifying glasses in order to detect social, ideological, cultural changes in Israel. There is no lack of questions. What role did/do sociopolitical factors play in the institution-alization of academic historical discipline? Are there "identity building" historians whose work bears the weight of Zionism and thus reflects a permeable continuum between scholarly elaboration of the past and the sociobiographic reality in which those historians live and operate? And were such historians to be found, would they enjoy scientific and/or pub-lic prestige and recognition? All these questions derive from the conceptu-alization of history-writing not as a closed perimeter of privileged intellectuals but as the continuous ampler interrelations within society. As asserted by Carr (1961/1990, p. 10–11),[3] historians face "raw materials" that are the basic facts, known and/or knowable, and whose accuracy is a necessary condition (Carr uses "a well-seasoned timber metaphor" of the historian as an architect) but not the essential function which is to call on these basic facts, order and contextualize them properly. This operation entails provisional, yet careful, selection by using "auxiliary sciences", such as archaeology, epigraphy, numismatics, chronology and others. All this takes form without forgetting that the "pulp" of history is, by no means, less rewarding than core facts. The historian's duty is, therefore, to inter-pret, mould, evaluate and provide historical significance and validity of a determined event.

In regard to Israeli historiography, a preliminary attempt to uncover some of the latter's dynamics was made by Conforti (2005), in a polemic over post-Zionism and post-modernism in Israeli academia. He showed that various historians researched Jewish history from both ideological "responsibility" and professional-pedagogical motivations. The idea, how-ever, is not new. Conforti's assessments, whose analysis spans to the 1960s, took much from Myers (1995) who had distinguished between political commitment and scientific commitment as expressed in the writings and actions of the so-called Jerusalem School, established by the first

---

[3] See Carr (1990). The book is a sort of study-manifesto against empiricism within histori-ography which in six chapters ("lessons") posits historians against historical facts, society, science and morality (bias), historical causation, human progress, historiographical developments.

generation of Jewish scholars at the Hebrew University in Jerusalem (1921–1948). His analysis revealed tensions, even academic schizophrenia, dual allegiances versus monolithic ideological insensitivities. Another, more recent, systematization of the relations between scholarly production and Israeli identity is offered by Ben-Amos and Shiff (2020) who co-edited a thematic volume on the subject.[4]

The case, nevertheless, does not differ from Jewish history per se, or from any other particularistic history (for instance, national, ethnic and religious). Jewish studies display similar, not to say analogous, tensions. The latter are undoubtedly a pivotal consequence of nineteenth-century nationalistic and positivistic academic training. As argued by Smith (1991, 25):

> [A]ny realistic account of ethnic identity and ethno-genesis must, therefore, eschew the polar extremes of the primordialist-instrumentalist debate and its concerns with, on the one hand, fixity of cultural patterns in nature and, on the other, 'strategic' manipulability of ethnic sentiments and continuous cultural malleability. [...] Collective cultural identity refers not to a uniformity of elements over generations but to a sense of continuity on the part of successive generations of a given cultural unit of population, to shared memories of earlier events and periods in the history of that unit and to notions entertained by each generation about the collective destiny of that unit and its culture.

These observations facilitate the traceability of identity-building processes in national historical writing. In the case of Jewish history, Brenner (2010) portrays such dynamics as he concentrates his efforts upon the intellectual and social genesis of Jewish history. In his book the author covers a period which ranges from the beginning of the nineteenth century to the beginning of the twenty-first century. There had been, of course, earlier Jewish history-writing, but it generally occurred in the context of theological observations. Only with the rise of modern scholarship, which enabled critical examination of Holy Scriptures that had previously been revered as sacred, did a distanced attitude with regard to the sources

---

[4] We refer to *Lines for Our Image: Exploring Israel, Writing About Ourselves* (2020). Ben-Amos, a historian of education, had published "Israël: La fabrique de l'identité nationale", Paris, CNRS Éditions, 2010 (elaboration of his 2002 book, published in Hebrew, on Israeli education). Shiff, a Jewish history specialist, is known for his research on Jewish American Diaspora and the historico-cultural connections between Shoah, Zionism and politics. Both scholars had been interviewed for the research presented in this book.

become possible. Brenner's aim is to uncover the complex relationship between pre-modern Jewish historiography and collective memory. As stated, he tackles the argument by focusing on a series of particular "master narratives" (defined as "a coherent historical account that has a clear perspective and is generally about a nation-state").[5] Although Brenner has paid great attention to Jewish historiography, not all the protagonists he exalts would be easily labelled as professional historians in contemporary terms, especially once he deals with the academic field as it was emerging at the already-cited Hebrew University (in this his categorization is quite similar to the one offered by Conforti).[6] However, neither of them provides the generational features of Israeli historians in relation to the "seasons" of country's state-building.

This book, based on long research dedicated to Israeli historians' contemporary role in shaping the country's national identity,[7] offers an analysis of Israeli historiography which takes into account personal biographies and (inter)generational features up to nowadays' Israel.[8] Israeli historiography is thus used as a window through which twenty-first-century academia, state, politics and society interrelate and intercross. The book's aim goes beyond the existent literature on Israel. Most of academic research lacks reference on what and how Israeli historians have been, more or less, "scribes" of Israeli national identity as well as social products stemming from it. This explains why so many, inside and outside Israel, pay more attention to presumably bigger interpretative issues. Topics such as ideology, geopolitical history and international relations are in vogue, especially

---

[5] Brenner (2010). See Introduction p. 9 and the following.

[6] "The protagonists to be discussed in a book on modern Jewish historiography doubtless include authors of large-scale works covering many periods, from Isaak Markus Jost and Graetz to Dubnow and Baron, as well as the founders and chief representatives of historical schools" (Brenner 2010, p. 11); yet Brenner also pursues the scholarly stories of intellectuals such as Martin Buber, Arthur Ruppin and Gershom Scholem who cannot be labelled as historians *tout court* but who radically "distinguish themselves from their predecessors" against the German, increasingly nationalistic, criteria of the *Wissenschaft des Judentums* as part of their Zionist activism (ibid., p. 158 and ff.).

[7] The research is based on a doctoral thesis, entitled "Engraving Identity: The Production of the Israeli 'Survival Unit' Through Its Historians", conducted at the Italian Universities of Turin and Florence and in co-tutorship with École des Hautes Études en Sciences Sociales (EHESS) (2014–2019), supervised by Prof. Gisèle Sapiro (EHESS) and Prof. Marco Tarchi (UniFi), and defended on 28 November 2019.

[8] The historical, social and cultural elements find both intellectual and generational dimension in the work of Sirinelli (1988) about French *Khâgneux* and *normaliens*; and Winock (1989).

in relation to the generation of the so-called *Nephilim*, that is, national heroic personages, Zionist leaders and entrepreneurs, and to venues such the kibbutz, school and the army as privileged arenas, where identity-consolidation policies have engendered different outcomes. The importance of the latter is, indeed, indisputable. Yet, it would be too simplistic to consider political figures alone as the only "exemplars" involved in the construction of Israel's national identity. The building of "Israeliness", considered to be a twofold process in which social agency is both creator and creation of social transformation, concerns the transversal stratification of a national habitus, in either Eliasian or Bourdieusian terms,[9] inasmuch as the "civilizing process" of national integration involves sociopolitical dispositions enable to mobilize the masses (Mosse 1974) as a relational self-explanatory "nationalizing nationalism" (Brubaker 1996). In other words, overt ideology and formal institutions aside, there exists an increasing general interest in how political identity is perceived by the ones who are socialized to it and the role of those who produce and codify it. Hence, the role of single actors has become crucial in understanding major phenomena concerning identity transformations and their long-term relevance. From this last point emerges what we may consider a meaningful analytical parallelism in key concepts. Moreover, in order to grasp the big picture, we need a perspective from within. Such a vantage point has found new emphasis especially in bottom-up approaches that aim to deconstruct master narratives and/or political discourse centred around the "new Jew" model, that is, the "Sabra" model [lit. *Opuntia ficus-indica cactus*], whose metaphoric analogy in Zionist thought ideal-typically encompassed roughness from the outside, hence the adaptation and resilience in relation to the hostile surroundings in Palestine (physical, societal and political) but whose fruit was sweet and abundant (a worthwhile effort).[10] The latter is no other than the attribution of status to identifiable social groups who are contemporaneously producers and products of the Israeli collective consciousness, therefore, active members of an "imagined community" (Anderson 2006).

Major inspiration for this research was found in Penslar (2007) who, although with different emphasis, had already delineated

---

[9] With habitus, both sociologists, despite differences in analytical sensibilities, refer to a set of codified dispositions and behavioural norms that are structurally (yet dynamically) interiorized by any socialized individual belonging to a certain social group. See Bourdieu (1998); Bourdieu and Wacquant (1992); Elias (2000, 2001); Roodenburg (2004); Sapiro (2015).

[10] Two classical texts in this regard are Almog (2000) "The Sabra"; and Kimmerling (2001) "The Invention and Decline of Israeliness".

generation-sensitive trends in Israeli historiography, based on the ideological and academic identities of historians. He suggests that "Israeli historians are, by and large, remarkably well traveled and well read, but, precisely because they live their lives in the small land about which they write, national history risks being reduced to local history" (ibid.). Given the multiple facets of national identity and its interrelations with historiography, there is a need to decipher the role of Zionist Jewish Israeli historians, insofar as scholars who are first-hand "providers" of identity-based discourse whilst inserting politics itself into national history.

In this book, the categorization of Israeli historians, as an advantageous magnifying glass, follows the rich sociological tradition by Pierre Bourdieu (1988), who viewed professional academics as a potential group whose affinities in terms of habitus (i.e., social dispositions and practical sense) and particular interests—scholarly and non-scholarly—are connected to their position in the social space. According to Bourdieu, not only do scholars act within the supposedly autonomous academic field but they also intercross the political, social and economic fields, since they situationally depend on the synchronization and temporal hierarchy of the former. In light of the latter, relevant diachronic and synchronic changes must be taken into account. One of the key elements permitting that sort of continuum is the dialectical relation between the historian as *homo politicus*[11] and his/her position as *homo historicus*.[12] In sociological terms, the two features may easily permeate the professional history-writing, while making of the latter a product of reflexivity of objectivized personal knowledge in the construction of scientific knowledge. The two, despite irreducible differences, are both finalized in a dialogue between the individual and the society he/she experiences, namely, the habitus, which bridges the national society, the personal background and the professional field. Once

---

[11] The term *homo politicus* implies an active democratic citizenry who exercises his/her individual sovereignty in the name of the ideal of popular sovereignty vis-à-vis the utilitarian individual-consumer, namely the neoliberal *homo oeconomicus* but also juxtaposed to the *homo juridicus* (rather dogmatic and legalistic for the sake of order and meaning). On the immense category, see Brown (2015): *Undoing the Demos: Neoliberalism Stealth Revolution*. However, one cannot ignore that citizenship as well as citizenry are strongly connected to the nation-state order.

[12] In this direction go two works by French scholars which reflect much of the symbiosis, tensions and changes in the figure of the professional historian and his role in greater society: Dumoulin (2003): "*Le rôle social de l'historien: de la chaire au prétoire*" and Charle (2013): "*Homo Historicus: Réflexions sur l'histoire, les historiens et les sciences sociales*".

again, not only do objective structures require investigation but also the interiorization of both national and professional habitus as incorporated by Israeli historians. Such an analytical approach, therefore, overcomes the dichotomies regarding politics and society, and enables to surpass the blurred boundaries stretching between objective historical factuality, the narration of events, power struggles and personal trajectories. That said, the apparently "meagre" historiography in terms of actual power and politics present conspicuous differences but also similarities, considered the contiguities between the two fields. According to Maza (2017): "[T]he 'where' of history is, by default, the nation [...]". Therefore, national history strengthens politics but is equally its direct product. That said, historians are part of society, as all other social agents, yet rarely do they come from a specific social group. Notwithstanding, their socialization encompasses the national narratives and the cultural codes of their time, regardless of specific sociological background. Professionally, however, they share scientific ambition aimed to reveal, and sometimes deconstruct, "historical truths".

The book socially reconstructs the sociopolitical history of Israeli historiography and contextualizes the different paths and fashions in which careers, roles and positions emerge in the historiographical discipline—starting from the establishment of local historiography in the pre-statehood period until nowadays Israel. The aim is thus to elaborate elements of change and continuity, while paying attention to historical and sociological contextualization.[13] The "reading" of the inner, subjective and contrasting nuances of Israeli historiography, situated within the structural and circumstantial frames which it occupies, is made possible by a generational periodization of historical "slices" related to both academic discipline and state. Only by adopting a transversal outlook, can one truly capture segments of social reality. In favour of greater and deeper understanding of Israeli society, the analysis introduces, periodizes and re-collocates the academic discipline of history, dedicated to the alloy of Jewish, Zionist and Israeli identity.

---

[13] Contextualization is of central concern for both Bourdieusian and Eliasian social analysis. The connections between power, behaviour, emotions and knowledge—which are conceptualized in "habitus", "field", "survival unit", "figuration" etc.—require long-term perspective. This involves a bridging of the supposed "macro-micro" divide to an extent that remains rather unusual in the social sciences, as it is sensitive to historical stratification of structures and dispositions.

The concept of "generation" helps to overcome the rather statistical notion of cohort and assumes what Karl Mannheim in his essay "The Problem of Generations" (1928/1952) formulated as "[A] rhythm in the sequence of generations [which] is far more apparent in the realm of the 'series'—free human groupings such as salons and literary circles—than in the realm of the institutions which for the most part lay down a lasting pattern of behaviour, either by prescriptions or by the organization of collective undertakings, thus preventing the new generation from showing its originality [according Mentré]" (ibid., p. 279). Consequently, one faces differently situated sequences of social groupings whose relationship plays a major role in interpreting societal strata, given the existence of an interior time (somewhat complementary to the concept of interiorized "habitus"), without neglecting general sociopolitical transformations which facilitate to delineate "general generational arithmetic" (Escudier 2016).

The case-study of Israeli national historiography and the historians who articulate it must be attentively contextualized, whilst bearing in mind the relevance of objective societal structures and conditions with which their subjectivity is confronted. The historical itinerary by itself does not suffice to explain the multiple interconnections between different fields and the interrelations between individual and society. Here the interconnection between the Israeli nation-state, conceptualized as a survival unit, and the stratification of national identity as interiorized through the habitus become significant.

The national habitus, with the dispositions through which collectivizing identification is made possible, is embodied by the state (the juridico-political vessel of social interactions), but is also subject to other normative behavioural codes, inasmuch as the nation-state figuration is interdependent on other forms (and scales) of social structures, such as other states, international organizations, non-state actors and so forth (one might intuitively think of the recognition of sovereignty, which is at the heart of the international system, but also of scientific cooperation and international academic acknowledgement). This theoretical framework bridges between the specificity of Israeli historians and the larger, more general, processes of state and nation-building. The book hopes to contribute to better understand the interplay between generations, national identity and state in Israel. It is therefore intended to a variety of scholars. It would be of interest for specialists in political sociology, nationalism studies as well as researchers in Middle Eastern and/or Israel studies. Considered its theoretical framework, the book seeks to address historical sociologists and sociologists of intellectual professions in light of Eliasian theory, while wishing to dialogue comparatively with future researches conducted in other countries which present similar contexts of conflict and societal complexities.

RESEARCH ITINERARY: AIMS, METHOD AND ANALYSIS

The analysis of the sociogenesis and development of Israeli historiography aims at providing key motivations and modalities through which the role and position of historians in their society have been constructed. The enquiry is the result of a four-year doctoral research which has been updated and re-elaborated since 2019. Inasmuch as the analysis aims to interpret the Israeli historiographical case starting from the structural and institutional autonomization of Israeli history studies, conceived as a privileged arena that delineates the processes of nation-state building in Israel. The enquiry places the scientific production in a stratified context under the twofold analysis of academia and state. In order to shed light upon these dynamics, there is need to adopt a dialectical methodological approach. On the one hand, the endeavour requires the deconstruction and reconstruction of the stratification of Israeli, namely Jewish and Zionist, historiography as an academic discipline. On the other, it is imperative to collocate and collectivize individual social agency, products and bearers of the Israeli survival unit and the habitus it engenders. This is made possible thanks to a sound theoretical toolkit which is accompanied and verified by empirical investigation. Chiefly qualitative, the research on which the book is based integrates some supplementary quantitative data.[14] Hence, the analysis escapes both "abstract empiricism" and "methodological formalism". It follows the footsteps of the "artisan intellectuel" (intellectual craftsman in French) and personalizes method and theory in order to obtain a more comprehensive understanding of the case-study at hand.

While the theoretical framework has been directly inspired by seminars and conferences attended during and after the doctoral research had taken form, the empirical data was accumulated and systematized via the realization of semi-structured in-depth face-to-face interviews with Israeli historians working on Israeli history and with scholars whose studies may be

---

[14] Quantitative data chiefly refer to statistics taken from secondary bibliographical materials or from institutional registries such as the Israeli Bureau of Statistics (sources are always mentioned in footnote).

considered "neighboring", mainly in the fields of Middle Eastern studies, Shoah and sociocultural sociology.[15] Some exchanges of information regarding academic development in Israel, disciplinary genealogy and archaeology only became possible through somewhat "accidental" small-talks in meetings around Israel studies conferences. Amongst those who provided informant-quality data, beyond the pure biographical information, we can mention: Anita Shapira, Yosef Gorny, Aviva Halamish, Israel Bartal, Zeev Tzahor, Dina Porat, Tuvia Friling, Yoav Gelber, Yaacov Shavit, Shalom Ratzabi, Shlomo Sand, Idith Zertal, Yechiam Weitz, Avner Ben-Amos, Benny Morris, Ilan Pappé, Daniel Gutwein, Hanna Yablonka, Ofer Shiff, Dan Michman, Motti Golani, Hillel Cohen, Orit Rozin, Yaron Tsur, Yehouda Shenhav, Rina Shapira, Itamar Even-Zohar, Rakefet Sela-Sheffy, David De Vries, Arieh Saposnik. Although most of the supplementary material was not systematically analysed and included in this book. The formal and informal exchanges of information were a valuable source to add oral witness quality to the more historical reconstruction of Israeli national historiography.

The crucial decision to treat these data as an empirical bridge between sociological processual analysis and oral history was taken in order to maintain a certain organicity of arguments in a shorter, somewhat denser, enquiry of Israel history in a generational perspective, whose epicentre was the juxtaposition of state-building and history-writing in Israel. Therefore, the original intent of the research, which aimed to analyse the trajectories of individual Israeli historians whose expertise directly centred on Zionist and Israeli history, was gradually widened into a generational one. The peculiar academic division of historical studies into the two history department system, namely general history and Jewish history, required this choice, despite its evident limits regarding the transversal nature of history-writing and some "sliding-door" effects in terms of personal academic careers. Topical issues and key events concerning Israel's national history can be researched from general, Jewish, Middle Eastern perspectives crossing not only history departments but also other departments in which research on Israel is conducted. Moreover, history is multidisciplinary by

---

[15] The construction of the object of research, as well as the realization of interviews, required of course a substantial field work in Israel. The latter was coordinated by prof. Sapiro, who mediated my stay in Israel, as a visiting scholar within the framework of the doctoral programme, with prof. Rakefet Sela-Sheffy, then head of the Unit of Cultural Studies (Faculty of Humanities) at Tel-Aviv University.

definition; hence, one can easily encounter scientific works written by professional scholars who are affiliated to humanities, social sciences, education and even law. The ample and fluid disciplinary boundaries are, consequently, quite difficult to trace. As stressed by a historian working at Tel-Aviv University and who was affiliated to the Labor Studies Program (Faculty of Social Sciences): "Historians are like parasites in academic terms. We can work almost everywhere in academia". Similar considerations can be made also with regard to the placing of Zionism as a European-oriented history vis-à-vis colonial history and its turbulent relations with any colonial/orientalist and post-colonial/post-orientalist approaches (though usually more relevant in universities outside Israel). As a result of the ambiguity and hardship in tracing all scholars interested in Israeli history, another decision was taken subsequently.

Consequently, the research took into account only scholars whose professional trajectories were anchored to academic research in Israeli public universities (Hebrew University of Jerusalem, Tel-Aviv University, Ben-Gurion University of the Negev, Bar-Ilan University, Open University), leaving aside colleges (in which history studies are much less institutionalized, since they offer no doctoral degree; whether they are public or private), and whose position within the Israeli academic system could be fully evidenced in terms of professionalization.[16] This made the generational categorization more easily verified, inasmuch as historians who were associate professors, full professors and emeriti—despite the inevitable heterogeneity between these categories—could show their "genealogical albums" between old masters and trainees. Though this choice may seem arbitrary, its rationale was to delineate institutional professionalization (i.e., solidity and acknowledgement of scientific production) as well as the reconstruction of biographies and careers.[17] Professors affiliated with Jewish history and Israel studies departments were contacted via email. The email stated:

---

[16] The research excluded the Technion—Israel Institute of Technology (IIT) for disciplinary reasons. Other two universities are excluded from the analysis: the private Reichman University (which was a college until its change in status in 2021) and the public Ariel University (which was recognized as a university in 2012 but which is situated in the West Bank, thus outside Israel's internationally recognized borders).

[17] According to available registries regarding Israel studies, the hermeneutic community of Israeli professional historians specialized in Israel's national history has never exceeded 30–40 individuals (non-academic, dilettante history-writers and biographers were excluded).

"Dear Professor X,

My name is Alon Helled and I am a PhD student in the field of political sciences at the Universities of Turin and Florence (joint program) in collaboration with the Paris School of Social Sciences (EHESS).

My doctoral thesis deals with the topic 'The path of a historian and the development of historiography in the Israeli academy'. I was invited by Prof. Sela-Shafi from the Department of Cultural Studies at Tel Aviv University to stay in the unit for several months in order to conduct a prosopographical field study on prominent intellectuals in the field of Israel studies.

I would be happy to meet with you and interview you in order to study, deepen and enrich my work on the topics indicated below:

1. Personal and professional background;
2. Transformations and trends in the study of general and Israeli history in particular;
3. The place of the historian in the academic establishment;
4. Public and state recognition of the historian's work and his status in Israeli society.

(the personal interview is planned to last for about an hour and a half, and will be recorded)

I would greatly appreciate your willingness to meet with me in order to contribute to my doctoral thesis.

Sincerely and thanks in advance,
Alon Helled"

Once availability was confirmed (often telephonically), most interviews took place at university departments, and sometimes at the interviewees' private households. Interviews were recorded, transcribed, translated from Hebrew (except for one, held in English) and progressively codified and thematized into generational categories (almost ideal-type descriptions). They lasted 45 minutes minimum with various exceptions which reached two hours and more. The in-depth semi-structured interview method enabled to cover a plurality of topics and a multitude of experiences (schematically outlined in the research plan). This type of interviews facilitated the intimate and open exchange of information (in a way of story-telling), while references such as names and events were noted. Such biographic-centred analysis characterizes a gradual and inductive course of research, suitable to processual analysis, once anchored to more structural general processes (historical, cultural, figurational etc.). Moreover, this methodological framework, adopted throughout fieldwork in Israel (2015–2019), permitted to approach the academic field by exploring its outsiders-insiders and the established versus non-established perceptions and descriptions of Israeli history. This enabled the understanding of the historians' social interactions in terms of professional epistemic community as well as politically relevant actors. It also traced the relations with other domains of scholarly work as well as to delineate processual trends in Israeli society.[18] Interviewees thus epitomized stimulating input on Israeli identity-building processes, beyond the classification of generational cohorts. The insights extrapolated from interviews furnished emphasis and precision to what had already been detected, and, furthermore, enriched the study with vivid personal anecdotes and interconnections, which added colour to available materials. Hence, the representation and socio-historical construction of Israeli Zionist historiography reached greater detail.

The on-field materials were framed within both Eliasian and Bourdieusian theories. Despite the differences between the two authors, the analytical anchors their works offer have enabled to detect the social and political features of Israeli historians through their interpersonal relations and interdependencies, either professional or public, through those interviews (accounted contemporaneously as exploratory and elucidatory). In this regard, the research places itself within the historical sociology while keeping an open eye on studies on nationalism and state-building processes, considering the central place national identity occupies in the study. Research materials also comprised examples of scientific production of Israeli historians as well as bibliographic references regarding interconnected issues relevant to Israeli history, society and politics. In addition, attention was paid to the local system of prizes and awards, namely the Israel Prize, the Yad Ben-Zvi Award, the Shazar Prize and others. The latter qualified the public acknowledgement of certain historians whose public engagement had been integrated, alongside activities outside academia (e.g., membership in scientific institutions, ministerial committees, civil society organizations, political parties etc.). The latter were searched beyond the personal account detailed in interviews. In this sense, the study

---

[18] In this regard, paramount was the need to maintain the interviewer's own personal detachment (*distanciation*) in order to provide inter-knowledge (*interconnaissance*). This element could not be any truer for this particular study, inasmuch as important factors (e.g., shared language, nationality and even academic interest) required attentive probe, and a high degree of self-awareness against any bias, to support congruent epistemic, but also pragmatic, adequacy. On the guidelines for fieldwork, see Beaud and Weber (2003): "*Guide de l'Enquête de Terrain*".

combined both primary and secondary materials which emerged from both interviews and fieldwork. Consequently, the content of the book examines the social history of Israeli historians from political, institutional and intellectual viewpoints. It focuses on the properties belonging to state-academia relations and to the generational change in what seems to be "national historiography" for topical merits, namely, Israeli Zionist Jewish history. As we shall see, the dichotomic detachment from pre-Zionist and Palestinian history accompanied the formation of Israel's national history-writing until rather later stages in the country's identity-construction.

The study brings to light the geopolitical and institutional circumstances, such as intellectual and ideological freedom and/or constraints, which have influenced Israeli historians in terms of mindsets, professional orientation and personal motivations. Truth be told, a balanced account on the plurality and singularity of biographies which stands at the heart of the enquiry might seem roughly sociological. Nevertheless, the need to historicize and produce primary and then secondary materials (which are reported in Chap. 3) is contemporaneously a starting point that enables the construction of interdependent social agency, as well as the exemplification of ideal-type trajectories, as contextualized by a distinctive generation. The latter approach was thus necessary in order to avoid two analytical risks: (1) a too synthetic character of (auto) biographical narratives, often interpreted as an absolute and irreducible destiny; (2) the too generic listing of societal phenomena without providing concrete historical examples.

In other words, the book aims to explore a puzzle, a map, which outlined the congruencies of the Israeli national habitus, the specific professional habitus of Israeli historians, as produced and reproduced in their field, given the transformations of the nation-state survival unit. A means to achieve such valid sociological foundations was the construction of a targeted prosopography of Israeli historians through time and place of work, while avoiding any illusory biographical traps which could end in false orientation (Bourdieu 1986). By critically following the dividing line between the world of academia, with all its institutions and inner dynamics, and the political (public) space, the generations of Israeli historians and their scholarly profession formed a solidly social unit to investigate, much beyond the general and rather trivial label depicting intelligentsia as a distant and detached "ivory tower".

The novelty in such an approach is the capacity to elaborate numerous Israeli histories with no determinism a priori, inasmuch as it stems from the problematization of the historiographical field (in the Bourdieusian sense). Additionally, critical aspects emerge in terms of generational significance, in light of sociopolitical and sociocultural state-driven processes. Generalizable interconnections and interdependencies are, therefore, revealed and make the specific Israeli case-study an extraordinary laboratory for processual social research. The study consequently provides an interpretative narration via the delineation of temporal concatenations and causal forms (Bichi 2000), which is different from existent literature on Israel's history, its sociopolitical dynamics and the century-old conflict. With that being said, the book is an attempt, anchored to empirical research inspired by processual sociology, to offer the social chronicles of Israeli historians, shaped by and through the Zionist Jewish nation-building in Palestine, then Israel.

The next chapter is dedicated to the framework of the historiographical field. It explains the concepts of habitus, survival unit and generations, as being tools for identity research before addressing the different generations of Israeli historians. The latter is followed by the chapters that describe and analyse the three generations of Israeli national habitus and the development of Israeli historiography.

References

Almog, O. (2000). *The Sabra: The Creation of the New Jew*, Berkeley [California], University of California Press.

Anderson, B. (2006): *Imagined Communities: reflections on the origin and spread of nationalism*, London: New York, Verso.

Beaud, S., Weber, F. (2003). *Guide de l'Enquête de Terrain*, Paris: La Découverte.

Ben-Amos, A., Shiff, O. (2020). "Kavim Le'Demuteinu: Lakhkor Et Yisrael, Likhtov Al Atsmeiu" (in English: "Lines for our image: exploring Israel, writing about ourselves"), Kyriat Sade: Tel-Aviv, Ben-Gurion Institute for the Study of Israel and Zionism, Yedioth Sfarim.

Bichi, R. (2000). *La Società Raccontata: Metodi Biografici e Vite Complesse*. Milano: FrancoAngeli.

Bourdieu, P. (1986). "L'illusion biographique" in *Actes de la Recherche en Sciences Sociales*, Vol. 62–63 [juin 1986], pp. 69–72.

Bourdieu, P. (1988). *Homo Academicus*, Stanford, Stanford University Press [CA].

Bourdieu, P., Wacquant, L.J.D. (1992). *An Invitation to Reflexive Sociology*, Cambridge, Chicago Press University &Polity Press.

Bourdieu, P. (1998). *Practical Reason: On the Theory of Action*, Stanford, Stanford University Press.

Brenner, M. (2010). *Prophets of the Past: Interpreters of Jewish History*, Princeton: Oxford, Princeton University Press (original edition in the German [2006]).

Brown, W. (2015). *Undoing the Demos: Neoliberalism Stealth Revolution*, New York, Zone Books: MIT Press.

Brubaker, R. (1996). *Nationalism Reframed. Nationhood and the National Question in the New Europe*, Cambridge, Cambridge University Press.

Carr, E.H. (1990). *What Is History?* [Second and revised edition of the 1961 edition], ed. R.W. Davies, Harmondsworth, London: New York [etc.], Penguin Books.

Charle, C. (2013). *Homo Historicus: Réflexions sur l'histoire, les historiens et les sciences sociales*, Paris, Armand Colin.

Conforti, Y. (2005). "Alternative Voices in Zionist Historiography", *Journal of Modern Jewish Studies*, Vol. 4, No. 1 March 2005, pp. 1–12.

Dumoulin, O. (2003). *Le rôle social de l'historien: de la chaire au prétoire*, Paris, Albin Michel.

Elias, N. (2000). *The Civilizing Process: Sociogenetic and Psychogenetic Investigations* (revised edition), translated by Edmund Jephcott, edited by E. Dunning, J. Goudsbfom and S. Mennell, Malden: Oxford: Carlton, Blackwell Publishing.

Elias, N. (2001). *The Society of Individuals* (edited by Michael Schroeter and translated by Edmund Jephcott), London: New York, Continuum.

Elias, N. and Scotson, J.L. (2008). *The Established and the Outsiders. A Sociological Enquiry into Community Problems*, Dublin, University College Dublin Press (1965 version London: Frank Cass & Co.).

Escudier, A. (2016). "Chapitre 4: La question des générations. Généalogie d'une notion", in Anne Muxel, Temps et politique, Presses de Sciences Po (P.F.N.S.P.), "Académique", pp. 87–104.

Kimmerling, B. (2001). *The Invention and Decline of Israeliness: State, Culture and Military in Israel*, Los Angeles and Berkeley, University of California Press.

Mannheim, K. (1952). "The Problem of Generations": in P. Kecskemeti, Essays on the Sociology of Knowledge: Collected Works, Volume 5. New York: Routledge. p. 276–322.

Maza, S. (2017). *Thinking About History*. London, Chicago: University of Chicago Press.

Mosse, G. (1974). *The Nationalization of the Masses: Political Symbolism and Mass Movements in Germany from the Napoleonic Wars through the Third Reich*, New York, Howard Ferting.

Myers, D.N. (1995). *Reinventing the Jewish Past: European Jewish Intellectuals and the Zionist Return to History*, New York: Oxford University Press.

Penslar, D.J. (2007). *Israel in History: The Jewish State in Comparative Perspective*, London: New York, Routledge.

Roodenburg H.W. (2004). "Pierre Bourdieu: Issues of Embodiment and Authenticity". *Etnofoor* 17(1/2): 215–226.

Sadri, A. (1992). *Max Weber's Sociology of Intellectuals*, New York: Oxford, Oxford University Press.

Sapiro, G. (2015). "Habitus: History of a Concept" in J.D. Wright (editor-in-chief), International Encyclopedia of the Social & Behavioral Sciences, 2nd edition, Vol 10. Oxford: Elsevier. pp. 484–489.

Sirinelli, J.-F. (1988). *Génération Intellectuelle. Khâgneux et normaliens dans l'entre-deux guerres*, Paris, Fayard.

Smith, A.D. (1991). *National Identity*, London: New York [etc.], Penguin Books.

Sand, S. (2000). "Ha 'Intelektual, h a'Emet ve' hakoah—Meparashet Dreyfus ve'Ed Milkhemet Ha'Mifratz" (in English: "The Intellectual, Truth and Power—From the Dreyfus Affair to the Gulf War"), Tel-Aviv, Am Oved Publishing (in Hebrew)

Sand, S. (2011). *The Words and the Land*, Los Angeles, Semiotext (English translation of the original French edition: "Les Mots et la Terre", Paris, Fayard, [2006]).

Weber, M. (1919 [original essay]). "Science as a Vocation" in Eisenstadt, S.N. (1968): *Max Weber: On Charisma and Institution Building*, Chicago: London, The University of Chicago Press.

Winock, M.: "Les générations intellectuelles", *Vingtième Siècle: Revue d'Histoire*, n°22, avril–juin 1989, pp. 17–38.

PART II

A Guide for the Journey: Conceptual Maps and Processual Tools

CHAPTER 2

Habitus, National Identity and State-Building

This chapter provides an analytical and conceptual overlook that will accompany our enquiry about Israeli historians and their interrelations with the national habitus who they interiorize and experience as individuals but also contribute to shape. The chapter opens with a section which follows the literature, chiefly based on Bourdieu's and Elias's works, that frames the study of Israeli national historiography. The conceptual tools of *habitus*, *survival unit* and *field* are applied in a two-way relationship between what are socially considered to be the objective structures (those of social fields and power-ratios and survival unit) and the incorporated structures (those of the habitus) in order to trace socially relevant dispositions. The goal is to combine the overlapping interpretation by the two scholars with the aim to unpack Israel's national identity in the chapters that follow. Furthermore, it includes sociopolitical observations about national identity and generations, as they have been used in the study.

The chapter's second part systematizes historical writing as a scholarly profession that is intrinsically linked to the making of national ideas for a collective identity to be formalized. By doing so, the chapter invites the reader to bear in mind that history-writing navigates "between the Scylla of an untenable theory of history as an objective compilation of facts [...] and the Charybdis of an equally untenable theory of history as the subjective product of the mind of the historian who establishes the facts of history and masters them through the process of interpretation, between a

© The Author(s), under exclusive license to Springer Nature Switzerland AG 2024
A. Helled, *Israel's National Historiography*, Palgrave Studies on Norbert Elias, https://doi.org/10.1007/978-3-031-62795-8_2

view of history having the centre of gravity in the past and a view having the centre of gravity in the present" (Carr, 1961/1990, p. 29). It thus provides a short sociological profile of intellectuals which is then applied to the context of national construction. The latter serves as the starting point of the generational analysis of Israeli historians, from which the categorizations are explored in Chap. 3 and the following derived.

THE FRAMEWORK OF THE HISTORIOGRAPHICAL FIELD: HABITUS AND GENERATIONS

Habitus, survival unit and field all denote structural, yet dynamic, relations between individuals situated within a spatio-temporal process, whose power-ratios undergo different moments of adaptation and resistance, integration and disintegration (the Eliasian civilizing processes of interrelational humanizing dependencies or the laws of attraction and repulsion that are at the heart of Bourdieusian field theory).[1] Habitus, an intrinsic psycho-sociological set of cultural norms, values and codes of behaviour, is embodied in socialized individuals who processually acquire these dispositions while becoming a collectivity. The latter, built through the integration of its members, enables group survival, since unity of dispositions facilitate non-violent relations and a common sense of belonging. The habitus, therefore, operates as the structuring mechanism of what has been sometimes referred to as bio-social survival.[2] In this regard, the Eliasian survival unit echoes the need to overcome difficulties in a sometimes-hostile environment. Not only does the survival unit mean a degree of interdependencies, as a specific collective social figuration, but it also means a dialectical space, occupied and experienced by individuals. In this book, the survival unit is Israel as the nation-state of the Jewish people. This constellation is justified by the fact that much of the

---

[1] Sapiro (2015a, b) retains that sociological adaptation of the "field" is made possible to "circumscribe individuals' action at the mesolevel, in differentiated social spheres with their own rules of the game and specific interests [...] implementing relational and topographical approach of the social world" (p. 140).

[2] The basic idea of traditional bio-sociology was, of course, that society like nature meant "a place of open competition, of struggle for survival in which only the fittest perpetuate their kind [...]", Dolby "On the Autonomy of Pure Science" (p. 282) in *Scientific Establishments and Hierarchies* (1982). Yet, a habitus can equally lead to self-sacrifice (such as in the case of soldiers falling in battle), thus opposed to survival of the single individual while prioritizing the endurance of the group.

collectivization force of Zionism, both ideologically and organizationally, aimed to concretize Jewish national unity in light of historical persecutions (culminated in the Shoah). The pursuit after a safe haven did not end with Israel's independence in 1948. The rationale of survival became the vulgate by which the state socialized its citizenry in light of never-ending perils (neighbouring Arab countries, the Palestinians, Iran etc.). This has influenced and conditioned much of Israel's national habitus. Not only has it trivialized and banalized Jewish nationalism (Billig 1995) but also routinized the existential threat, thus enhancing the common feeling of collective insecurity. The latter, consequently, triggers a double effect: on the one hand, it results in a "revisionist sieged society", capable of producing only securitarian-led politics (Del Sarto 2017), and on the other, the sociopolitical and sociocultural compartmentalization of non-Jews (de Swaan 2015), which creates barriers in terms of trust, deficient democratic citizenship and sectorial cleavages (as we shall see in Chap. 5: "*Artziyut*").

Needless to say, the Israeli survival unit is also the "vessel" in which Israeli historians interact, as citizens and members of the national collectivity. In order to differentiate the conceptual emphatic strength of the macro sociological notion of "survival unit"—referred to the unit of Jewish Israelis—we will use the concept of "field" in order to demarcate the objective relations between positions of individuals within the specific domain of academia, applied to Israeli historiography. The latter suits the conceptual, either symbolic or material, struggles of stakeholders who confront each other, with differentiated means and ends according to their position in an institutionalized autonomous structure, while their interactions (similar to Elias's figurational dynamics) contribute to conserve or transform the former (Bourdieu 1988, 1998). In this sense, Israeli national historiography, defined as Zionist and Jewish, demonstrates both objective and subjective distinctions (Bourdieu 1984), inasmuch as it marks out the established canons of Israel in relation to the otherness of Arab-Palestinian history. These dynamics, of course, engender social practices and representations, which present themselves as indelible and natural reality and, as such, are easily reproduced (Bourdieu and Wacquant 1992). As such the field dialectically competes and dialogues with the Eliasian idea of human figurations that conceptualizes interactions and evolving networks of inter-group independencies in terms of power, behaviour, emotions and knowledge (Elias 2000; Loyal and Quilley 2004).

Either conceptualized as fruit of positionings within a determined field, or the stratification of integrational collectivization of a survival unit, the habitus plays a role in our enquiry of Israeli historiography, since it implies the profound and unconscious existence of psychologically disciplined socialized "selves" (Elias, "The society of Individuals"), hence, self-restraint, not only vis-à-vis short-term emotional impulsiveness but in relation to the prescriptively determined social conduct, as well. Featuring durable and generalizable dispositions that suffuse human action, the often-cited multi-layered "psychic make-up" is a dynamic process beginning from "the soil from which grow the personal characteristics through which an individual differs from other members of his society", or the "unmistakable individual handwriting that grows out of the social script" (Elias 2001a, b, 182).[3] Nevertheless, and despite the fact that every single individual is different from the other, there are specific marks which are shared by all in-group members (the Durkheimian institutionalized social facts, or Maussian incorporated anthropological bodies),[4] therefore, enabling to observe and classify different aspects of we-I balances (Elias 2001a, b). Furthermore, the habitus is generationally "deposited" and, consequently, form mental schemata that collectivity bears for itself but also hands down to future members. It is thus a strategic "structuring mechanism" of sedimented social orientation (Bourdieu and Wacquant 1992). The habitus constructs as it is constructed. That does not mean that the habitus does not undergo long-term variations to influence its development and social specificity. Some configurational properties might remain unaltered, whereas others might differ significantly depending on the conditions of (dis)integration within the group of reference as well as on external constellations to it (e.g., threats, competition, homologation with other groups etc.). It is dialectically relational.

The dynamicity of the habitus in structuring the mental dispositions and conduct within collectivity is shaped and contained in the figurational survival unit. The latter encounters "spurts and counter-spurts" along its way, while "[A]gain and again a rising outsider stratum or a rising 'survival unit' as a whole, a tribe or a nation state, attains the functions and characteristics of an establishment in relation to other outsider strata or survival units which, on their part, are pressing from below, from their position as oppressed outsiders, against the current establishment" (Elias 2000, 382).

---

[3] This metaphor dialogues with the Bourdieusian definition of the "habitus" as "feel for the game" or "practical sense"; see Bourdieu (1990).

[4] See Desrosières (1991). "Social Science, Statistics and the State" in *Discourses on Society: The Shaping of the Social Science Disciplines—Sociology of the Sciences.*

According to Elias, the survival unit's persistence, in time and space, is made possible only if it keeps securing structural durability through a meaningful social unit vis-à-vis external and internal social units alike. Whatever shapes and is shaped through the process of habitus formation, it is the result of the interdependencies inside or outside the boundaries of the survival unit. Their gradual formation in history is the reason for their relative primacy, their durability and resistance (namely, self-reliance and self-regulation which guarantee inner integration and conformity to a solid social habitus).[5] Here the modern nation-state seems to be the superior kind of survival unit, according to Elias, since it monopolizes the means of violence and subjects individuals to its rules by homologizing and demarcating them via a unifying principle; a dominant pressure "urging people towards state integration now usually leaves the pre-state units, such as tribes, only the choice between preserving their identity as a kind of museum piece, a stagnant backwater on the periphery of a rapidly developing humanity, or renouncing a part of their identity and therefore the traditional social habitus of their members [...]" (Elias (2001a, b). "Society of Individuals", 214). Therefore, the nation-state efficiently succeeds in embedding and embodying societal integration, at least in theory. The nation-state "ossifies" we-images as ineluctable, providing a common social habitus which is "immovably tied by a strong affective charge" (ibid., 220).

The psycho-social stability of different survival units, as well as their relational character, either conflictual or pacific (Kilminster 2007), becomes a key element in the "frontlines of civilization" (van Vree 2002). This process is, of course, possible due to "we-feelings", associated with family, ethnicity, religion, economics and so forth.[6] It is the astute sense of belonging which is taken for granted as the interiorized habitus presents almost behavioural automatism. Consequently, the sphere of historical geopolitical events and changes, shaping the interactions between habitus

---

[5] As argued by Elias: "[O]ne of the characteristics which make this connection between the size of and pressure within the network of interdependence on the one hand, and the psychological make-up of the individual [the 'habitus'] on the other particularly clear, is what; we call the 'tempo' of our time. This 'tempo' is in fact nothing other than a manifestation of the multitude of intertwining chains of interdependence which run through every single social function that people have to perform, and of the competitive pressure that permeates this densely populated network, affecting directly or indirectly every single individual act" (Elias 2000, 379).

[6] This has been shown by Mennell (2007). *The American Civilising Process.*

and survival unit, influences the narration and codification of events as solid "facts" to be then interiorized. That is to poise the concepts at both the level of nation-state-based politics, where macro phenomena take place thanks to states' organizational capacity and its ideological penetration, on the one hand, and that of micro-social lives, such as solidarity networks and national identity-bound personal experiences, on the other.[7]

In this regard, the magnifying glass of "generations" becomes useful. Since the habitus contained by the survival unit shows both continuity and change, over rather long spans of time, different generations mirror the transformation in interdependencies, whilst providing a temporal dimension to the habitus in intergenerational chains (Van Krieken 1998). What and how future generations would feel and act in relation to the survival unit and the habitus can thus be traced. One might even assume a certain correspondence between the set of social conditions and the habitus, as developed within people from childhood onwards, much beyond any anagraphical identification. The generational transmission process of the habitus, however, is by no means linear and may even face noteworthy fractures and countertendencies in the chain, depending on the compatibility of sociopolitical context and other, more or less, objective situational conditions.[8] As pointed out by Escudier (2016), "generation", as a concept, acquired its meaning during the second half of the nineteenth century, once it gained the status of "history-science" (French, *histoire-science*), which empirically explained and periodized what were perceived as the great sociopolitical transformations of the time, while offering a "generational arithmetic" (Escudier 2016, 89). Similar to the critical reflections by Karl Mannheim ("*The Problem of Generations*", 1928/1952), generations are more than the formulation of sequential groupings engaged in interrelational dynamics (cooperation, indifference but also intergenerational and intra-generational competition between individuals). Generations are also fruit of institutional organizations, educational techniques and patterns of collective behaviour in historical perspective, that is, the habitus. Yet, each and every generation sets the surroundings

[7] On the successful mechanisms of the "national" to ground society, see Malešević S. (2019). *Grounded Nationalisms*. On the personal experience changing in relation to society, see Elias (2001a). *The Loneliness of the Dying*.

[8] When this kind of sociological sensibility is deployed, it opens any sort of analysis to "the connection between the survival value of knowledge and its usefulness; social reality as perspectival; the relation between interdependence and integration; the distinction between interaction and interdependence [...]" (Kilminster 2007, 44).

for the succeeding one.[9] The ability to (re)act to these surroundings largely depends upon "[T]he transmission of group understandings from generation to generation [which] is an interpretative as well as a selective process. Each act of transmission sifts, interprets, and selects certain elements from past experience [...]" (Mannheim 1956, 83). The main aspect is, therefore, experienceable time, namely interiorized experiences and reciprocal influences, perceived not as a simple chronological datum but as a unit of history consisting in intellectual evolution and social structures. Consequently, the succession of generations implies continuity and/or discontinuity of thought, hence, open the path to the invention and re-invention of traditions, as demonstrated Hobsbawm and Ranger (1983), as well as to the social construction of collective memory (Traverso 2005, 2010).

The interplay between generations witnesses the importance of history. The latter is the playground of tendencies of convergence and divergence affecting the dispositions and interdependencies within the survival unit and the habitus it fosters. Structural conditions are of great impact. These provide metahistorical strata which further strengthen the depth and breadth of any generational analysis. Koselleck (1989), for instance, links mankind's life-circles to the immense continuum of history.[10] Generations exist within socio-historical realities whose context differs, while history continues. Cohorts of social agency who present similar attitudes, world-views, beliefs and goals in life are grounded in a shared historical-biographical past. However, social formation is not all-inclusive, considering that variables such as class, religion, ethnicity and gender cannot be fully comprised and might reveal differential degrees of agency. Not only do such dialectics set the identification by others, as opposed to self-identification (which many contemporary individuals are allowed to claim in post-modernist thought), but they also entail continuous negotiations between individual and collective social legitimacy. The case of the

---

[9] According to Mannheim (1998, pp. 12–13): "[O]ne set of educational influences is preparing the new generation to practise and defend their rational self-interest in a competitive world, while another lays the emphasis on unselfishness, social service and subordination to common ends. One set of social influences is guided by the ideal of asceticism and repression, the other by the wish to encourage self-expression".

[10] "The succession of generations leads to the existence of a plurality of experiential spaces that overlap each other and, like different strata, are distinct from each other and exclude one another" (Koselleck 1989, 650): "Linguistic Change and the History of Events", *Journal of Modern History*, Vol. 61, No. 4 (Dec., 1989), pp. 649–666.

national sense of belonging which is "injected" and produced by the habitus in order to secure the survival unit of the nation-state exemplifies generational variation, despite the pursuit after continuity and stability. In this sense, the role of historians seems highly relevant. But what makes it so special? The next section will examine history as an intellectual profession which encapsulates an inherent degree of politicization in its capacity to disseminate national identity.

History as a Profession: Making National Ideas for Collective Identity

Intellectuals are considered to have had a special role in offering schemas of interpretation to social reality. The construction of national identity, as a part of a seemingly generalized and universalized forma mentis, exemplified the contribution of intellectual professions to the collectivizing effort in the eighteenth century onwards. Either through naturalist positivism or through emotion-driven romanticism, scholars attempted to historicize ideas and events in light of the supposedly collective and omnipresent *Zeitgeist*. By subdividing a presumed universal history into different epochal generations, these scholars attributed "historic conscience" to the past in relation to the present, way beyond any chronographic function.[11] Political subjects such as clans, religious and ethnic groups were morphologically historicized and categorized, providing cultural, racial and political hierarchy to nascent nations and states, while reflecting their unique *Volksgeist*, that is, "Spirit of a people" (Gellner 1983, 1997). The meticulous work of historians, philologists, archaeologists, anthropologists and others sets the ground for people's cooperation, contrast or indifference under the aegis of the nation-state (Malešević 2019), once history was perceived as rationally scientific (the legacy of European Enlightenment embodied by scholars such as Johann Gottfried Herder, Johann Gottlieb Fichte, Jules Michelet, John Richard Green). History-writing thus aimed to give sense to the past through the reconstruction of earlier representations in their irreducible precise specificity and concreteness. The interpretation of materials (mostly archival)

---

[11] Starting from the traditional biblical models, constricted in their geographical and chronological parameters, through the Eurocentric Hegelian notion of presumed "universal history" (meaning reason's self-realization in history) to the recent attempts to define a perspective of "global history" regarding the realm of ideas beyond that of cosmopolitanism or that of capital-based colonialism. See Sartori and Moyn (2012): "Approaches to Global Intellectual History" in *Global Intellectual History*.

was, and has been, the main challenge for historians. According to Skinner (2002), history-writing must not fall into any paradigmatic traps of parochial bias or personal prejudice. Yet, only few would assert that history is weight-free of everything which deals with subjective meaning and experience, text and context. After all, the elaboration of facts is conditioned by both language and ex post construction, since only rarely does the historian process history in actu (Chartier 1982; Koselleck 1989). Hence, the thematization of history as an actual processual sequence of events and what is said about it are two different things, though indistinguishable in their interaction.[12] This consideration emphasizes the key role of personal perspective, conditioned by social and political status (fruit of position in the field and socialized habitus), but which does not necessarily determine historiographic quality. That said, there is no doubt that national historiography presents different sentiments and sensibilities, anchored to a certain type of "peoplehood" in a certain period of time, especially since it articulates and moulds a proper historical vocabulary.[13] This last point raises the question of how to address and delineate national history, in relation to its intellectual sociogenesis. In Eliasian terminology (Elias 2000), the latter concept refers to the primal social action and codes of behaviour as they are carried out within the boundaries of affectively neutral impersonal criteria. These standardize and moderate forms of expression which shape the dispositional features of the collective habitus (hence a distinctive yet related aspect from what Elias denotes as "psychogenesis", that is to say, the processes of developing individual self-control and self-discipline). In our case, we shall see that the intellectual codes and zeitgeist of each and every historiographical generation are rooted in the political sphere from which the Zionist national identity-building process originated.

---

[12] In his treaties on history and philosophy, Raymond Aron (2011) articulated the problem of history-writing vis-à-vis the world (both inner and external) of the historian in charge of elaborating the sense of consequential events into historical conscience.

[13] In Israeli historiography, terms such as "Arabs\Palestinians", "Aliyah\Immigration", "terrorists\freedom-fighters", "Mizrahi Jews\Easterners" and others, show the complexity in selecting a proper terminology. It is a twofold challenge. On the one hand, historians neither wish to provoke the public 'politically correctness', nor to confront political sanctions that might hinder their careers; whereas, on the other hand, the choice in wording always reveals their historiographical sensibility and the political stand they wish to express in a determined context (the period about which they write but also that in which they write). By consequence, terminology combines both personal and structural elements in the academic profession.

More broadly, politicization and/or doctrinal mythicization, some-times causing de-contextualization for the sake of national (artificial) coherence of crucial events, such as great battles of independence,[14] are parts of habitus formation, when applied to the creation of collective identities based on the nation-state. National identity is to be experi-enced by collectivity. It is not fruit of accidental spontaneous senti-ments, inasmuch as its construction entails the selection of cultural segments from the past, such as events and personalities, texts and myths (intimately related to the formalization of national language and literature), later to be celebrated by generations in the form of public commemorations and national epopees. Either the fruit of proto-histor-ical, symbolic and ethnical genealogies (Connor 1990, 1994; Smith 1986, 1991) or of collectivizing imaginary materialized in rituals, praxis, common knowledge and heritage within modern identities (Anderson 2006; Hobsbawm and Ranger 1983; Thiesse 1999), national identity requires to be mapped and organized. Not only is history-writ-ing the dispositive that represents the starting point for national identity to be reasoned and accomplished, but it is also a codifying channel for the *mythomoteur* to achieve scientific legitimacy and gain institutional relevance (Thiesse 2007; Smith 1986).

In this sense, the effort of thinking history and systematize it (already questioned by Georg Simmel in his 1905 essay "How is History Possible?" [see Simmel 1971]) are the same questions applied to nationhood (Brubaker 1996). Consequently, the attribution of status to any so-called national history cannot avoid politicization. As summarized by Matonti (2012, 98): "[B]oth ideas and history do not advance autonomously". The two depend on the reception and decision-making of politics. The intellectual challenge is, therefore, to gain epistemological self-awareness, or better yet, self-reflexivity, with regard to the studied event. No histori-cal facts are to be considered "pure" because they are subjectively refracted through the mind of the historian. This becomes exceptionally relevant, once historians work on their own national history, considering the dispo-sitions of the national habitus which they interiorize as members of the survival unit. In other words, national historians find themselves in a situ-ation in which they are compelled to critically bridge between objectivity and subjectivity, and "react" to their own mental pictures and "national

---

[14] Matonti (2012) refers to these key events as "ruptures of intelligibility", "critical moments" and "multi-sectorial mobilization", showing the intellectual weight conveyed by such a speculation of political ideas.

character" (Elias 2008, 2013; Mennell 2020[15]). Notwithstanding, the legitimacy of this scholarly operation can only be evaluated by peers who work on similar topics in the same field (this is why the categorization of Israeli national historians is anchored to Israel studies and Jewish history departments). Rarely do inexpert readers have the ability to deal with the analysis of a past which is unknown to them. History-writing is first of all a hermeneutic effort which enables and legitimizes a plurality of interpretations, sometimes contradictory and not always equally consistent. Many are the challenges in this regard.

According to E. H. Carr (1990)[16] historians face "raw materials", sometimes partial, which thus necessitate the use of "auxiliary sciences", namely, archaeology, epigraphy, numismatics, chronology and so forth, while looking to fill in gaps. Even stronger in his description of the craft was Le Goff (1988), who confessed that historians have to "invent" materiality as well as imagery. That is to say that there is no real imaginary antithesis between single individuals and their social world, as Eliasian theory clearly shows. With regard to the specific task of history-writing, the relation between material objectivity and individual subjectivity further delineates that historiography has much in common with social sciences and psychology.[17]

In this respect, contemporary history-writing has already denounced most of the empirico-positivistic heritage of nineteenth-century historiography (often with direct references to German historian Leopold von Ranke) (Sand 2017). Nevertheless, the role played by nationalism has been kept somewhat unchanged in academia. National history remains a divider, which defines "We" and "Others" through the determination of the universal all-devouring, multi-functional, all-embracing features of the

---

[15] Elias, N. (2008). "National peculiarities of British public opinion". in *Essays II: On Civilising Processes, State Formation and National Identity*, vol. 15, 230–55. Dublin: UCD Press; ibid., (2013). *Studies on the Germans: Power Struggles and the Development of Habitus in the Nineteenth and Twentieth Centuries*, vol. 11. Dublin: UCD Press; and Mennell, S. (2020). "Power, Individualism, and Collective Self Perception in the USA".

[16] Carr, E. H. (1990): *What Is History?*. The book is a sort of study-manifesto against empiricism within historiography which in six chapters ("lessons") posits historians against historical facts, society, science and morality (bias), historical causation, human progress, historiographical developments.

[17] All these disciplines are interactive in their process of thinking, namely the formulation of hypotheses via periodization, "geographical" partition between individual and collectivity, generalizable analogies.

modern nation-state.[18] The habitus, which it codifies, may be linked to either democratic and republican patriotism (in terms of civil religion) or social exclusion and intolerance (Viroli 1995). Yet, beyond the frequent—some would say inevitable virulent nationalistic drifts—the aim of any national history has been fostering political congruence in terms of both sentiment and movement (Gellner 1983), which can be considered either as the mobilization of the nationalist sentiment or as a historically predestined development. The idea of predestination presents no novelty. Western history had been much influenced by the religious belief in the Holy Scriptures. Jews and Christians alike had postulated a going-forward theological history with a deep theodicean sense which implied the eventual tangible end of history itself.

Even seemingly enlightened and modern historians, such as Edward Gibbon (*The History of the Decline and Fall of the Roman Empire*, 1776–1788), had emphasized human (Hegelian) progress, strictly linked to the notion of civilization. Hence, despite the opposite perspectives (godly salvation vs. conquest of reason), traditional history-writing gave importance to more or less collective past experiences by conserving, elaborating and handing down chronicles which served as focal elements to facilitate the social acquisition of national identities. Therefore, history-writing had to be based upon general causes and effects over men (legacy of thinkers such as Montesquieu and Tocqueville). This rationale made long-term analysis the core task of historians, suitable to the search after continuity, change and quasi-repetitions within "holistic" structural coherences (Braudel 1958).[19] Consequently, history became useful to politics. The cooperation between the two enabled to obtain socially normative and pervasive "fusion of culture and polity which is the essence of nationalism" (Gellner 1983, p. 13), based on the triadic construction of people, state and territory. This selectively combined national habitus implied the engagement, both material and emotional, in the construction of a self-evident and entropy-resistant collective identity (Kuzmics et al. 2020).

---

[18] This feature seems to be historically ineluctable. Even Lord Acton, who had envisaged a distinct universal history and pronounced an apparently total disagreement with national histories, left some relevance to nations, viewed as subordinated and subsidiary to history in its entirety. *The Cambridge Modern History: an account of its origin, authorship and production* (1907).

[19] One may even be tempted to consider Braudel's view contiguous with Eliasian figurational sociology, since both seek to understand the profound stratifications in history itself (much against anachronistic historiographies).

This point is the core of this book, as already illustrated in the introduction. The case of political Zionism (Jewish nationalism) which identified the land of Palestine with the land of Canaan (once the unified biblical realm of Israel and Judea), as formalized by the Hebrew Scriptures, gradually became an alternative to Jewish assimilation (caused by legal emancipation and secularization in nineteenth-century Europe), since the latter could not escape the racial (and racist) ideological hold of anti-Semitism. Nevertheless, by actualizing an ancient past beyond effective historicity, religion became an instrumental repository of historic continuity to revive Jewishness as a political national project. That is not to say genuine ancient traditions lacked from Jewish practices, namely Kashrut laws, Hebrew as the liturgical language, the Torah ark facing Jerusalem etc., but it means that their nationalization and adaptability to the Zionist enterprise reinvented a symbolic usage which had neither been inherent to Judaism nor been socially "inherited" beforehand. In the construction of national Jewish identity symbols, such as the national anthem (the *Hatikvah*, lit. English "The Hope"),[20] the emblem of the state (i.e., the Menorah)[21] and the national flag (a reinterpretation of the Jewish *tallit*) (the prayer shawl) combined with the star of David, are all products of an invention which is no other than the objectification of myths aiming to provide a solid national identity to the, terminologically "invented", Jewish people (Sand 2009).[22] These politico-cultural products formalized a cosmic order in

---

[20] The *Hatikvah* (originally *Tikvateinu* ["Our Hope"] is a nine-stanza poem which was written by Jewish poet Naphtali Herz Imber (1856–1909) and whose melody was composed by Samuel Cohen (1870–1940). It was inspired by several folksongs, mainly from Eastern Europe. It had been chosen as the anthem by the members of the First Zionist Congress in 1897, and was unofficially proclaimed as the national anthem of the State of Israel in 1948 (officially sanctioned as such only in 2004). The text reads: "As long as the Jewish spirit is yearning deep in the heart; With eyes turned toward the East, looking toward Zion, then our hope—the two-thousand-year-old hope—will not be lost: To be a free people in our land, The land of Zion and Jerusalem". The text is available in both Hebrew and English at: http://www.stateofisrael.com/anthem.

[21] A menorah surrounded by an olive branch on each side, and the writing "ישראל" (Hebrew for Israel) below it. Designed by brothers Gabriel Shamir (1909–1992) and Maxim Shamir (1910–1990), the shape took inspiration from passages from the book of the prophet Zechariah, and later partially modified, according to the will of the national symbol and flag commission (1948–1949). The image of the relief of the Arch of Titus in Rome for the symbol was inserted to emphasize the return to the "Promised Land".

[22] The categories of "Jewish nation" and "Jewish people" soon acquired interchangeable meaning. See Sand (2009), p. 256–271.

which God guides and protects his "chosen people" from any possible harm; while, Zionist politics juxtaposed the catastrophes of pogroms and the Holocaust in Diaspora to independence and survival in the land of Israel. Of course, "nationally" speaking, this process becomes viable only when a sufficiently shared collective habitus succeeds in maintaining a solid survival unit.[23]

In conclusion, the chapter sought to provide conceptual overview of the sociopolitical "geography", that is, the sociopolitical map with which to address the thematic macro-topics of our enquiry. Habitus and generations help to contextualize nationalism and nation-building processes, history-writing as both a personal experience and a scholarly profession, useful to formalize collective identities. The latter may be reflected through the former, as much as the other way round. The historical interpretation is never exclusively confined to the sole consideration of means, context and knowledge at disposal. It consists in linguistic and cognitive elements which are based on ideas (and ideologies), on trend and fashions as well as on the way each and every historian situates him-/herself within a specific contextualization vis-à-vis "facts". By introducing "habitus", "generations" and "survival unit" as parts of processual socialization, the intellectual *milieu* of Israeli historians will show itself not only under a purely academic profile but primarily as a sociopolitical and cultural field that crosses, as it is crossed by Israeli society at large. In the next chapter we shall dive into the generational social history of Israeli national historiography in relation to the history of Israel as a state in process. We will thus reconstruct the historiographical profession, starting from its sociogenesis (prior to Israeli independence), and will place it on the junction where national processes shaping the Israeli Zionist habitus cross changes in the identity of the Jewish survival unit. The chapter will offer the reader three historiographical, and national, generations from which one might generalize different aspects of the nation-state.

---

[23] Here national memory, as the set of representations of the past (museums, memorials, honorary foundations etc.), plays an essential role. However, any self-asserted images of the past, national symbols or ritual commemorations of remembrance will not be possible without historians' contribution, as well as those of other scholars such as archaeologists, anthropologists, pedagogists etc.

REFERENCES

Anderson, B. (2006). *"Imagined Communities: Reflections on the Origin and Spread of Nationalism"* [revised edition], London: New York, Verso.

Aron, R. (2011). "Dimensions de la Conscience Historique" [préface de Perrine Simon-Nahum], Paris, Les Belles Lettres.

Billig, M. (1995). *Banal Nationalism*, London: Thousand Oaks: New Delhi, Sage Publications.

Bourdieu, P. (1984). *Distinction: A social Critique of the Judgement of Taste* (translated by Richard Nice), Cambridge [MA: USA], Harvard University Press.

Bourdieu, P. (1988). "Homo Academicus", Stanford, Stanford University Press [CA] (original edition in French (1984), Editions Minuit, Paris).

Bourdieu, P. (1990). *The Logic of Practice*, Stanford, Stanford University Press.

Bourdieu, P. (1998). *Practical Reason: On the Theory of Action*, Stanford, Stanford University Press.

Bourdieu, P., & Wacquant, L. J. D. (1992). *An Invitation to Reflexive Sociology*, Cambridge: Chicago Press University & Polity Press.

Braudel, F. (1958). "Histoire et Sciences Sociales: La Longue Durée", in *Annales. Économies, Sociétés, Civilisations*. 13ᵉ année, N. 4, 1958. pp. 725–753.

Brubaker, R. (1996). *Nationalism Reframed. Nationhood and the National Question in the New Europe*, Cambridge, Cambridge University Press.

Carr, E. H. (1990). *What Is History?* [second and revised edition of the 1961 edition], ed. Davies, R.W., Harmondsworth, London: New York [etc.], Penguin Books.

Chartier, R. (1982). *"Intellectual History or Sociocultural History"* in Modern European Intellectual History [eds. LaCapra, D., and Kaplan, S.L.], Ithaca: London, Cornell University Press.

Connor, W. (1990). "When is a Nation?". *Ethnic and Racial Studies* 13(1): 92–103.

Connor, W. (1994). *Ethnonationalism. The Quest for Understanding*. Princeton: Princeton University Press.

Del Sarto, R. A. (2017). *Israel under siege: the politics of insecurity and the rise of the Israeli neo-revisionist right*, Washington: Georgetown University Press.

De Swaan, A. (2015). *The Killing Compartments: The Mentality of Mass Murder*, New Haven: London, Yale University Press.

Desrosières, A. (1991). "Social Science, Statistics and the State" in "Discourses on Society: The Shaping of the Social Science Disciplines—Sociology of the Sciences": A Yearbook-Volume XV, 1991, edited by Wagner, P., Wittrock, B. and Whitley, R., Dordrecht: Boston: London, Kluwer Academic Publishers.

Dolby, R. G. A. (1982). "On the Autonomy of Pure Science" in Elias, N., Martins, H., and Whitley, R. "Scientific Establishments And Hierarchies" [edited by], Sociology of the Sciences: A Yearbook 1982, D. Reidel Publishing Company: Springer Netherlands Dordrecht: Holland/Boston: USA/London: England.

Elias, N. (2000). *The Civilizing Process: Sociogenetic and Psychogenetic Investigations* (revised edition), translated by Jephcott, E. with some notes and corrections by the author and edited by Dunning, E., Goudsblom, J., and Mennell, S., Malden: Oxford: Carlton, Blackwell Publishing.

Elias, N. (2001a). *The Loneliness of the Dying* (translated by Jephcott, E.), New York: London.

Elias, N. (2001b). *The Society of Individuals* (edited by Schroeter, M. and translated by Jephcott, E.), London: New York, Continuum.

Elias, N. (2008). *On Civilising Processes, State Formation and National Identity*, Vol. 15, 230–55. Dublin: UCD Press.

Elias, N. (2013). *Studies on the Germans: Power Struggles and the Development of Habitus in the Nineteenth and Twentieth Centuries*, vol. 11. Dublin: UCD Press.

Escudier, A. (2016). Chapitre 4: "*La question des générations. Généalogie d'une notion*", *in* Anne Muxel, *Temps et politique*, Presses de Sciences Po (P.F.N.S.P.), "Académique", pp. 87–104.

Gellner, E. (1983). *Nations and Nationalism*, Oxford, Basil Blackwell.

Gellner, E. (1997). *Nationalism*, London, Weidenfeld & Nicolson.

Hobsbawm, E., Ranger, T. [ed.] (1983). *The Invention of Tradition*, Cambridge: New York, Cambridge University Press.

Kilminster, R. (2007). *Norbert Elias: Post-philosophical Sociology*, Abingdon: New York, Routledge.

Koselleck, R. (1989). "Linguistic Change and the History of Events", *Journal of Modern History*, Vol. 61, No. 4 (Dec., 1989), pp. 649–666.

Kuzmics, H., Reicher, D., & Hughes, J. (2020). State, Emotion, Authority, and National Habitus. State-Related Problems of Our Time and Methodological Discourses in Sociology and Historical Sociology. *Historical Social Research/Historische Sozialforschung*, 45(1 (171)), 7–41.

Le Goff, J. (1988). *The Medieval Imagination* (trans. Goldhammer, A.), Chicago: University of Chicago Press.

Loyal, S. & Quilley, S. [edited by] (2004). *The Sociology of Norbert Elias*, Cambridge: New York [etc.], Cambridge University Press.

Malešević, S. (2019). *Grounded Nationalisms: A Sociological Analysis*, Cambridge, Cambridge University Press.

Mannheim, K. (1956). *Essays on the Sociology of Culture* [Collected Works, Vol. VII], Abingdon: New York, Routledge.

Mannheim, K. (1998). "*Diagnosis of Our Time: Wartime Essays of a Sociologist*" (collected works vol. III), New York, Routledge.

Matonti, F. (2012). "*Plaidoyer pour une histoire sociale des idées politiques*", *Revue d'histoire moderne et contemporaine*, 5/2012 (n° 59–4bis), pp. 85–104.

Mennell, S. (2007). *The American Civilising Process*. Cambridge: Malden, Polity Press.

Mennell, S. (2020). Power, Individualism, and Collective Self Perception in the USA. *Historical Social Research*, 45(1), 309–329.

Sand, S. (2009). *The Invention of the Jewish People* (translated from the Hebrew by Yael Lotan), London and New York, Verso.

Sand, S. (2017). *History in Twilight: Reflexions on Time and Truth*, London, Verso.

Sapiro, G. (2015a). "Field Theory", in Wright, J. D. (editor-in-chief), International Encyclopedia of the Social & Behavioral Sciences, 2nd edition, Vol. 9, Oxford: Elsevier. pp. 140–148.

Sapiro, G. (2015b). "Habitus: History of a Concept" in Wright, J. D. (editor-in-chief), International Encyclopedia of the Social & Behavioral Sciences, 2nd edition, Vol 10, pp. 484–489.

Sartori, A., Moyn, S. (2012). *Global Intellectual History*, New York, Columbia University Press.

Simmel, G. (1971). *On Individuality and Social Forms* (selected writings edited and with an introduction by Levine, D. N., Chicago: London, The University of Chicago Press.

Skinner, Q. (2002). "Meaning and Understanding in the history of ideas", in *Visions of Politics*, Vol. 1. 'Regarding Method', Cambridge, Cambridge University Press.

Smith A.D. (1986). *The Ethnic Origins of Nations*. Oxford: Blackwell.

Smith, A.D. (1991). *National Identity*, London: New York [etc.], Penguin Books.

Thiesse, A.-M. (1999). *La Création des identités nationales : Europe XVIII-XX Siècle*, Paris, Editions du Seuil.

Thiesse A-M (2007). "The Formation of National Identities". In: Demossier M. (eds.) "*The European Puzzle. The Political Structuring of Cultural Identities at a Time of Transition*". New York & Oxford: Berghan Books, pp. 15–28.

Traverso, E. (2005). *Le passé, modes d'emploi. Histoire, mémoire, politique*, Paris, La Fabrique.

Traverso, E. (2010). *L'histoire comme champ de bataille. Interpréter les violences du XXe siècle*, Paris, La Découverte.

Van Krieken, R. (1998). *Norbert Elias* [Key Sociologists], London: Routledge.

van Vree, W. (2002). "The development of meeting behaviour in modern organizations and the rise of an upper class of professional chairpersons" in van Iterson, A., Mastenbroek, W., Newton, T. and Smith, D. [edited by] *The Civilized Organization Norbert Elias and the future of Organization Studies*, Volume X, Amsterdam: Philadelphia, John Benjamins Publishing Company.

Viroli, M. (1995). *For Love of Country: An Essay on Patriotism and Nationalism*, Oxford, Oxford University Press.

The Three Generations of Israeli National Habitus and The Development of Israeli National Historiography

PART III

The Three Generations of Israeli
National Habitus and The
Development of Israeli National
Historiography

CHAPTER 3

Komemyiut: Pre-statehood and Historiographical National Enterprising

Tikvatenu (Our Hope); lyrics: Naftali Herz Imber
Our hope is not yet lost,
The ancient hope,
To return to the land of our fathers;
The city where David encamped.
As long as in his heart within,
A soul of a Jew still yearns,
And onwards towards the ends of the east,
His eye still looks towards Zion.

The two first stanzas of the poem by Jewish poet Naftali Herz Imber represent Jewish yearnings for the "Promised Land". Through the sentiment of ancient hope (and claim) of return to Zion (one of the seventy-two names of Jerusalem), the poem depicts an eternal and unbreakable bond between the Jewish people and the land of its forefathers. It places Jerusalem as a universal pillar, a meeting point for all Jews, an axis mundus, that is a cosmic umbilical world axis, where they are to mould anew their collective fate (Eliade 1954, 1957, 1961). The poem thus regains possession and recomposes both biblical and symbolic narratives which characterized Jewish longings in Diaspora. It consists in the ancestral lineage to the biblical Hebrews and in the extra-temporal divine promise on the land of Israel, promised to Hebrew patriarchs and ruled by Israelite

A. Helled, *Israel's National Historiography*, Palgrave Studies on Norbert Elias, https://doi.org/10.1007/978-3-031-62795-8_3

kings. Its plea endorses a spiritually driven national revival, hence, a resurgence of the Jewish people through personal and collective sacrifice, aimed to be a remedy-action, a thaumaturgy gathering all Jewish exiles.

Inasmuch as the poem attributes an almost prophetic role to those who are about to take part in the mystic return, it situates the gathered Jewish people within the logics of European nationalism, perceived as a civilizational process which requires the entrance of the Jews into an emancipatory modernity, promoted by the nation-state Zionist model.[1] Every Jew must thus free himself/herself from the precarious conditions of statelessness (the so-called negation of Exile). The sentimental sense of commonality, combined with personal fulfilment and social engagement, lay at the heart of Jewish political, social and cultural rebirth and was the driving force of national Jewish/Israeli habitus. As the territorial anchor was culturally identified with the Ottoman province of Palestine, political Zionism gradually developed a collective habitus, based on the principles of *Komemyiut*. The Hebrew term means "standing erect, holding ones' head high fearlessly, proudly", as well as "independent existence, sovereignty, independence, renewal and revival".[2] *Tikvatenu* is thus exemplary in conveying the emotionally charged dispositions contained by the Zionist habitus, and from which Jewish national originates (for instance, common history, faith and kinship).

Nevertheless, Zionism as a European-born national movement never embodied ideological homogeneity (as many other national movements, such as the Italian Risorgimento etc.). It consisted in a multitude of voices, creeds and experiences which Zionist organizations attempted to epitomize with a rather limited and fluctuating success. Diversity had already been part of the *Hovevei Zion* (lit. "Lovers of Zion") whose movement *Hibbat Zion* was founded in 1881 in response to anti-Semitic pogroms in the Russian Empire, and constituted the first Jewish international political conference in 1884 in Katowice (Upper Silesia, then part of the Kingdom of Prussia). Its members discussed proto-Zionist heralders such as

[1] The term "Zionism", *Zionismus* in German, was coined in 1890 by Austro-Hungarian Jewish thinker Nathan Birnbaum (1864–1937), co-founder of the first national Jewish student association A.V. Kadima Wien (lit. Onwards), established on 25 October 1882. Birnbaum published an article on 1 April 1890 on Jewish self-emancipation and national determination as viewed and practiced by the forerunners of Zionism, namely, *Hovevei Zion* on the periodical *Selbstemanzipation!*

[2] Even-Shoshan: *The New Comprehensive Hebrew-Hebrew Dictionary* (1987 edition), Jerusalem, Kiryat Sefer Ltd [see Vols. 3/4, p. 1176, p. 1473]. The 1948 War of Independence has often been referred to as *Milkhemet* [War of] *Ha'Komemyiut*, using this term.

Sephardic Rabbi Judah ben Solomon Hai Alkalai (1798–1878), author of the book *Minhat Yehuda* ("The Offering of Yehuda", 1843), and Orthodox German Rabbi Zvi (Zwi) Hirsch Kalischer (1795–1874), author of *Drishat Zion* [lit. "Seeking Zion"] published in 1862. The viewpoint of the two Rabbis differed from the vision of German Jewish socialist Moses Hess (1812–1875), author of the influential book *Rome and Jerusalem* [originally *Rom und Jerusalem, die Letzte Nationalitätsfrage*], Leipzig (1862), in which the ideologist advocated for emancipation through agrarianization (the redemption of the soil), fruit of the deep influence of the French Revolution, Hegelian dialectics, Spinozian pantheism and contemporary Marxism on Hess's observations. Yet, the status given to these Zionist precursors was mainly attributed in retrospect, since their ideas did not engender concrete political action. This was different in the case of ideologists such as Leon Pinsker (Tomaszów Lubelski 1821-Odessa, 1891) and Moshe Leib Lilienblum (1843–1910), who inspired Jews to organize the first *Aliyah* (1882–1903), during which 25,000–35,000 mostly Eastern European Jews immigrated to Palestine. Both thinkers emphasized the need in the practical progressive implementation of Jewish immigration to the land of Israel, regardless of any international charter acknowledging Jewish right to the land.

The development of a collectivizing habitus, based on enthusiastic utopian youth finding seemingly practical solutions to anti-Judaic and anti-Semitic stances in Central and Eastern Europe, reached its ideological codification in the rational liberal, thus typically middle-class, national thought of Theodor Herzl (1860–1904). Herzl popularized Zionism by making the Jewish question a visible political concern to be dealt with diplomatically. He thus dedicated himself to diplomatic lobbying. He was successful in meeting with Restorationist Anglican clergyman, Reverend William Henry Hechler, who was serving as Chaplain to the British Embassy in Vienna, who arranged him an extended audience with Frederick I, Grand Duke of Baden, in April 1896, which led to three audiences with the German Emperor Wilhelm II (18 October, 28 October, 2 November 1898). Herzl also met King Ferdinand I of Bulgaria (July 1896), as he continued advocating for a solution for European Jewry across Europe and the Ottoman Empire (he was received by Sultan Abdulhamid II on 17 May 1901). He met with Jewish philanthropists such as Moritz (Zvi) von Hirsch and Edmond James de Rothschild, and kept promoting the Jewish question amongst Czarist authorities and British ones. In January 1904, Herzl met the Vatican's Secretary of State,

Cardinal Rafael Merry del Val, the Italian Monarch King Victor Emmanuel III and subsequently Pope Pius X. However, most of his diplomatic efforts bore limited fruits. Yet, his impact was, first and foremost, an inner-Jewish matter.

Herzl combined his journalistic skills (as a former correspondent for the Viennese daily *Neue Freie Presse* in Paris, where he had covered the Dreyfus Affair, 1894–1906) by disseminating his ideas through writing. His political pamphlet *Der Judenstaat* (German, literally "The Jews' State" or more commonly "The Jewish State"), published on 14 February 1896 in Leipzig and Vienna,[3] circulated and became the driving force for the First Zionist Congress (Basel, Switzerland, 29–31 August, 1897) in which 208 Jewish delegates and 26 press correspondents were present from all parts of Europe. His utopian novel "The Old New Land" (German: *Altneuland*), published in 1902, gave further impetus to the Zionist cause. Herzl's interpretation to Zionism gathered romantic, socialist and secularist ideas which were coalesced with political pragmatism. The ideal of revolutionizing Jewish history, while juxtaposing it to realpolitik and national statehood, bestowed Herzl with the honour of being the "visionary of the Jewish State", as commemorated in Israel by law (The Benjamin Ze'ev Herzl Law, 29 June, 2004).

Despite ideological differences within Zionism, oscillating between socialism and conservatism, secularism and national messianism, all early Zionists espoused the entrepreneurial transformation of individual action into a collective national effort. The complementarity in terms of identification with Judaism and the land of Israel facilitated the construction of a Jewish national habitus to be nurtured in a territorial survival unit. The so-called synthetic Zionism, an epithet officialized in a speech by Chaim Weizmann (1874–1952, future first President of Israel) at the Eighth Zionist Congress in The Hague in August 1907, advocated a pragmatic combination of the immediate emancipation of Jews in Palestine (the practical stand of Hibbat Zion) and Herzl's prioritization of political and international understandings. It therefore applied a two-fold Zionism. It contemporaneously sought the execution of the Jewish national cause de facto in loco, alongside continuous diplomatic efforts.

---

[3] This was followed by the foundation of the weekly newspaper *Die Welt* (lit. "The World") in May 1897 and whose first issue appeared on 4 June 1897 (the weekly was published both in Vienna and in Cologne and became the official magazine of the Zionist movement in 1903; its publication ceased in 1914).

This was to become the dominant modus operandi of the Zionist movement until Israeli independence.[4]

Another feature of that stage of Zionist production of a national habitus was the revival of the Hebrew language to accompany Jewish settlement and labour (never prioritized as such by Herzl). The 1913 public "War of the Languages" around the language of instruction at the nascent Technikum in Haifa manifested the importance of formalizing the linguistic choice for Jews immigrating to Palestine to create a new type of Jewish life.[5] It was a debate between the non-Zionist Jewish aid agency *Hilfsverein der deutschen Juden* (1901–1939, *de jure* until 1941), which endorsed for German, and Zionist supporters of the revival of Hebrew who were against the Technikum's Berlin-based board of trustees which had decided to establish German as a language, due to its scientific, academic and technical relevance (26 October 1913).

Their decision was followed by strikes and protests led by the teachers' union (*Histadrut*). Eliezer Ben-Yehuda (1858–1922), Hebrew linguist, lexicographer and newspaper editor, considered to be the "reviver of the Hebrew language", as well as Ahad Ha'am and other intellectual figures supporting Hebrew, overtly criticized the decision. The strife delayed the opening of the academic institution, which was put on hold by the outbreak of WWI. The latter embittered relations between the two factions. In the end, the Jewish German philanthropic organization surrendered and approved Hebrew as a teaching language on 22 February 1914. This meant a significant consolidation and social acceptance of the Hebrew language reaching a status of a worthy academic and scientific vernacular. The debate strengthened an autonomous education in Hebrew under Zionist organizations with the opening of Hebrew Reali School of Haifa and of the Jerusalem-based Hebrew teachers' training college (both

---

[4] A more intellectual and philosophical form of Zionism, namely Cultural Zionism, or spiritual Zionism, is to be found in the writings of its founder Ahad Ha'am (lit. "One of the People"; pen-name of Asher Zvi Hirsch Ginsberg, 1856–1927). The latter envisaged a secular Jewish "spiritual centre" in Palestine that would be based on humanist education in Hebrew and on Jewish revitalization, not necessarily in terms of national statehood. This current Zionism aimed to resolve the problem (the decline) of Judaism (due to assimilation) by the "revival of the hearts". See Ahad Ha'am's *This Is Not the Way* (1889), available on the website of the Ben-Yehuda Project (in Hebrew).

[5] Till then Hebrew had been used as the language of instruction only in several Jewish schools, while most schooling was held and organized by international organizations such as *Alliance Israélite Universelle* and the Jewish German *Hilfsverein*.

already established in 1913). The Hebrew-speaking schools were soon acknowledged by Ottoman and later British authorities, and laid the foundations for the nascent national education system.

The "War of the Languages" was also an important part in the linguistic conflict between Yiddish and Hebrew that had begun in the late nineteenth century and was influential in the culturalization process of the Jewish settlement in Palestine (the Jewish Yishuv). While opponents to Yiddish considered it a diasporic, degenerated, dialectical jargon destined to disappear (namely, Herzl, Ahad Ha'am, Eliezer Ben-Yehuda), some writers and intellectuals, such as Sholem Aleichem (pseudonym of Solomon Naumovich Rabinovich (1859–1916)), Nahum Sokolov (1859–1936) and Yehoshua Hana Rabnitskij (1859–1944), sought to maintain Yiddish as a literary language. Noteworthy is the case of Hebrew "purists" throwing a stink bomb in a Jerusalem theatre during the premiere of the Yiddish operetta *Shulamith* (also known as *The Daughter of Jerusalem*) written in 1880 by playwright Abraham Goldfaden (1840–1908).[6] The debate exasperated with the so-called Battalion for the Defence of the Language (1923–1936). This small but militant group of Jewish students attending the Herzliya Hebrew Gymnasium (established in 1905) divulged, diffused and propagated for the sole use of the Hebrew language (their slogan: "Jew, speak Hebrew!" became widely known and was later used by Ben-Gurion).

The Hebrew-speaking national cause received further endorsement with the foundation of the Hebrew University,[7] which is the place of the sociogenesis of our enquiry on Israel's national historiography. The Hebrew University was the first universal, multidisciplinary academic establishment in Palestine (unlike the purely technical Technion), and whose establishment had already been agreed upon by Zionist delegates in

---

[6] Other manifestations of Hebrew zeal took place on various occasions at the Hebrew University of Jerusalem after its foundation, such as Martin Buber's lecture in German in May 1927, and the controversy over the institutionalization of an academic chair of the Yiddish language, eventually established in 1949.

[7] On the status of the Hebrew language at the Hebrew University and the role of the latter in the consolidation of the former, see Efrati, N.: "*The Hebrew University and the Hebrew Language*", pp. 305–336, in Lavsky [ed.] (2005): "*The History of The Hebrew University of Jerusalem: A Period of Consolidation and Growth*", Jerusalem, The Hebrew University Magnes Press (in Hebrew).

the early years of the Zionist enterprise.[8] The ceremony of the university's foundation took place on 24 July 1918 on its future grounds on Mount Scopus, Jerusalem. Thirteen cornerstones were solemnly laid in presence of British military officers Edmund Henry Hynman Allenby and Chaim Weizmann in front of circa 6000 guests, including the Grand Mufti of Jerusalem, Kamil al-Husseini, the Anglican Bishop to Palestine and the city's Rabbis. The ceremony concluded with the singing of *Hatikvah* and *God Save the King*. Functional to the realization of the project was Albert Einstein's visit in early 1923. The nascent university established two institutes: one for chemistry and microbiology; the other for Jewish studies, as well as a library, only few months before its official inauguration. The dedication ceremony took place on 1–3 April 1925 (seven years after the ceremony of foundation). It was a meaningful step in the ongoing Zionist nation-building. Speeches were held by Chaim Weizmann, president of the Zionist Organization (who also became the first chairman of the board of governors[9]), Rabbi Abraham Isaac Kook, Hebrew poet Hayim Nahman Bialik (1873–1934) and the British First High Commissioner for Palestine Sir Herbert Louis Samuel. About 7000 guests participated in the ceremony (including Lord Arthur James 1st Earl of Balfour, as the guest of honour [given the famous declaration of 1917], Field Marshal Allenby, Ahad Ha'am, Sir Patrick Geddes [who had planned the campus], poet Shaul Tchernichovsky, Meir Dizengoff, scholars, artists and other cultural and political dignitaries). Despite the apparent solemnity of its establishment, the academic staff of the nascent university comprised only seven professors and about thirty research assistants. Yet, it soon concentrated on research and commenced frontal graduate teaching as early as 1928 (undergraduate curricula developed much later on, since students had

[8] The foundation of a university in *Eretz Israel* had already been discussed in November 1884 during the Kattowitz (Katowice) conference of the Hovevei Zion movement. Yet, no decision was taken in this regard. The issue was raised again during the First Zionist Congress (1897) by Jewish scholar and mathematician Hermann Hirsch Schapira (1840–1898). The project's construction was assigned to Scottish biologist, sociologist and town planner, Sir Patrick Geddes (1854–1932).

[9] Members of the Hebrew University Board of Governors also included Albert Einstein, Sigmund Freud and Martin Buber (the latter joined the faculty of the Hebrew University in 1938, following the rise of the Third Reich as a full professor of anthropology and philosophy of sociology).

already been trained in Europe).[10] Dr Judah Leon Magnes (1877–1948) was nominated first chancellor of the Hebrew University (a position gathering both academic and administrative decisional power). Magnes served as the university's president till his death in 1948, while prof Samuel (Schmuel) Hugo Bergmann (1883–1975) was appointed the institution's rector.

Both Magnes and Bergmann were prominent members of the lay and Universalist Jewish intelligentsia. They shared a German central European culture which deeply had influenced their ideals prior to their Zionist involvement. Both supported a binational autonomy as the desired form of polity for Jews to live in Palestine. Magnes believed that the university itself was the ideal place for Jewish-Arab cooperation, and he worked tirelessly to advance this goal. The association of *Brit Shalom*, lit. "Covenant of peace", founded in 1925, advocated for ideological and intellectual positions. Amongst its members we find economist and sociologist Arthur Ruppin (co-founder; who held a senior position within the Jewish Agency as Director of the Palestine Land Development Company [1933–1935]); philosophers Hugo Bergmann (co-founder), Martin Buber (co-founder), Hayim Jehuda (Leon) Roth and Ernst Simon; historian Hans Kohn (later pioneer in the research on nationalism); Kabbalah scholar Gershom Scholem; ethnographer and orientalist Shelomo Dov (Fritz) Goitein; educator and social activist Henrietta Szold; pacifist Nathan Hofshi (Frenkel); Hebrew educator and linguist Yitzhak Epstein; microbiologist Israel Jacob Kligler; agronomist Haim Margaliot-Kalvarisky; librarian Felix Weltsch and his cousin journalist Robert Weltsch; Hebrew educator and publicist Joseph Luria and even Rabbi and author Yehoshua Radler-Feldman Ha-Talmi etc. However, the intellectual group disintegrated by the early 1930s, mostly as a consequence of the 1929 Palestine riots (for which Ruppin abandoned the group). In the aftermath of its disintegration and in the increasingly violent and uncertain situation in Palestine, while the Zionist Congress was striving for Jewish national statehood, some of the former Brit Shalom members (e.g., Scholem, Buber, Szold, Simon) followed Magnes in forming the political association *Ihud* (Hebrew, lit.

---

[10] Two-hundred and fifty students commenced their studies in the first academic year 1928–1929 at the Hebrew University; all enrolled in humanities. Whereas, in the academic year 1946–1947 1027 students attended the university (35% enrolled in natural sciences classes, almost 9% in agriculture and the rest in humanities). See Nachum T. Gross: "*Social Sciences Until 1948/49—Plans and Beginnings*", pp. 503–541 (especially p. 518) in Lavsky [ed.] (2005) [in Hebrew].

"Union"), established in 1942 as a response to the Biltmore Conference (May 1942, New York City), which demanded Palestine to become a sovereign Jewish Commonwealth.

In more general terms, the binational viewpoint was becoming increasingly unconvincing in light of the dramatic events concerning Jewish-Arab Palestinian relations. Such stands were perceived as radical elitist intellectualism. Moreover, members of binational associations were accused of knowing very little about local politics as well as having only a remote sense of Eastern European Judaism, which represented the demographic majority of Jewish immigrants in Palestine (Ratzabi 2002). That said, Brit Shalom exemplifies that the supposed nationalization of Jewish intellectuals as part of the greater nation-state building process had very different interpretations, even when Zionism seemed to have already become politically monolithic.

THE SOCIOGENESIS OF ZIONIST JEWISH HISTORIOGRAPHY IN ITS GRADUAL INSTITUTIONALIZATION

These inherent complexities characterizing Judaism, Jewish identity and the multiple stances in Zionism within the nascent academic field in Mandatory Palestine motivated the inauguration of the Institute of Jewish Studies.[11] It was consequential to the sociocultural zeitgeist and the lessons learned from Europe's national revivals, which well-equipped societies with a national knowledge disseminated and spread throughout collectivity. That is to say that the sociogenesis did not come out of nothing. Some canons had already been experimented, stabilized and even standardized. In addition, the osmosis between vibrant ideological debates, active politics and intellectual entrepreneurship facilitated the institutionalization of ideas, sprouting out from the fertile grounds of local intelligentsia.

Founded in late 1924, the institute had been preceded by the establishment of the society of history and ethnography of *Eretz Israel* the same year (based on the model of Jewish society of history and ethnography, founded by Samuel Klein in Saint Petersburg, Russia, in 1908). The institute aimed at acting as a driving force for the rebirth of the Jewish nation by combining

---

[11] Following the "War of the Languages" in 1913, the Hebrew and Jewish character of the nascent university had already been envisaged and programmed by its first chancellor Judah Leon Magnes, together with Chaim Weizmann and Samuel (Schmuel) Hugo Bergmann. Hence, the institutional prioritization of establishing the Institute of Jewish Studies among the first realities within the Hebrew University.

studies on Jewish culture and history in both the land of Israel and Diaspora through academic scientific research. The abovementioned society, which pushed forward interdisciplinary research of *Eretz Israel* and the Jewish population in situ (thus geographical and archaeological), much influenced the vantage point of the Jewish Studies Institute. The institutionalization of academic research on the land and its local history marginalized the more transversal study of Jewish history in its entirety. The geographical distinction, therefore, neglected the macro-history of the Jews. The death of the society's founder Klein (1940) subsequently left a void chair at the Institute of Jewish Studies, which was filled in by Second Temple and Talmud historian Gedaliah Rogoznitski ([later Alon] 1902–1950) and by biblical archaeologist/historical geographer Benjamin Maisler [later Mazar] (1906–1995) in 1943 (neither the first nor the second had initially been recruited on tenure-track positions). Yet, reality gradually changed, as the weight of Zionism grew, at least within the Jewish Yishuv. More and more people, lecturers and students alike, demanded to unify the millennial existence of the Jews with the national project. The Institute of Jewish Studies had to comply with this form of political protagonism. In addition, the scientific knowledge produced at the Hebrew University began to reflect some intellectual ramifications. The mere philological study of Jewish scriptures and the archaeology of the land lacked the more general contextualization which only historiography seemed to provide. The situation changed with the arrival of historian Yitzhak (Fritz) Baer (1888–1980) in 1930. As Baer had already obtained a position as a full professor, he helped in the recruitment of another historian, Ben-Zion Dinaburg (later Dinur), for the academic year 1935–1936.

The latter, who would become Minister of Education and Culture in the third to sixth Israeli governments (1951–1955; under Prime Ministers David Ben-Gurion [III, IV] and Moshe Sharett [V, VI][12]), was an educator

---

[12] Among Dinur's political achievements as Minister of Education: the 1953 State Education Law, which neutralized factionist and competing education networks based on the existing party-system (the formalization of *Mamlakhtiyut*), the initiation of the Israel Prize in 1953 (he himself was awarded twice: in 1958 for Jewish studies and in 1973 for education), the establishment (and headship as chairman) of Yad Vashem (1953–1959) and the law of the "supreme institution for scholarship on the Hebrew language in the Hebrew University of Jerusalem" with which the Academy of the Hebrew Language was institutionalized in 1953 (before it an association founded in 1890). He was also involved in legislating the law of state archives (1955) and the establishment of the Council for Higher Education of Israel (1958). In addition, he was elected member of the nascent Israel Academy of Sciences and Humanities (1959) and received the *Yakir Yerushalayim* Award ("Worthy Citizen of Jerusalem") in 1967, the year of the award's inauguration.

in the Hebrew language, and was appointed the first lecturer of modern Jewish history at the Hebrew University. Both Baer and Dinaburg signalled the starting point of the scientific and autonomous development of historical studies regarding the Jewish people. Structural circumstances at the Hebrew University facilitated this trend. The 1933 Hartog committee played a significant role in addressing structural scientific inner debates. It recommended the unification of all history studies under the same department as part of the university's organizational reform. Accordingly, in May 1935 historians Victor (Avigdor) Tcherikover (1894–1958), Yitzhak Baer and the recently recruited Richard (Michael) Koebner (1885–1958) promoted the unification of general history and Jewish history into a sole department within the Faculty of Humanities (established in 1928; while the division of the faculty into different departments took place in 1930), in order to overcome disciplinary limitations. Nonetheless, their proposal was rejected by their peers, mostly Bible and Talmud scholars and members of the Institute of Jewish Studies who wished to keep all research on Jewish life within the walls of the institute. The parties eventually reached a scientific and organizational compromise. Jewish history was kept as a particular field of research vis-à-vis the general historical research. It resulted in the institutionalization of two separate history departments: a model that would be adopted by Israeli universities and would remain unchanged for decades to come. The general history department was founded in 1936 by historians Yitzhak Baer, Richard Koebner and Victor Tcherikover. Koebner, who was to head the department, and Tcherikover had been trained and supervised by the same scholar, namely historian and Egyptologist Eduard Meyer (1855–1930) in Berlin. Their common professional training contributed to the promotion and institutionalization of historiography on the mediaeval Latin Kingdom of Jerusalem and the Muslim conquest of Palestine within the general history department, thus, attesting the inevitable contamination of topics between the two departments.

Such subject-matters received scholarly attention in the works of academics as philologist Moshe (Max) Schwabe (1889–1956); Second Temple historian Abraham Haim Schalit (1898–1979), trained in Vienna, immigrated to Palestine in 1929 and recruited in 1950 (future recipient of the Israel Prize in Jewish studies, 1960); and subsequently by Joshua Prawer (1917–1990) who was trained in history by Professors Baer and Koebner and would become one of Israel's prominent experts on Crusader's Jerusalem. In this regard, the seemingly mediaeval

Palestinocentric interest in the nascent general history department did not
disincentivize the contemporaneous establishment of the Jewish history
department. The department, however, was not established as a monodis-
ciplinary academic structure. In fact, it initially comprised both Jewish
history (*Toldot Israel*) and Jewish sociology. It was headed by Baer,
Dinaburg and Ruppin (1876–1943).[13] Though Baer and Dinaburg considered the establishment of the Jewish history department a cornerstone
in the nation-building process and as an important part of the revival of
the Jewish people (under the aegis of the Zionist movement), it took a
great deal of effort to select, formulate and propose a clear academic
programme.

The formal administrative and academic division of history studies was,
indeed, the founding and defining moment in the scholarly professional
differentiation which engendered a specific scholarly system. The creation
of two history departments was the sociogenesis of the professional habitus of the nascent Hebrew/Israeli historiography. The institutionalization
of these academic fields engendered two parallel intellectual domains. The
decision settled the field of powers. It structurally separated academic
positions and curricula in terms of university governance. This model supported historiographical particularism with respect to Jewish national history (against the minority opinion expressed by Tcherikover, Baer and
Koebner) vis-à-vis the apparent universalism of general history (initially
connoted as purely European, yet gradually differentiated into
Mediterranean, transnational and in more recent years global/world history). The partition of resources determined the hegemonic position of
the Institute of Jewish Studies in all Jewish topics, inasmuch as the new
department and the programmes it offered prioritized biblical, philosophical and philological works over archival historiography tout court. It thus
anchored Jewish humanities onto an institutional and intellectual status
quo which distanced Jewish history from general history, despite the disciplinary common grounds of the two. The consequential trajectory of
Jewish history concerned historiographical endeavours by Hebrew
University scholars who studied the European societies and modern states

---

[13] Sociology was supposed to become an autonomous discipline but the lack of resources
did not enable it. Consequently, the dual-discipline department remained as such till
Ruppin's death in 1943. The department of Jewish sociology and demographics was inaugurated in November 1946 and was definitively established in January 1947.

in which Jews had lived, rather than dedicating their works to what would later become local (territorial) history.

In practice, the institutional demarcation of the distinct history departments, establishing the structural specificities of the academic knowledge, had little to do with the study of Palestine/*Eretz Israel*. This was evidently the case of the book, *The History of the Jewish Settlement of Palestine, from the Redaction of the Talmud to the Palestine Settlement Movement* (1935), which had been ideated by Dinur but was subsequently written and edited by historical topographer, Rabbi Samuel Klein (1886–1940). The latter had been a member of the university since 1924, and was in charge of topographical/geographical enquiry over *Palaestina Judaica* (the Institute of Land of Israel Studies, established in 1933). Inasmuch as neither Dinur nor Baer prioritized historical studies of the land of Israel per se, the scholarly interest shifted and found more fertile grounds among archaeologists and geographers (all members of the Jewish Palestine Exploration Society established in 1913). Scholarly works on the land of Israel thus became interdisciplinary and general in respect to Jewish history. The exploration of the land, which echoed the vantage point of settlers' society in the making, dealt with prehistory, classical history, mediaeval crusades and the Arab conquest.

Initially, the academic interest was not exclusively "nationalised" by the Jewish Zionist identity in the sense that the geographical and archaeological mapping of the land represented (and reproduced) a more European "civilizational" rationale. The discovery of the Levant as part of the greater orient had already adopted colonial and orientalist standards which reflected the combination of European modern sciences, hence an ontological and epistemological distinction, with power-driven instruments of domination, alongside intermingled mythical abstractions, fantastical and fictional mental pictures (Said 1978). This was purely an artificial operation, both intellectually and politically, since "contents and histories [were] too interdependent and hybrid, for surgical separation into large and mostly ideological oppositions like Orient and Occident" (Said 1996, p. xii). However, this was soon to change. As asserted by Said (1996, 26): a "narrowing focus and localization in the way we look at intellectuals [and thus their work] is also due to the fantastic proliferation of specialised studies, which has quite justifiably tracked the expanding role of intellectuals in modern life". This is also due to the nationalization of knowledge in the latter's capacity to strengthen and expand both macro and micro networks of solidarity (Malešević 2019). In fact, during the period of the

British Mandate in Palestine (1920–1948), *Eretz Israel* witnessed its expansion in the field of Biblical and Second Temple research as part of the more general interest in Near-East ancient history and languages (especially with the recruitment of Harry Torczyner [later Hebraicized in Naftali Herz Tur-Sinai, 1886–1973]) who co-founded the Hebrew Language programme and that of Semitic languages. This was another step in the progressive particularization of national dispositions to be accumulated: territory, history and language.

In tandem with the development of neighbouring disciplines, historians Yitzhak Baer and Ben-Zion Dinaburg, both members of the society of history and ethnography of *Eretz Israel,* took steps to further consolidate the Jewish history department and the discipline they wished to push forward. They commenced to pave and construct much of what is considered today to be the "Jerusalem School". Dinaburg, especially, emphasized the centrality of *Eretz Israel* in the history of the Jewish people. He fostered a teleological connection between the Jewish nation and the land, hence, between the collectivized individuals and their survival unit. In this sense, Dinaburg appears to be an exemplary habitus-provider, since he laid the foundations for an institutional psycho-social construct for future citizens to interiorize, beyond the political sociogenetic apparatus of the state already in nuce (administered by the Jewish Agency for Palestine, founded in 1929). His conviction in the intimate and constant relation between Diaspora and the Promised Land brought Dinaburg to serve as a coeditor of the periodical *Zion: Collection of the Historical and Ethnographic Society* (established in 1926). Nevertheless, the Palestinocentric interest in the land of Israel alone was considered somewhat inadequate by the cofounders of the Jewish history department.

They privileged a more general historiographical approach. Yet, the transformation and changing status of the discipline vis-à-vis the Jewish population in Palestine from the Middle-Ages to the late nineteenth century did occur. It meant a shift from the perception of the native Ottoman old Yishuv (pre-1882) to that of the new Yishuv (with the rise of Zionism and the first Aliyah 1881–1903), which clearly attested the centrality of Ben-Zion Dinaburg (Dinur) in advocating for the new and methodical Zionist historiography. That is not to say, however, that Dinaburg was not interested in the proto-Zionist history of the Jewish population in Palestine (Barnai 1995). In addition, Dinaburg and his colleagues academically institutionalized new programmes and curricula by recruiting permanent academic staff (in the beginning classes were held by temporary non-tenure visiting scholars). Unlike Baer and other professors, Dinaburg presented a different intellectual temperament. He used his intellectual charisma and soon became a public figure. Moreover, he was committed to scientific popularization, whereas Baer maintained a more restrained personality, both academically and publically (Ben-Arieh 2005).[14] While Baer dedicated his research to mediaeval Spain, its Jewish population and general history related subjects such as the crusades (he co-founded and taught at the history department), Dinur showed a growing interest in modern Jewish chronicles and their attachment to the land of Israel. His scholarly interest reflected his national-Zionist ideological stand, especially detectable in his works on *Hibbat Zion* (1932, 1934, 1946) and Herzl (1946). Yet, both shared similar scholarly interests, having been trained and influenced by German Jewish historian Eugen Täubler. These common grounds were expressed in the initiation of the quarterly *Zion* (1935) which replaced the former collection of essays. As the editorial aim and purpose of the quarterly reads (Dinaburg & Baer, 1935).

"In addressing the foundation of the historical quarterly 'Zion'—which is to replace the collections 'Zion', that had mostly been dedicated to the examination of the chronicles of *Eretz Israel*, its Jewish settlement and the chronicles of the Jews in Eastern countries—we wish, henceforth, to satisfy *two fundamental needs of the contemporary Jewish historical science*: the need in *a common floor* to all those who endeavour in Jewish history in order to participate in the *discussion regarding the problems of Jewish* [*Israeli* in the original] *chronicles*, and the need in *a special floor* to the *uniqueness of investigation* of '*Khochmat Israel*' [Hebrew lit. "The Wisdom of Israel"; with clear reference to the German *Wissenschaft des Judentums*] *from a historical perspective.*

The recent Jewish historiography, as all Jewish sciences in this time, was created and developed, to a large extent, out of defensive needs and conditions in the polemic concerning the naturalization and political* [state-related] *equality on all its processes and revelations, collateral effects and echoes; internal and external alike.* This polemic is that which established the theological and literary character of Jewish historiography; it signaled some fields of life as 'points of interest' for our scholars, and it is that which also delineated, either consciously or unconsciously, their fashions of research and method.

[14] Ben-Arieh, Y. (2005). *Developments in the Study of Yedihat Ha'aretz at the Hebrew University, 1925–1948*, pp. 347–409, especially p. 366; in Lavsky [ed.] (2005): "*The History of The Hebrew University of Jerusalem: A Period of Consolidation and Growth*", Jerusalem, The Hebrew University Magnes Press.

Though *in the last generation there was an attempt to correct some of the fundamental deficiencies in these ways and methods*; thus, *demanding a clean and independent work*, some aspired *to liberate the historical research from the burden of theology*, whilst advocating the grounding of issues *following documentation and its examination through the founding principles of scientific critic*; hence, *paving the way to the ample study of economic conditions* and widening to a great extent the breadth of perception of the interest in the past. In other words, the *needed fundamental transformation of Jewish history from being [a form of] general knowledge and a domain of the past, as for the Jewish perception of reality by former generations*—significantly falling short of *the domain of historical action*, following the public distinction of the Jewish reality of our time. In light of this public distinction, given its conclusions, it has established foundations and summarised theories. Thus, there ought to find *criteria to historical research*, to *clarify the perception and understanding of the past*.

The fundamental assumption in the perception of our past, which should be the starting point also to *investigate the roles of Jewish historiography* as well as for the *establishment of the historical object of research*, which is—in our view—a simple and binding assumption: *Jewish history is, indeed, the chronicles of the Israeli nation that had never desist and whose importance never waned*. Jewish history is unified by the *homogenous unity surrounding all eras and all places*; all come to teach [us] about one another [...]".[15]

Zion clearly set novel criteria in the study of Jewish history. It was an intellectual manifesto that called for a sort of an avant-garde critical scientific discussion of the Jewish past, following a traditionally positivistic documentation-based analysis. In addition, it exalted the autonomous nature of historical research vis-à-vis theology not only by method but also by defining a new object of interest, that is to say, the material conditions of the Jewish nation in terms of political equality and economic conditions. The quarterly sought to provide contributions that aimed to scientifically explain the domain of historical (human) action, while leaving aside the theological perspective, anchored to the category of the divine. By so doing, it sought to emancipate the historiographical discipline from other branches in Jewish studies at the Hebrew University. Furthermore, by referring to contemporaneity (such as in the expressions "our time", "recent generations"), *Zion* suggested that historiography had more than one role to play. Scientificity aimed at research that would provide political

---

[15] Dinaburg B.-Z., Baer, Y.: *"Editorial Aim and Purpose"*, Zion, October, 1935, Vol. 1, N. 1, pp. 1–5 (in Hebrew; citation p. 1 [my translation; words in italics are my emphasis]).

tools to be used outside academia. Hence, the scientific journal explicitly professed its own engagement in espousing the Zionist cause, particularly in its ideologically socialist stream.

In this respect, Dinaburg's own conviction becomes a valuable element whilst exploring the breadth of depth of the historiography he so fervently developed. The guidelines *Zion* had set stood against Jewish assimilation/ naturalization into the greater civil society as well as against the opposite trend of leaving Diaspora aside and concentrate on Palestine alone. Dinaburg considered the national imperative in terms of the political collectivization of Jewish identity (as all Zionists), and emphasized the special connection between Jewish dispersion and the biblical land. Out of his academic and political creed, he asserted that Diaspora and *Eretz Israel* were to be placed onto the same continuum in the national history of the Jewish people. The intimate historical link between people and land demonstrated an organic unity as well as an interplay between internal and external forces (an Eliasian survival unit par excellence). The historiographical paradigm, he developed, set common grounds which were necessary foundations for national con- science and state-building. By advocating new parameters to Jewish histori- ography, Dinaburg and Baer formulated a demand of secularization of Jewish *historia sacra*. Not only was it a methodological demand but an ideo- logical one as well. This standpoint entailed that Jewish national identity was a stable, yet dynamic, collective habitus, based upon common historical experiences, chiefly exile and Diaspora, which had to be emancipated from the seemingly monolithic religious component. That said, the barycentre remained a continuous reference to the biblical lost territory. It averred that Jewish history and the history of the land were two faces of the same coin and, therefore, could not be studied separately (alongside the philological research of sources). This national-based intellectual choice would gradually become the habitus of the state of Israel and the meta-narratives which stemmed from it ever since.

Notwithstanding, the establishment of the new periodical was the out- come of an ongoing ideological and intellectual struggle. The quarterly portrayed a twofold stand. On the one hand, it, overtly and immediately, delineated the "history of the Israeli nation" at any age and in any place as the core assignment of scholarly work, thus claiming the continuum and unity of Jewish history with no particular localist or orientalist stand.[16] On

---

[16] This assertion finds evidence in the only article published in the first volume of the *Zion* which directly addressed *Eretz Israel*, namely Shohat, A.: "*The Jews in Jerusalem in the XVIIth Century*" (1936) Zion, Vol. 1, Issue N. IV, pp. 377–410 (further developed and republished in "Cathedra" 13, Oct. 1979, pp. 3–45).

the other, it autonomized historical research not only from the realm of theology but also from that of competing academic disciplines, namely philology, literature, archaeology, geography etc.

As in many others domains of human knowledge and action, the inauguration of *Zion* did not occur in a void within the Institute of Jewish Studies. The institute, in fact, had already merged, together with the Institute of Oriental Studies, into the novel Faculty of Humanities, starting from the academic year 1929–1930. This change permitted the latter to establish another scholarly periodical, the quarterly *Tarbitz* (lit. "a place of study"), promoted by Talmud philologist Jacob Nahum Halevi Epstein (1878–1952), the head of the Institute of Jewish Studies. The first issue of the novel quarterly was published the same year. It was the first intellectual platform for scholars to share and discuss their research on Judaism, biblical and Talmudic exegesis, Kabbalah and Jewish mysticism, Hebrew religious bibliography, etc.[17] Yet, despite its impact on Jewish studies at the Hebrew University, *Tarbitz* exclusively covered Jewish thought, philosophy and philology, whereas *Zion* maintained a purely historiographic editorial line. Therefore, the two periodicals translated the Institute's intellectual differentiation and nurtured scientific complementarity, rather than scholarly antagonism. This significant sociogenetic process in terms of standardization and formal recognition of Jewish historiography as a worthy autonomous academic discipline could not have taken form without the adaptation of the German Jewish *Wissenschaft des Judentums* model to the locally Palestinocentric process of nation-state building.[18]

Scientific paradigms were chiefly imported from the Lehranstalt für die Wissenschaft des Judentums (subsequently renamed Hochschule für die Wissenschaft des Judentums) in which numerous Jewish scholars had been trained. Furthermore, the history of the Jews as a unified, consequently

[17] Amongst the periodical's prominent contributors: Jacob Nahum Epstein (1878–1952, founder of the Institute of Jewish Studies and first editor-in-chief of the quarterly till his death), Gershom Gerhard Scholem (1897–1982, Israel Prize Laureate 1958), Saul Lieberman (1898–1983, second editor), Simha Assaf (1889–1953, rabbi, historian of Jewish thought, rector of the Hebrew University (1948–1950) and judge of the Supreme Court of Israel (1948–1953)), Hanoch Albeck (1890–1972), Hayyim (Jefim) Schirmann (1904–1981, editor of *Tarbitz* Israel Prize recipient 1957) etc. The quarterly has been published by Magnes Press.

[18] Noteworthy is the admiration of Dinaburg (Dinur) to the historiographical work of Dubnow as well as to the latter's contribution to Jewish public life. See Dinaburg (1936): "*Simon Dubnow: on the occasion of his 75th Birthday*", *Zion*, Vol. I, N. 2, pp. 95–128.

"national", history had been already attempted by Jewish intellectuals cul-
minating in the historiographical works of Heinrich Graetz (1817–1891)
and Simon Dubnow (1860–1941): both sensitive to the Zeitgeist in
Jewish millennial history.[19] According to Brenner (2010, 158): "Zionist
historians set a radical distance between themselves and earlier representatives of the discipline, although despite these efforts to distinguish themselves from their predecessors it is also clear how much they were influenced
by them and that they were able to develop their own positions only in
contrast to those already available. This twofold relationship may help
explain the vehemence of the conflict". Both continuity and rupture,
therefore, found different combinations within Jewish studies at the
Hebrew University in Jerusalem. In addition, Dinaburg, more than his
colleagues, knew how to crystallize his perspective on the past in light of
current affairs in the spirit of Zionism's objective to "normalize" the
Jewish people (Myers 1988).

Slightly different is the interpretation that traces an overt Zionist impetus towards political and cultural sovereignty in Palestine in Jewish historical scholarship, as headed by the same Dinaburg. Their engagement
benefitted from the ongoing normalization of the Jewish people, as it
occurred to them, while affording a unique sociopolitical opportunity
(Ram 1995, 1996).[20] Either way, Dinaburg represented an exemplary
sociological type, whose specific character merged with a Mannheimian
life-situation that revealed and condensed the habitus of his generation.
The latter actively attributed to his professional category the role of fostering national conscience, collective will and transversal identification

---

[19] A complete historiographical construction of the Jewish past was first made by Prussian
Jew Heinrich (Zvi) Graetz in his comprehensive history of the Jewish people from a
historical-positivist perspective (i.e., *Geschichte der Juden von den ältesten Zeiten bis auf die
Gegenwart*) (lit. "History of the Jews from Ancient Times to Present Day"), 11 volumes,
Leipzig, published in 1853–1875, while the second one was written by Dubnow, a
Byelorussian Jewish scholar and activist, who published *Weltgeschichte des jüdischen Volkes* (lit.
"World History of the Jewish People"; previously written and published in Russian), 10
volumes, Berlin published in the years 1925–1929.

[20] See Ram, U. (1995): "Zionist Historiography and the Invention of Modern Jewish
Nationhood: The Case of Ben Zion Dinur", *History and Memory*, Vol. 7, No. 1, Israeli
Historiography Revisited (Spring–Summer, 1995), pp. 91–124. The article was almost con-
temporaneously published in Hebrew: Ram (1996): "Those Days and This Time: The
Zionist Historiography and The Invention of The Jewish National Narrative: Ben-Zion
Dinur and His Time", in "*Zionut: Pulmus Ben Zmanenu*" [Zionism Controversy], *Iyunim
Bitkumat Israel*, 1996 (thematic issue edited by Avi Bareli Pinhas Ginossar), pp. 126–159.

between Jewish Palestine and their brethren in Diaspora. By conceiving, combining and placing his personal inclinations into his historiographical effort, he inaugurated the season of engaged scholarship whose twofold aim was to fruitfully serve Zionism and later the nation-state. Hence, not only did Dinaburg capitalize his position in promoting himself to the status of an exemplary "national historian" in pre-/post-Israeli independence, but he created and codified future standards and expectations in terms of cooperation between politics and scholarship. As an authoritative intellectual, deeply sensible to the role of education in shaping the collective sense of belonging, he moulded an ideal-type of an intellectual who was professionally and politically in tune with power. This makes him an absolute "sociogenetic" inventor of public intellectualism in Israel's history, a *homo faber suae tempore*, whose architectural project was carried out and still stands, in spite of changing circumstances.

Although this perspective certainly corresponds to the somewhat univocal categorization of the first generation of scholars as national public intellectuals, given the gradual Zionization of Palestine,[21] the case of the Dinaburg-Dinur seems to be an exception amongst his peers. His political engagement surely outstood and outreached that of his peers (namely, Baer, Tcherikover and Koebner), as well as that of disciplinary adjacent scholars such as Gershom Scholem (1897–1982), founder of the modern academic study of the Kabbalah, Josef G. Klausner (1874–1958; Second Temple historian and Hebrew literature scholar) and Yehezkel Kaufmann (1889–1963, philosopher and biblical scholar). Yet, despite conspicuous ideological divergences which characterized these scholars (Scholem was a binationalist, Dinaburg a socialist and Klausner a rightist revisionist etc.). All these founders of Israeli academia were celebrated as national civil servants by the state. Klausner, Kaufmann, Scholem, Baer and Dinur were all awarded the prestigious Israel Prize for Jewish studies in 1958, alongside another recipient, Martin Buber, awarded in the field of humanities.[22]

---

[21] Here the term "Zionization" means the numerical increase of Jews living within the borders of British Palestine (approx. 56,000 Jews at the end of WWII in comparison with the estimated number of 431,000 Jews on the eve of WWII) as well as the accumulative success of Zionism as a national movement among the Jewish population of the yishuv.

[22] Since the prize had previously been ideated by Dinur himself, then Minister of Education (1953), it is more than intuitive to believe that this institutionalized public acknowledgement—well-ritualized and routinized as part of each Israeli Independence Day—was due to a certain form of companionship between these scholars in a somewhat modern mimicry of the mediaeval Latin title *comites palatini*.

Notwithstanding, Dinur's public intellectuality, visibility and resourceful ambition to shape Jewish national identity, under the aegis of Zionism, only reached its fullest completion after Israeli independence. That said, one cannot ignore Dinur's ability to professionally "invent" himself several times. He had initially worked as a Hebrew educator (in Imperial Russia and during his first years in Palestine), then as a university professor showing an animated political interest which resulted in his candidacy to the first Knesset, while enjoying Ben-Gurion's endorsement. Though never reelected to the second Knesset, Dinur capitalized his professional curriculum in light of politics as he joined the Israeli government, becoming Israel's fourth Minister of Education (08.10.1951–03.11.1955) at the rather old age of 67.

This point is essential as it confirms the particularity of Dinur's personal trajectory. He presented a unique experience that consisted in the public role and social status he reached in comparison with other intellectuals belonging to his generation, less able in serving as expert intellectuals. In his capacity of Minister of Education, Dinur decided the history curricula be taught in Israeli schools. Either directly—by issuing ministerial orders—or indirectly by nominating experts (mostly close colleagues from the Hebrew University) to education policy committees, he played a high-profile political role. Not only did his decisions implement the socialist Zionist *Mamlakhtiyut* (Israeli civic consociational republicanism) as ideated and projected by Ben-Gurion but they also formalized and disseminated the historical interconnections between Jewish history and the Israeli nation-state. The categorization of Dinur's biographical and public trajectories, exhaustive as might ever be, did not find any substantial equivalences. That's what makes Ben-Zion Dinur somewhat of a *unicum* in the Zionist, later Israeli, intellectual field (Zameret 1998; Kaplan, 2003; Rein 2003).[23]

---

[23] Zameret, Z. (1998): *"Ben-Zion Dinur: A State-Building Intellectuall"*, *HaTzionut* (eds. Carpi, D. and Ratzabi, S.), N. 21, pp. 321–332 (in Hebrew) which concentrates on Dinur's ministerial actions, and to Rein, A. (2003): *"Patterns of National Historiography in B. Dinur's Works"*, *Zion*, Vol. IV, pp. 425–466 [preceded by Kaplan, Y.: "Ben-Zion Dinur (1884–1973)" [70th Anniversary of Dinur's death], pp. 411–424], ibid. (in Hebrew) which analyses Dinur's academic writings.

After all, apparent disciples such as Jacob Katz (1904–1998),[24] Menahem Stern (1925–1989), Haim Hillel Ben-Sasson (1914–1977) and Yisrael Heilprin (1910–1971) enjoyed no similar sociopolitical synergy. That said, other historians belonging to the "Jerusalem School" later bridged between the first generation of Jewish Zionist historians ("proto-Israelis") and those who would eventually become Israeli historians tout court, inasmuch as they were indeed handed down with a toolkit containing widely accepted historiographical paradigms (at least till the mid-1980s).

The fact that the historiography produced at the Hebrew University did not engender another synergic combination of academia and politics, should not be the sole criterion of judgement when assessing the collective weight of this sociogenetic phase in the development of Zionist (Israeli) historiography and scholarship. The impact of the training provided by Dinur and his colleagues is better examined in the general perception of those who were to follow the formers academic footsteps. All trainees and successors coped with a specific scientific legacy anchored to paradigms, rooted in European positivism and Jewish Haskalah, as practiced by their professors. The Jewish history department maintained much of its central European, especially German, historico-philological traditions; an approach that was heavily criticized by the socialist factions of the Yishuv. Hence, the seemingly starting point of the historiographic discipline in Palestine was not a sharp detachment from previous Jewish Central European historiography but a rather geographical relocation, that is, a sort of intellectual scientific transplantation that had been concretized by Dinur and his colleagues but which remained solid, regardless of the single historian (bright and charismatic as he might be).

The nascent national historiography, however, produced neither a sole mode nor a sole voice. As a matter of fact, it provided the means to avail one's historiographical expertise of both factual academic and educational

---

[24] As asserted by Porat (2003), in spite of Dinur's and Katz's clear interest in education as a means to propagate national sense of belonging, the two former educators had a very different perception with regard to how and in what fashion to promote this particular goal. Whereas Dinur continually mixed educational and academic activities in order to achieve political goals, Katz gradually moved from education to history and kept the two fields apart, especially in the case of writing school textbooks for pedagogic purposes (following Israeli independence). See Porat, D.A. (2003): "*One Historian, Two Histories: Jacob Katz and the Formation of a National Israeli Identity*", Jewish Social Studies, New Series, Vol. 9, No. 3 (Spring–Summer; 2003), pp. 56–75.

narration of history, according to aim and position. A variety of "national historians" gave continuous, yet different, meaning to the national Jewish existence. Following Israeli independence, with an already consolidated "Jerusalem School", a tangible shift in the academic and social creed took place. It reached culmination in the 1950s–1960s and was traceable in one of Dinur's pupils: Shmuel Ettinger (1919–1988), a historiographical case worth mentioning. In this sense, the sociogenetic norms and codes of the professional habitus of historians exemplified its adaptational capacity vis-à-vis societal changes.

ETTINGER: THE EVOLVING HISTORIOGRAPHICAL CONCEPTS OF UNITY AND CONTINUITY IN JEWISH HISTORY

Shmuel Ettinger, born in Kiev under the Czarist Empire, descended from a religious Hassidic family and was raised in Yiddish and Hebrew. He immigrated in Palestine with his family in 1936. His family legacy influenced him, as he attended a yeshiva in Hebron, alongside his studies in philosophy, economics and general history at the Hebrew University in the 1940s. After a short period of political militantism as founder of the "Hebrew Communist Association", he abandoned the leftist ideology in 1946 and fought in the 1948 War. He also changed university curriculum and was trained by Professors Yisrael Heilperin, Yitzhak Baer and Ben-Zion Dinur in the field of Jewish history. He later studied at the Institute of Slavic Studies at the University of London in 1951–1952 and acquired mastery of the Polish language and culture. In 1952 he returned to Israel and joined the Hebrew University. In 1956 Ettinger was awarded a doctorate and was appointed a professor in 1965. At the Hebrew University he developed a radical approach to modern and contemporary Jewish history that reformulated the associative affinity (in Hebrew: 'זיקה') between Diaspora and *Eretz Israel*, as disseminated by Dinur and other founders of the university. As one of the ultimate representatives of the Jerusalem School in Jewish studies at the pre-state Hebrew University, Ettinger kept emphasizing the conceptual framework revolving around the unity and continuity of Jewish history vis-à-vis periods of dispersion, meaning centripetal and centrifugal tendencies. Deeply influenced by Dubnow, he commenced to attribute the unifying role of gathering the Jewish people not to the Promised Land but to the somewhat deterministic primordial sequence of anti-Semitism (specifically Hellenistic) which reproduces anthropological stereotypes, as engendered by the inner contrast between Judaism and Western civilization (Gutwein 2013).

This thesis, consequently, expropriated Zionism (in its proto-modern forms) from being the constant historical sequence in Jewish existence. In contrast with the Zionist *leitmotif*, namely the connection between people and lost territory (encountered in the works and teachings of Dinur), Ettinger considered Zionism to be a modern socially radical phenomenon which could not characterize any national feature. Therefore, the periodization and interpretation of Jewish national sentiment strongly differ. Not only did this divergence indicate contrasting modes in exploring the national feature in Jewish history, but it revealed political dissent between Ettinger and Dinur which soon placed them on antagonistic ends. The difference is rather noteworthy regarding the setting of habitus and survival unit. The core of the collective habitus finds a diverse, possibly dual, sociogenetic source. Whereas Dinur stressed the primordial constant intergenerational yearnings of the Jewish people to the land, and thus fostered historicization unifying the people and the land via the Jewish nation-state, Ettinger refuted the association and offered a different historiographical interpretation centred on the sequence of anti-Semitism. Ettinger, therefore, defined and periodized the collective sentimental Zionist disposition as the consequence of the land's central image and role in nineteenth-century Europe, originating in the "old" diasporic survival unit. In other words, while Dinur situates the national habitus in the realization of utopian ideal of return to the lost land, Ettinger qualifies the perils of anti-Semitic persecution as the sociogenetic stratum of the Jewish habitus, later "nationalised" by the nation-state.

Based on this generalization, some scholars considered Ettinger to be a proto-post Zionist ("new historian"; see the specific chapter), or at least, as a critical historian within the Jerusalem School (Barnai 2011; Tzahor 2013).[25] Nonetheless, both trainer and trainee, Dinur and Ettinger, converged on the corrective negation of exile, meaning the restoration and normalization of the Jewish people in its land of origin through the attainment of sovereignty. In addition, the two shared significant aspects

---

[25] This is the interpretation promoted by Barnai Y. (one of Ettinger's trainees) (2011): "*Shmuel Ettinger: Historian, Teacher, and Public Figure*", Jerusalem, Shazar Center Press. The latter is discussed in Gutwein (2013) but seems to be dismissed, although indirectly, by another of Ettinger's trainees. Tzahor, Z.: "*A Biography on Another Historian*", Cathedra, N. 148 (June 2013), p. 194–197 (a review of Barnai's book).

regarding their intellectual profession. Both envisaged Jewish history as a particularistic field of research, due to the sacral national character of the Jewish people (though interpreted differently). Hence, they privileged mechanisms of public visibility such as divulgation and popularization of their work via public debates. Given these differences and similarities, the case of Ettinger may feature a habitus-building in motion, as stratified by a shift in perspective, as the generation of founders of the state and national historiography faced its immediate successors. Dinur and Ettinger were two extremes of the national habitus in the making. In spite of interpretative sensibilities, the survival unit in the land of Israel/Palestine was a common endeavour.

Regarding the historiographical method, there is little doubt about the rigour with which Hebrew University historians scrutinized the extensive documentation they accumulated. Inasmuch as they prioritized primary resources, they practiced and applied a philological method to historical research. They espoused the scrupulous empirical verification of written documents to be collected and carefully woven into each other. This historico-philological approach succeeded in reproducing the meticulous efforts by Dinur's generation to orderly delineate the long-term development of Jewish life. It thus consolidated the interconnection between Diaspora and the Promised Land, without the latter being exclusive in terms of topicality. The approach, identified with the "Jerusalem School", did not simply enable a linear historicization, neither in terms of anthological compilation, therefore pedagogical, nor in those of de-mystification by the examination of what had largely been considered *historia sacra*. It permitted the emergence of a local *historia profana* that was not necessarily Palestinocentric. The general effort, nevertheless, ensured the continuous link between the Jewish people with its land as an existential framework. A committed historical account in a momentous turning point in Jewish history under the aegis of political Zionism.

In this process of nation-state building, striving for an equilibrium between the independent universal character of academic knowledge, considered the limitations of an embryonal university governance, and the contextual political circumstances could not be tension-free. The tension between the problem of the Jews, according to political Zionism, and the problem of Judaism, as conceptualized by cultural Zionism (and binational pacifists), remained unescapable. The focus on the pedantic and articulated work of collecting and organizing archival resources did not attenuate the scope of their historiography within politics but only enabled its own solidity and finesse. According to Penslar (2007, 106):

Zionist ideology was well served by the Jews' unusually high level of textual production and by the long history of Jewish communal autonomy, which provided Zionist historians such as Ben-Zion Dinur ample evidence, reproduced in his multi-volume anthology *Yisrael Bagolah* (Israel in Exile), that the Jewish collectivity had, throughout the historic depth and geographic breadth of the diaspora, comprised a coherent national body, which, through Zionism, was merely fulfilling its longstanding and inevitable destiny.

Within the historiographical, evidently essentialist, paradigm, almost all members of the "Jerusalem School" delineated the centrality of a redemptive principle in Jewish chronicles.

The historical driving force permitted to trace an organic, ontological continuity even in contingencies such as the secular manifestations of the social and national radicalism of modern Jewish history. Nevertheless, the alignment of past events into a coherent linear spatio-temporal frame also presented variations in the extent of objectivization of history itself. History students combined both general and Jewish curricula, and encountered different sensibilities and approaches to history-writing (as asserted by historian Yisrael Bartal, trainee and professor of the Hebrew University, interviewed on 22 May 2017). On the one hand, there was the path, paved by Dinur and Baer, characterized by the tension between a broad teleological view of Jewish history and its central tendencies, a rare command of critical investigative methods directed towards detailed elements of historical reality in a wide variety of areas. On the other, some confronted the present-day subjective approach, professed by historians such as Richard Koebner, who overtly declared his self-reflective relative stand within the meaningful universe of history, thus pioneering a sort of conceptual history at the Hebrew University (Selzer 2013).[26] Koebner's rather individualistic stand was juxtaposed with the more collectivistic vision of politically engaged Zionist historians.

With this regard, one may rightly ask which academic curricula enjoyed greater success in numerical terms covering the period 1925–1947. General history or Jewish history? Significant data are those indicating the percentage of students who graduated with a general or Jewish

---

[26] See the pages on Richard Koebner (p. 158–162) in Selzer, A. (2013): "*The History of the Hebrew University of Jerusalem: Vol. IV: Who's Who Prior to Statehood: Founders, Designers, Pioneers*", Jerusalem, The Hebrew University Magnes Press (in Hebrew), 2013 (especially pp. 160–1) [also reported in the English version published in 2015].

specialization: history (23.2%; 551 in absolute number) and Jewish history (6.4%; 151 in number). The latter mean an absolute preference for general history by Hebrew University trainees over the specialization in Jewish history. Yet, Jewish history enjoyed relative popularity amongst students vis-à-vis other Jewish/Hebrew academic curricula, as other statistical data clearly indicate: *Eretz Israel* studies (1.2%; 28 in number); archaeology (1.6%; 38); Semitic languages (0.7%; 16); Hebrew language and literature (21%; 498 [combined]); Talmud and Mikrah (5.1%; 121 [combined]); Jewish philosophy (0.3%; 8) out of the total of 4492 students (on 47% lack statistical information).[27] Therefore, the impact of Jewish history within the walls of the Hebrew University seems to be somewhat marginal, since the discipline trained a much lower number of students in comparison with general history and Hebrew language and literature curricula (disciplines which may attest a true cultural revival among the Jewish population in Mandatory Palestine).

In addition, these data depict an intellectually rich, yet fragmented, academic field. The latter was not free from neither structural problems nor inner struggles over resources and prestige, which influenced the capacity to attract students and provide valid academic curricula. According to the abovementioned Bartal (2009),[28] struggles on nominations and competition over budgets, ideological conflicts and scientific disagreements did not cease after 1948. The not-so-new academic institution imported its ideas, plans and actions from Europe and the US, as it was operated by staff coming from Jewish Diaspora in those countries. This academic generation gradually transformed into "Eretz Israeli", meaning identified with the land of Israel. That is to say that the long process of establishing Jewish, later national, academic life in Palestine/Israel was a process towards the institutionalization of a nation-state, where ideology, identity and scholarship intercrossed. The model of the two history departments confirms such dynamics. In this respect, the foundation of the Hebrew University and the "Jerusalem School" was a true sociogenetic moment, since its teachings would leave footprints along the way of the

---

[27] The figures are re-elaborated from the data collected in Ben-Avot, A. (2009): "*Hebrew University Students and Graduates, 1925–1947: A Social and Academic Profile*", pp. 303–342 in Lavsky, H. [ed.] (2009): "*History of the Hebrew University of Jerusalem: Academic Progression in a Period of National Struggle*", Jerusalem, The Hebrew University Magnes Press. See the table N. 12: "Graduates from the Hebrew University 1925–1947 according to Academic Specialization", p. 323–324.

[28] Bartal, Y. (2009): "*Postscript: Academic Nation Building*", p. 488–491 in Lavsky (2009).

academic institutionalization of other establishments in Israel (despite the limited numbers of both staff and students).

After all, the Hebrew University, to which Jews came to teach and study from Central and Eastern Europe, was the first universal high education institution which codified and formalized the prevalence of the Zionist ideology through academic training. The appropriation of Jewish history resulted in a particular autonomous field: a support to the fledgling Jewish national movement. The Jewish past shifted away from its original religious terms and matched the new national context. It served Zionism in the nation-building process, through top-down social integration. The establishment embodied both generational and national rebellion vis-à-vis diasporic Jewry, while keeping alive the biblical myth of the Jewish people as the chosen people ("Light unto the Nations", as asserted in Dinur's essay of 1975[29]). This scientific historiographical exemplifies the effort to foster a unified historical consciousness that was socially acknowledged by the state, via the political ambitions of the same Dinur as Minister of Education. In other words, the professional habitus, combined with the nascent national one, placed engagement and involvement in the Jewish res publica. These two aspects, namely Jewish particularism and the public role of historians, were the first layer in the Israeli national, collective and public habitus. The standardization of professional canons, alongside the elaboration of knowledge, useful to the writing of a national history, contributed to the double process of identity-building and state-building by political Zionists. The combination of the two sets the sociogenetic dispositions that significantly transformed the nascent Jewish polity into a successful enterprise. The professional habitus and the national habitus mutually strengthened their hold on the Jewish society in Palestine and consequently consolidated the foundations of the survival unit, anchored either to the spiritual yearnings regarding the biblical land of Israel or to the dangers of Diaspora (in light of Dinur's or Ettinger's interpretation). Ideology, territory and history merged. A novel societal figuration was engendered: the Jewish nation-state.

Israel was established, and with time passing by, the scholarly cohort of the "Jerusalem School" was gradually replaced by another generation of historians. The latter, though academically socialized and professionalized by the first generation, expressed new ways of thinking and new fashions

---

[29] Dinur, B.-Z. (1975): "*Ha-Mered Be Galut Hu Ha-Yasod Be-Ma'avak Ha-Dorot*" (lit. "The Rebellion is the Foundation in the Struggle of Generations"), Jerusalem: Mossad Bialik.

in historiography. New criticism and historical imagination brought change to the understanding of Jewish history in post-Independence Israel, as we shall see in the next chapter.

REFERENCES

Barnai, Y. (1995). *Historiography and Nationalism: Trends in the Research of Eretz Israel and Its Jewish Settlement, 634–1881*, Jerusalem, The Hebrew University Magnes Press.

Barnai Y. (2011): *Shmuel Ettinger: Historian, Teacher, and Public Figure*, Jerusalem, Shazar Center Press.

Bartal, Y. (2009). "Postscript: Academic Nation Building", pp. 488–491 (cit. p. 488, p. 490) in Lavsky, H. [ed.] (2009). *History of the Hebrew University of Jerusalem: Academic Progression in a Period of National Struggle*, Jerusalem: The Hebrew University Magnes Press.

Ben-Arieh, Y. (2005). "Developments in the Study of Yedihat Ha'aretz at the Hebrew University, 1925–1948", pp. 347–409, (especially p. 366); in Lavsky, H. [ed.] (2005): *The History of The Hebrew University of Jerusalem: A Period of Consolidation and Growth*, Jerusalem: The Hebrew University Magnes Press (in Hebrew).

Brenner, M. (2010). *Prophets of the Past: Interpreters of Jewish History*, Princeton: Oxford, Princeton University Press (translated from the German original [2006] by Rendall, S.).

Dinaburg B.-Z., Baer, Y. (1935). "Editorial Aim and Purpose", *Zion*, October, 1935, Vol. 1, N. 1, pp. 1–5 (in Hebrew).

Dinur, B.-Z. (1975). *Ha-Mered Be Galut Hu Ha-Yasod Be-Ma'avak Ha-Dorot* (lit. "The Rebellion is the Foundation in the Struggle of Generations"), Jerusalem: Mossad Bialik.

Eliade, M. (1954). *Cosmos and History: The Myth of the Eternal Return* [translated by Trask, W.R.], New York, Harper Torchbooks.

Eliade, M. (1957). *The Sacred and the Profane: The Nature of Religion* [translated from French: Trask, W.R.], New York, Harvest/HBJ Publishers.

Eliade, M. (1961). *Images and Symbols; Studies in Religious Symbolism* [translated by Mairet, P.], New York, Sheed & Ward.

Gutwein, D. (2013). "Shmuel Ettinger: Anti-Semitism and the Thesis Beyond Zionism: Historiography, Politics and Status", *Iyunim Bitkumat Israel,* Vol. 23, pp. 83–175 (in Hebrew).

Kaplan, Y. (2003). "Ben-Zion Dinur (1884–1973)" [70th Anniversary of Dinur's death], *Zion*, Vol. IV, 2003, pp. 411–424 (in Hebrew).

Lavsky, H. [ed.] (2005). *The History of The Hebrew University of Jerusalem: A Period of Consolidation and Growth*, Jerusalem, The Hebrew University Magnes Press (in Hebrew).

Lavsky, H. [ed.] (2009). *History of the Hebrew University of Jerusalem: Academic Progression in a Period of National Struggle*, Jerusalem, The Hebrew University Magnes Press.

Malešević, S. (2019). Grounded Nationalisms: A Sociological Analysis. Cambridge: Cambridge University Press.

Myers, D. (1988). "History as Ideology: The Case of Ben Zion Dinur, Zionist Historian "Par Excellence"", *Modern Judaism*, Vol. 8, No. 2 (May, 1988), pp. 167–193.

Penslar, D-J. (2007). *Israel in History: The Jewish State in Comparative Perspective*, London: New York, Routledge.

Porat, D.A. (2003). "One Historian, Two Histories: Jacob Katz and the Formation of a National Israeli Identity", *Jewish Social Studies*, New Series, Vol. 9, No. 3 (Spring–Summer; 2003), pp. 56–75.

Ram, U. (1995). "Zionist Historiography and the Invention of Modern Jewish Nationhood: The Case of Ben Zion Dinur", *History and Memory*, Vol. 7, No. 1, Israeli Historiography Revisited (Spring–Summer, 1995), pp. 91–124.

Ram, U. (1996). "Those Days and This Time: The Zionist Historiography and The Invention of The Jewish National Narrative: Ben-Zion Dinur and His Time", in *"Zionut: Pulmus Ben Zmanenu"* [Zionism Controversy], *Iyunim Bitkumat Israel*, 1996 (thematic issue edited by Avi Bareli Pinhas Ginossar), pp. 126–159 (in Hebrew).

Ratzabi, S. (2002). *Between Judaism and Zionism*, Leiden: Academic Publisher Brill.

Rein, A. (2003). "Patterns of National Historiography in B. Dinur's Works", *Zion*, 2003, Vol. IV, pp. 425–466.

Said, E.W. (1978). *Orientalism*, New York, Pantheon Books.

Said, E.W. (1996). *Representations of the Intellectual*, New York, Vintage Books.

Selzer, A. (2013) [ed.]. *The History of the Hebrew University of Jerusalem: Vol. IV: "Who's Who Prior to Statehood: Founders, Designers, Pioneers"*, Jerusalem, The Hebrew University Magnes Press (in Hebrew).

Tzahor, Z. (2013). "A Biography on Another Historian", *Cathedra*, N. 148 (June 2013), pp. 194–197.

Zameret, Z. (1998). "Ben-Zion Dinur: A State-Building Intellectual", *HaTzionut* (eds. Carpi, D. and Ratzabi, S.), N. 21, pp. 321–332 (in Hebrew).

CHAPTER 4

Mamlakhtiyut: The Silver Platter and Consolidation of Israel's National Habitus

The Silver Platter
Lyrics: Natan Alterman
… and the land will have rest. The heavens' eye crimsons
And dims away slow
Over borders still smoking.
And the nation will rise, torn-hearted but breathing …
To accept the one miracle
There is no other coming …
She prepares for the rite. She wakes with the moon
And stands, ere the dawn, swathed in joy and in awe.
Then before her appear
A boy and a girl
Marching, ever slowly, towards the fore of the nation.
Wearing full kits, and heavy of boot,
They rise in the path
Silent proceeding.
Their clothes are unchanged, water's not yet erased
A trace of days' toil and nights spent under fire.
Tired without end, ascetics from rest,
Dripping with Hebrew youth's dews—
The two approach quiet,
And motionless stand.
Not a sign if they're living, or if they've been shot.

© The Author(s), under exclusive license to Springer Nature Switzerland AG 2024
A. Helled, *Israel's National Historiography*, Palgrave Studies on Norbert Elias, https://doi.org/10.1007/978-3-031-62795-8_4

75

Then the nation will ask, washed in wonder and tears,
"Who are you?" And their silent reply:
"We are the silver platter
Upon which you were handed the state of the Jews."
So they shall say. And fall to their feet in a shadowy veil.
And the rest shall be told in the annals of Israel.

"The state will not be given to the Jewish people on a silver platter" ran the saying attributed to Chaim Weizmann, already President of the Zionist Organization (1920–1946) and soon first President of Israel (1949–1952), published by *Ha'aretz* newspaper on 15 December 1947, soon after the UN decision to endorse the partition of Palestine (adopted by the UN General Assembly as Resolution 181 on 29 November 1947). The poet Nathan Alterman (1910–1970) put into words the tragic understanding of the sacrifices that everyone understood would have to be made for Jewish independence. The poem first appeared in the Alterman's column "The seventh column" on 19 December 1947 in *Davar* (the newspaper of the Zionist left; owned by the Histadrut, that is, the Zionist Labour Federation of Hebrew workers in *Eretz Israel*).[1] This poem juxtaposes the gruesome and heavy sacrifice the Zionist Yishuv, namely the "*makhtarot*" (the Jewish paramilitary organizations, i.e., Haganah, Irgun and Lehi), had to make with the independence of the state: a miracle which is born out of sweat, fire and blood.

The dramatic combination of "wonder and tears" prefigures an emotional attachment and sense of belonging that supposedly transcends differences and intestine rivalries within the Jewish entity which has just become a polity. It calls for the need of national unity and endurance vis-à-vis all hardships and adversities. As the poem presents the emergence of a novel survival unit, it seems appropriate to open this chapter with the assumption of a unified front containing the various animas of the newborn Israeliness. Neither the sociological and cultural diversity that had been part of Jewish life in Diaspora nor the hierarchy of different agents could produce a collective Israeless. The survival unit in the making had to be realized through the ultimate sacrifice by each and every individual. The latter dictates the construction of a national habitus (as the poem

---

[1] The poem was later set to music by Israeli composer Nurit Hirsh and sung by Israeli singer Yehoram Gaon in 1973. Consequently, the lyrics that had echoed the imminent sacrifice of the 1948 War of Independence were updated to that of the Yom Kippur War in 1973.

itself suggests in the myth of heroism in the form of the "silver platter") to be handed down to posterity by the generation of Nephilim, meaning the heroic veteran pioneer-settlers in the pre-statehood period, who are the legitimate founders of the Israeli survival unit, as if "[T]hey are equal in relation to the fate awaiting them" (Canetti 1962, 274). The political intention, therefore, as in all nations, was to provide structure and ground rules to citizens, render them complicit in their fate and identification with power, while the price of survival and self-preservation was being labelled as a heroic sacrifice. Moreover, the construction of the national habitus also entailed a sense of belonging, anchored to the inherent power of the collective. It thus diluted existent social cleavages, at least in appearance, and in out-to-do and ought-to-be mode.

Though political power was highly identifiable and definable in the persona of David Ben-Gurion (Shavit 1992) and some other power-brokers and bureaucrats (for instance, Pinchas Lavon, Golda Meir, Levi Eshkol etc.) within the centre-left political party MAPAI (the Hebrew acronym for the Workers' Party of Eretz Yisrael), the national habitus that was striven for had no partisan ideological specificities (which did not mean any lesser institutional activism). The nascent Israeli national habitus delineated the rite and form of the sovereign nation-state in its daily presentability, solemnity and honourability. The approach consisted in the unification between state and the ethical and moral values of Judaism, hence the two feet of political Zionism, embedded and shaped by Ben-Gurion's civic thought. The aim was to guarantee the formal nationalized republican tenet of public life in the new state (Kedar 2007a, b, 2013). This institutional frame centred around two principles: the centralist role of the national system and its institutions, and the dignity and respectful conduct of institutional officeholders and functionaries. This approach was soon termed *Mamlakhtiyut*.[2]

---

[2] Hebrew-English dictionaries often translate the term as "statehood" or "sovereignty" with the adjectival form *mamlakhti* rendered as "officially of the state" (thus institutional or public, such as *mamlakhti* education). The term, and concept, was coined by Ben-Gurion as its main guiding principle from the Hebrew radix m-l-kh (the basic letters from which the verb "to reign" is composed, hence the words: "king" [*melekh*], "queen" [*malkah*], "kingdom" [*mamlakhah*] and "monarchy" or "kingship" [*melukhah*]. Accordingly, the term epitomized both the biblical and messianic idea of Eretz Israel and the modern model of national sovereignty. However, *Mamlakhtiyut* as a concept can find its origin in the Russian word *gosudarstvo* (literally "kingdom" or "empire"; adjective: *gosudarstvenni*), as Ben-Gurion was deeply familiar with both Russian culture and politics.

According to Kedar (2002), Ben-Gurion did not opt for the adjective "national" in expanding Israel's state-building, inasmuch as there was no demographical correlation between the Jewish state and the Jewish nation (at that time of its independence, the majority of Jewry still lived in Diaspora).[3] This grand ideology imbued significance to the sacrifice and hardships of Israel's early independence (1948–1953), and thus contained strong civic-republican and consociational forms in terms of political power. It aimed to construct a democratic regime and to establish a comprehensive recognition and identification of citizenry that viewed the sovereign state as the centre of authority to be respected. Public policies sought to construct a symbolic-conceptual-moral framework for the Zionist state to provide its citizens with common civic ground rules. This was an imperative, since the Jewish settlement in Palestine had been founded on voluntary adhesion. Therefore, the (intensive) completion of nation-state building had to devise state-based apparatuses in order to enforce common civic national culture through its organizational capacity, ideological penetration and networks of micro-solidarity in the sovereign yet prevalently immigrant society (Malešević 2019). The *Mamlakhtiyut* of the state also meant an institutional transition from party-led bodies (the various factions of Zionism) to state-centric public institutions.[4]

This transition took place via novel normative procedures. The latter expressed common-law and civil-law mixedness, as Israeli jurisprudence was fashioned by Hebrew-Jewish juridical heritage, the Ottoman past, the imported British colonial jurisprudence during the Mandate, as well as by continental Europe's juridical principles (Kedar 2007a, b; Mautner 2011). Like any modern nation-state, Israel institutionalized its status as the central provider of order and security, especially embodied by the universal military

---

[3] See Kedar, N. (2002). "Ben-Gurion's Mamlakhtiyut: Etymological and Theoretical Roots", *Israel Studies*, Vol. 7, No. 3 (Fall, 2002), pp. 117–133.

[4] This change was not due to the construction of *Mamlakhtiyut* per se but to the incessant decrease in appeal of old ideologies (chiefly Zionist socialism). As the framework of ideological currents became less, the capacity to attract and recruit new followers was "expropriated" by the state. The latter reached its peak in the 1970s when party-institutions such as Beit-Berl (named after Berl Katznelson, the spiritual leader of the Labour movement in Mandate Palestine), Ben-Zvi Institute, the Ben-Gurion Heritage Institute etc. were transformed into independent (supposedly apolitical) research centres whose administration and material resources (namely, archives, libraries, collections etc.) were affiliated to public universities.

conscription (Kedar 2008).[5] That said, the process of Israeli state-building shaped the Jewish polity as a regulated welfare democracy with a well-defined hierarchical structure, thus manifesting a rather elitist position.

According to Bareli (2009), this implied a rather top-down Ashkenazi "paternalistic and patronizing" system which was not able to peacefully integrate those who were not identified with Zionism (namely the Arab minority as well as the Jewish immigrants from Arab-speaking countries, identified collectively as *Mizrahim*, lit. "easterners"). The so-called Second Israel was gradually born.[6] This was in contradiction with Ben-Gurion's immigration policy of *Kibbutz Galuyot* (lit. "The Ingathering of the Exiles"), which aimed to facilitate the Jewish melting-pot in new-born Israel, alongside the other state-based tools of public education.[7] Tensions,

[5] There is no doubt Ben-Gurion was a security-conscious leader who put in his mind the importance of an efficient army. Israel's first prime minister and minister of defence founded the Israel Defence Forces, while emphasizing its protective duty as "*Tzva Ha'Am*": the people's army, based on compulsory military service and not on professional mercenaries. The Security Service Act of 1949 and the Military Justice Law, promulgated by the Knesset in 1955, outline the *mamlakhti* imperative to formalize and uphold discipline and justice among the ranks of the IDF. Kedar, N. (2008): "A Civilian Commander in Chief: Ben-Gurion's Mamlakhtiyut, the Army and the Law", *Israel Affairs*, Vol. 14, N. 2, p. 202–217.

[6] The mass immigration of oriental Jews—with scarce structures for integration to take place—also engendered the so-called second Israel and moulded for generations the "ethnic demon" in Israeli politics. See Tsur, Y. (1997). "Aliyah from the Islamic Countries", pp. 57–82 in Zameret and Yablonka [ed.s] (1997): "*The First Decade: 1948–1958*", Jerusalem, Yad Izhak Ben-Zvi Publications.

[7] The old Yishuv, which numbered circa 650,000 individuals in 1948, carried out a cultural and spiritual integration in order to forge the new nation, namely through a uniform education. The 1953 State Education Law replaced the pre-statehood educational currents that had been linked to political factions (namely, the general current: centre-right Zionism, the socialist worker's current, the religious-Zionist Mizrahi current). Nonetheless, the "sectorialization" of Israeli education kept the parallel religious *mamlakhti* education system (anchored to the state but exclusively administered by the national religious faction), the Haredi orthodox yeshivot (Jewish Talmudic educational institutions) and the public Arab education (with evident and unresolved contradictions). See Zameret, Z. (2002). *The Melting Pot in Israel: The Commission of Inquiry Concerning Education in the Immigrant Camp During the Early Years of the State*, Albany, State University OF New York Press; ibid. (2003): "*The Education in the First Decade*", Tel-Aviv, Open University Press (in Hebrew); Hacohen, D. (2010). "*The 1953 State Education Law: A Missed Decision?*" in Hacohen, Lissak [ed.s] (2010). *Decisional Crossroads and Key Matters in Israel*, Kiryat Sedeh-Boḳer, Ben-Gurion Institute: Ben-Gurion University Press (in Hebrew: "*Tsomte hakhra'ot u-farshiyot mafteaḥ be-Yiśra'el*"); and Tadmor-Shimoni, T. (2010): *A Homeland Lesson: National Education and State-Building* 1954–1966, Kiryat Sedeh Boker, Ben-Gurion Institute: Ben-Gurion University Press.

therefore, emerged from these elitist bourgeois stances which were pushing aside the socialist spirit of *halutziyut* (Kabalo 2009) that had previously characterized Zionist's egalitarian and agrarian pioneering, and were at the heart of Mapai's hegemonic position in politics. The professional and academic middle class, product of veteran settlers, and the chiefly Mizrahi agrarian proletariat in the 1950s already showed sociological cleavages in terms of wage gap and social status with which Mapai had difficulty to cope with (Bareli and Cohen 2008a, b and ibid. 2012).

The consequence was a somewhat blatant correspondence, in the early 1950s, between Mapai's head-figures and the composition of ministers, elected not through democratic procedures but dependent on Mapai's internal party-system "with virtually no interference", while recruiting civil society via propagandistic discourse (Bareli 2007a, 2017). That hyper-structuration of state mechanisms around the ruling *Mapainik* element clearly showed the relevance of inner-party affairs and the go-getter, wheeler-dealer nature of its politics. The latter shaped the path of Israel's public life and its sociopolitical habitus for decades to come. Institutional stakeholders thus became the embodiment of decision-making and concrete implementation of public policies (till then part of the Jewish Yishuv's semi-autonomous institutions), not without fundamental ideological contradictions (Bareli 2007b). The transversal presence of the state shaped and conditioned a national habitus which aimed to place social cohesion and collective consciousness at the centre of the Jewish society. The processual institutionalization of the nation-state-based survival unit concerned the army, welfare services, health and education systems, but also the expansion of local academia (Tzahor 2001). Yet, the figuration of the Jewish democratic state, sanctioned by the 1948 Declaration of Independence,[8] excluded non-European and non-Zionist citizens from state strongholds or at least obstructed their

---

[8] The term "democracy" does not appear explicitly in the declaration. However, it lists the values and freedoms which are intrinsically identified with democratic rule: "THE STATE OF ISRAEL will be open for Jewish immigration and for the Ingathering of the Exiles; it will foster the development of the country for the benefit of all its inhabitants; it will be based on freedom, justice and peace as envisaged by the prophets of Israel; it will ensure complete equality of social and political rights to all its inhabitants irrespective of religion, race or sex; it will guarantee freedom of religion, conscience, language, education and culture; it will safeguard the Holy Places of all religions; and it will be faithful to the principles of the Charter of the United Nations". For the official text of the declaration in English, see the Israeli Knesset website: https://main.knesset.gov.il/en/about/pages/declaration.aspx.

integration into the high ranks of public bureaucracy and civil service. This exclusion was neither overt nor necessarily systematic but it did, in fact, trace "established" and "outsider" positions. Ashkenazi Jews, especially those who were sabras, mostly descendants of pre-1948 Jewish immigration into Palestine,[9] became integral active members of Israeli citizenry, whereas other components of society remained on its margins. A clear case of such an exclusion was that of the Arab Palestinian community. Once englobed into the borders of Israel after the 1948 War, the Arab population of Israel was granted citizenship, but was subject to martial law. The latter administered Arab villages and individual activities such as work and travel permits, curfews, administrative detentions etc. until 1966.

All that being said, after its Independence, the young state had to follow its promise, as proclaimed in the 1948 Declaration: "[...] bringing the blessings of progress to all the country's inhabitants, and aspiring towards independent nationhood". Government needed, therefore, to secure its political achievement, guarantee the basic wellbeing of its population and plan its path towards growth and progress among modern nations. It had to develop infrastructures, both material and symbolic, design projects and policies to be implemented. Within this framework the element of expertise and scholarship found a role to play.

Mamlakhti Intelligentsia

The complexities and contradictions of *Mamlakhtiyut* are also reflected in the ambiguous role of Israeli intelligentsia. In the first two decades of Israeli independence, the Jewish state consolidated and codified the

---

[9] A special social status was reserved to the members of the "Second Aliyah" that took place between 1904 and 1914, during which approximately 35,000 Jews, mostly from the Russian Empire, immigrated into Ottoman Palestine. For decades to come, the Zionist ethos identified the second Aliyah with socialist pioneering and strong charismatic leadership, which set the foundations of worker's organizations, and the health and education systems. Moreover, although this group was a quantitative minority among other Jewish immigrants during the same period, it produced a formidable self-consciousness and greatly influenced the Zionist enterprise. On the issue, see Neumann, B. (2009). "Teshikat a'Halutzim" (The Passion of Pioneers"), Tel-Aviv, Sapir: Am Oved; and Alroey, G. (2014). "An Unpromising Land. Jewish Migration to Palestine in the Early Twentieth Century", Stanford, Stanford University Press.

so-called scientific strategists (Lissak and Cohen 2010, 2011)[10] who were recruited from the three pre-state-established academic and scientific institutions (the fourth academic, though not scientific, pre-state establishment was the Bezalel Academy of Art and Design, founded in 1906). The Hebrew University of Jerusalem, the Weizmann Institute of Science in Rehovot and the Haifa-based Technion were the scholarly stock from which Israeli decision-makers could recruit experts in order to implement their public policies. Scientific strategists prevalently came from natural sciences and exact sciences (namely, chemistry, physics, mathematics, biology/medicine, agronomy), with few exceptions of scholars specialized in other disciplines (such as philosopher Nathan Rotenstreich, demographer Roberto Bachi and sociologist Shmuel N. Eisenstadt [sociology]). Their dialectical engagement was based on loyalty versus the political establishment, state mechanisms as well as on the pioneering positions of these scholars within the academic milieu. This group became representative of a new kind of social agent/intellectual figure: the Israeli public expert. They were not simple administrative functionaries but civil servants who were directly or indirectly sponsored and "officialised" by the state (Bourdieu 1990; id. 1998). These experts obtained a monopolistic position in collaborating with state authorities and ministries. Their peculiar professional position had a give-and-take nature.

The group pushed *Mamlakhtiyut* forward as its members helped the state to shape policies and institutions, and in exchange to their advice, their academic careers and public prominence were promoted. The institutionalization of the scientific domain in Israel exemplifies this development. The establishment of the Council for Higher Education in 1958 (with its powerful policy-leading organ of the Planning and Budgeting Committee [PBC], the Israel Academy of Sciences and Humanities in 1961) codified the parameters and criteria of the academic collective. Consequently, Israeli scholars, once entering academia, were (and still are) socialized into a professional habitus which has a well-stratified public system at its core. This intersection, made of collegiality and social responsibility in exchange for prestige (organizational entitlement), sets state

---

[10] See Lissak and Cohen (2010). "The Scientific Strategists in the Period of Mamlakhtyiut: The Symbiotic Relations between the Academic Community and the Centers of Power", *Iyunim Bitkumat Israel*, Vol. 20, pp. 1–27 (in Hebrew), and the English version of the same article: "Scientific Strategists in the Period of Mamlakhtyiut: Interaction Between the Academic Community and Political Power Centers", *The Journal of Israeli History*, Vol. 30, No. 2, September 2011, pp. 189–210.

patronage as the main stakeholder of academia. Without the need to give any ethical judgement regarding the intercrossing of interests, the state consolidated the Israeli academic system and allowed its rapid expansion.

Four public universities were founded: Bar-Ilan University in Ramat-Gan (1955), aimed to provide higher education, alongside Jewish and Talmudic studies, to the religious-national stream in Israel;[11] University of Tel-Aviv (1956), established despite the overt opposition of the Hebrew University;[12] University of Haifa (1963), aimed to provide academic accreditation in social sciences and humanities in complementarity to the well-established Technion at the initiative of Mapainik Haifa Mayor Abba Hushi (1898–1963) and the head of the city's education department Moshe Rinot (1921–1984) who had later became a professor of history of education at the same university (he headed the school of education in the period 1968–1974); and the University of Beer-Sheva (1969), renamed "Ben-Gurion University of the Negev" in 1973, while seeking to promote the development of the Negev.[13] The entry of the scientific community into politics and that of politics of *Mamlakhtiyut* into the field of academia seemed to have been quite beneficial, inasmuch as the cooperation between the parts contributed to develop a well-educated civil society, which bridged the gap between the new state and its model of reference, namely the "Western world" (Europe, and later the US).

It enabled Israeli society to constitute standards of universal scientific culture as well as to obtain the status of a "credential society" (Collins

---

[11] On the history of Bar-Ilan University, see the three volumes written by staff members of the university (all in Hebrew): Klein, M. (1997). *Bar-Ilan: Academy, Religion and Politics* [Bar-Ilan: Academia, Dat u'Politica], Jerusalem, Hebrew University Magnes Press; Schwartz, D. [ed.] (2006). *Bar-Ilan University: From Idea to Action* [Universitat Bar-Ilan: MeRah'aion le'Maas], 2 volumes, Ramat-Gan, Bar-Ilan University Press; Iram, Y., Friedlander, Y., Ohaion, S. (2013). *The Mission of a Religious University* [Yiuda shel Universita Datit], Ramat-Gan, Bar-Ilan University Press.

[12] For further reading regarding the struggles and difficulties in founding the university: Cohen, U. (2014). *Academia in Tel- Aviv: The Making of a University*, Jerusalem, The Hebrew University Magnes Press (in Hebrew).

[13] For further reading (in Hebrew), see: Hadari, Z., Tal, H. (1984). *Chapters in The History of the University* [Prakim be'Toldot ha'Universita], Beer-Sheva, Ben-Gurion University Press; Gardos, Y., Nevo, I. [eds.] (2014): *Science and Scholarship in the Negev: The Story of Ben-Gurion University in the Negev*, Vol 1: "The Founders" [Mada u'Ruakh ba'Negev: Universitat Ben-Gurion ve'Toldotea be'Reyi ha'Mekhkar], Beer-Sheva, Ben-Gurion University Press.

1979; Cohen 2001).[14] Noteworthy is that the expansion and variegation of institutions of higher education in Israel was no different from that in other countries during the post-WWII period. Academic education meant modernization of society, economic growth through the diversification and qualification of the local labour market. In spite of the tight affinity between politics and the abovementioned scientific strategists, the cadre lacked almost entirely the development of humanities, history included (with the already discussed exception of Dinur, see the previous chapter).

May the explanation be the recent constitution of national history within the borders of a sovereign state which preferred investing in security, infrastructure, health and agriculture, rather than in the somewhat politically inconvenient issue of its national genesis, namely the factious and fragmented Jewish society of the Yishuv and/or the consequences of the 1948 War. According to Tzahor (2001), Israeli historians, who mainly belonged to the Hebrew University, did not take part in constructing and disseminating the national narrative, since they had not been involved in the political field, and if so, only in marginal fashions "ex-cathedra", outside the walls of university. The decision by the Jerusalem School to establish an institute for studying contemporary Jewry ("Avraham Harman Institute of Contemporary Jewry" founded in 1959 by prof Moshe Davis: the first American Jew to receive a PhD from the Hebrew University) and not for the study of Zionism and Israel would exemplify the mild scholarly interest in Jerusalem. The void would be filled in by the University of Tel-Aviv that would inaugurate a specialized institute for the study of Zionism in 1962. Consequently, the "hub" for academic research of Zionism and Israel, slowly but inevitably, shifted from the Hebrew University of Jerusalem to Tel-Aviv. However, there was one topic whose importance to Israeli identity and politics supposedly transcended the inner divisions of Israeli academe and was to be placed at the heart of the Israeli national survival unit, its *mamlakhti* conscience and acquire intergenerational significance: the Holocaust and its impact on Israeli statehood.

[14] Collins, R. (1979). *The Credential Society: An Historical Sociology of Education and Stratification*, New York, Academic Press. On the Israeli case, in which the Hebrew University of Jerusalem played a key role in the constitution and establishment of a powerful (Ashkenazi) elite of state-bureaucrats, see Cohen, U. (2001). "The Hebrew University of Jerusalem from Yishuv to State: initial Perspectives on the Development of the Credential Society in Israel", *HaTzionut*, N. 23, pp. 297–329.

Israeli Mamlakhtiyut, the Shoah
and Its Historiography

The awareness and interest in the Shoah in Israeli society, and consequently in academia, was gradual. It developed in phases. The first one included the period between the years 1945 and 1949 which testified the unfolding of the tragedy. It was pushed aside by the struggle for independence and the precarious social and psychological readiness to confront the Holocaust. This was also bound to material reasons. Despite hard evidence that had already emerged from the Nuremberg Trials (1945–1949), testimonies and information about the destiny of Jews during WWII were only partial, if not scarce, due to the unavailability of documentation. Furthermore, the trials took place in the tense geopolitical context of the Cold War, which prioritized military issues such as aggression, crimes against peace, prisoners of war, massacres and crimes against civilians and humanity (related to Nazi Germany) over issues related to the Jewish population. Noteworthy was also the Zionist prism through which the Yishuv judged the Shoah. The ideological attitude by many Zionists was the so-called negation of Diaspora that considered the refusal of European Jews to adhere to Zionism as what actually brought extinction upon them, with the exception of Ghetto fighters to whom the myth of heroism was immediately attributed. Moreover, the survivors themselves were busy in reconstructing their lives in the revived Jewish society. The latter quickly adhered to national survival unit, after the violent decivilization experienced in Europe.

According to Yablonka (1994/1999), Zionist ideological prejudice met neither victimization nor heroism but forms of entrepreneurship (e.g., the majority of medicine students graduating from the Hebrew University were in fact Holocaust survivors as well as most of Israel's first professional aviators). The second phase in affronting the Shoah in Israel span in the years 1950–1962. During that period the new state started to appropriate the Holocaust in terms of historical factuality. The political establishment considered the Shoah as a central component of Israel's national identity to be reconstructed. This process reached culmination in the Eichmann Trial (1961). Hence, throughout these first decades of statehood, Israel lacked historical perspective on the Shoah. The tragedy was too fresh for it to assume any critical, at least distanced, dimension. Any information was still "raw" and not properly organized, thus easily manipulated for political purposes (as attested by the 1952 Reparations Agreement between Israel and West Germany and the wave of protest against it[15]).

The state centred its actions on the legislation of laws: Law for the penalization of Nazis and their helpers (1950), the legal basis of the abovementioned Eichmann Trial; the "Holocaust and Heroism Remembrance" Law (1951) and the Yad Vashem Law (1953), establishing the Martyrs' and Heroes' Remembrance Authority, aimed to institutionalize "the commemoration in the Homeland of all those members of the Jewish people who gave their lives, or rose up and fought the Nazi enemy and its collaborators" and to set up "a memorial to them, and to the communities, organizations and institutions that were destroyed because they belonged to the Jewish people [...]" (Shoah and Heroism Commemoration-Yad Vashem Law, 1953, Israeli Law Book, N. 132, p. 144); followed by the "Holocaust and Heroism Remembrance Day" Law (1959), which assumed its official and commemorative character only in 1962, after the Eichmann Trial. Therefore, it was the ample legislation and the mediatic Eichmann Trial that resulted in a substantial transformation of relations amongst Israelis (and Jews living in Diaspora) and the perception of the Holocaust. As personal testimonies were recorded, transcribed and organized in official archives, the trial permitted not only immediate, somewhat impressionistic, evaluation of the breadth and depth of the Holocaust but a comparative juxtaposition of different historically valid documentation providing evidence for years to come. The latter elicited questions about how and why it happened, while inextricably linking it to the Jewish state whose independence inaugurated the beginning of a new era for Jews all over the world. Through this process, which inevitably stretched between juridical and historical facts (and public perception), Israel fused together Zionism and Holocaust remembrance. By doing, so, the state collectivized and nationalized another element to its habitus. Israeli statehood formalized its supremacy as the sole remedy to the tragedies in Diaspora, and further placed itself as the protector of the Jewish people by using the Eichmann Trial as well as the abovementioned legislation. The Jewish

---

[15] The agreement, together with the Kastner trial (1955), challenged the conflictual and politicized atmosphere with regard to major Holocaust-related events, testifying bitter struggles between the leftist Mapai and rightist Herut, as well as with the vocal opposition by the communist Mapam and Maki parties.

nation-state was the only survival unit to defend the Jewish collectivity. In order to provide this kind of identification, and therefore to be able to hand it down to future Israelis, historiography became a significant domain for the elaboration of the Shoah in relation to Jewish history and to the growing interest in Zionist history.

Two Israeli historians, though not the only ones, seem to have influenced and institutionalized most of the study of the Shoah in Israel: Israel Gutman (1923–2013) and Yehuda Bauer (born in 1926). Both faced in person the perils of the Holocaust and drew younger scholars at the Hebrew University to deal with this emotionally charged history. Historians such as Dalia Ofer, Sara Bender, Tuvia Friling, Hanna Yablonka, Yehiham Weitz and Daniel Blatman were direct students of the two "giants" of Shoah studies in Israel. Many others, who had not been directly trained by the two, followed their lead (namely, University of Tel-Aviv historian Dina Porat and Bar-Ilan University historian Dan Michman). That is not to say, of course, there were no inner disputes and controversies within this group of Shoah scholars, as in any other academic and intellectual field. Yet, the emphasis they put on the Holocaust influenced the whole field of Israeli historiography. Their works not only addressed the Jews as victims of tragic events but also combined macro features and long-term processes, namely, anti-Semitism (traditional and modern, alike), the conditions of exile, German society and the rise of Nazism. Moreover, Bauer himself, in his book *Rethinking the Holocaust* (2002), reevaluates, and somewhat downsizes, the influence and conjunctures of geopolitical circumstances in relation to the Shoah and Israeli independence. The precursors of Holocaust studies in Israel viewed the Shoah as a historical unicum that could not be compared to other genocides but which couldn't (and cannot) be exclusively defined by and through its impact on Zionism and Israel. Nevertheless, as shown by the academic production of their trainees, an almost transversal academic interest shifted from studying the Holocaust tout court to exploring the Yishuv leadership's role in rescue attempts during the Holocaust and the impact of the tragedy on issues and questions pertaining to Israeli identity. The Jewish nation-state, its inner Zionist motivations and its sociogenetic legacy became a lodestone for various generations of Israeli scholars.

WRITING ISRAELI HISTORY: THE GENESIS
OF CONTEMPORARY NATIONAL HISTORIOGRAPHY

The personal and intellectual interactions between the background of the researcher and the facts as first-hand experiences moulding his/her own self-consciousness in relation to the challenge of history-writing lie at the at the heart of the historiographical scholarly work on Israeli national history. Unlike the sociogenetic legacy of first-generation historians who based their works at the "Jerusalem School" on the macro, secular and millennial interdependence between Jewish history and the land of Israel, the novel generation of historians had to confront the Jewish nation-state as a living historical fact, while facing the almost inevitable mirroring-effect of being part of his or her personal biography. According to Gorny (1997), one of Israel's first historians to specialize in Israeli history tout court, he himself, and perhaps the entire generation of fellow historians, was "torn between [my] personal experience and [my] evaluation of historical facts [...] no viewpoint is alternative, both are parts of a somewhat more comprehensive viewpoint".[16] For sure, the tremendous changes and challenges faced by people around the years of Israeli independence (the aftermath of the Holocaust, the end of the British Mandate and the difficulties of integration into the Zionist melting-pot) found some stability in the principles of *Mamlakhtiyut*, as the latter provided institutional and sociopolitical order. However, whereas the study of the Holocaust had a historiographical anchor in Jewish studies and was instrumental for adding another pillar to the Israeli national habitus, Israeli national history had to develop "step-by-step". It had to be autonomized as a discipline vis-à-vis both Jewish history and history of the Middle East, whose "Arabist" and "Orientalist" specializations had already been institutionalized at the Hebrew University. Tel-Aviv University became an alternative in terms of content and academic interest.

A scholarly journal that demonstrates the extent to which Israeli researchers espoused *Mamlakhtiyut* and Zionism as their disciplinary beacon is undoubtedly the *HaTzionut* (lit. "Zionism"). Formally named *HaTzionut: Ma'assef Le'Toldot Ha'Tnuah Ha'Zionit ve' HaYishuv*

---

[16] Gorny, Y. (1997). "The Decade of Wonder: Reflections on the First Decade of the State in the Jubilee Year" in Zameret & Yablonka [ed.s] (1997), pp. 363–370, citation p. 353 (my translation). The latter opens a debate over the self-reflective nature of national historiography (see the introductory chapter).

Ha'Yehudi be'Eretz Israel (lit. "Collection of the History of the Zionist Movement and the Jewish Settlement in Eretz Israel") was founded in 1970 and published by The Chaim Weizmann Institute for the Study of Zionism and Israel at Tel-Aviv University. The journal was an academic interdisciplinary platform that had been initiated by a group of Zionist scholars, mainly historians from Tel-Aviv University, who had begun to show academic interest in Zionism, its history and politics. Their initiative was ultimately formalized. It was established in 1962 as the university's first research institute by prof Gavriel Cohen (1928–2021), who served as its first director, in partnership with the World Zionist Organization and the Lester and Sally Entin Faculty of Humanities.[17] *HaTzionut* was first edited by prof Daniel Carpi (1926–2005) with the aim to present and address ongoing critical historiographical research on the political, social, cultural and organizational transformations in Zionism in Jewish Diaspora and in Israel, alike. The journal was divided into three sections: essays, archival documentation, bibliography and book reviews. It was published by the HaKibutz HaMeuchad Publishing (the publishing house of the United Kibbutz movement, founded in 1939 by socialist Zionists).[18]

The journal programmatically announced the ongoing changes in Jewish historiography vis-à-vis the Zionist enterprise. It gave centre stage and critical interpretation to multiple facets of Israel's pre-statehood. As the journal's first editor-in-chief, Daniel Carpi (1926–2005) asserted in its inaugural premise:

> The Chaim Weizmann Institute for the Study of Zionism of Tel-Aviv University presents to the public of readers a first collection of researches on the history of the Zionist movement and the Jewish Yishuv in modern times.

[17] The Institute was headed by professors Gavriel Cohen, Daniel Carpi, Matitiahu Mintz, Yosef Gorny, Ron Zweig, Shalom Ratzabi and Anita Shapira; sustained by an academic committee whose members (in the past and present) are professors Alexer Bein (biographer of Herzl, Israel Prize Laureate, 1987), historians: Yehuda Niny, Dina Porat, Yaacov Shavit, Yaron Tsur and Bilha (Billie) Melman, Meir Hazan, as well as literary scholar Dan Laor etc. As declared by the Chaim Weizmann Institute, it is "devoted to advancing scholarly research of the Zionist idea, the Zionist movement, the Yishuv (Jewish community in Palestine), and the State of Israel, from a multidisciplinary approach and a critical perspective". The Institute is currently chaired by historian prof Motti Golani.

[18] Closed in 2002, the journal "resurrected" under the name of *Israel: Journal for the Research of Zionism and the State of Israel-History, Culture, Society* (also in Hebrew). The latter is published biannually and is specialized in interdisciplinary research of Israeli society (such as literature, sociology, gender, art, diplomacy etc.).

[…] Our hope is that this collection, with the ones that will follow—as we presume—will contribute to *widen our knowledge and understanding* of this period in the history of [the people of] Israel (originally: "Toldot Israel" [chronicles of Israel]) which is so essential, not only as a scientific subject of research but also to the *deepening of our conscience as a people coming back to its land and to its cultural heritage* […] we do not claim the right of being pioneers of such a research, as many fine and prominent scholar have already published works and bibliographic materials. However, it is highly doubtful that in these times of *tremendous political and cultural transformations* befalling the people of Israel in the last generation […] once many historiographical convictions have been questioned, renewing opinions and currents. […] The works the Institute for the Study of Zionism has initiated and will initiate aim at uncovering the roots, the framework as effectuated by the Jewish national movement; on all its sides: achievements, failures, actions and scandals. […] What is *the place and part of the state of Israel in general history of the Jewish people?* What has it to offer? And how will it know to integrate and express the *immanent forces*, which have befallen the generations of Jews in Diaspora, and have been a subject and a driving-force to the history of the people in its days of exile? […].[19]

In other words, the editorial premise was a manifesto calling for a historiography that would be capable of placing and reconstructing relations in Jewish contemporary history between the diasporic past and the far-reaching phenomenon of Zionism and its greatest accomplishment: the constitution of a national home in the land of Israel.

The growing interest in Zionist history and the autonomization of the academic field within the faculty of Humanities at Tel-Aviv University reproduced the model of the Hebrew University (as all the rest of Israeli universities) with the structural separation of general history and Jewish history as distinct historiographical realms (and eventually departments). However, it came to terms with the peculiarity of Zionist Israeli history as a new subfield of specialization within the already established Jewish history. The aim was to gain research specificity and thus autonomize the scholarly interest within an existent institutional frame. This humble scope achieved the consent of prof Shlomo Simonsohn (1923–2019), known for his conservative and elitist views on higher education which meant not only the dichotomous division between university and professional schools

[19] Carpi, D. *HaTzionut*, N. 1, pp. 7–8 (original in the Hebrew; both translation and *italics* are mine). The first number of the journal was dedicated to the memory of Dr Galia Jardeni-Agmon (1924–1968), a socialist Zionist who had been a literary critic, journalist and editor and who joined the founders of the Chaim Weizmann Institute as a researcher in 1963.

but also his opposition to the systematic enlargement of universities (inauguration of new fields of research as well as providing public subsidies to low-income students). At any rate, Tel-Aviv University inaugurated a novel scientific path, centred around the historical and cultural process regarding Zionism. This exemplifies the multi-layered reality of any national habitus in relation to time. The application of historical research shifted, both thematically and geographically, inasmuch the development of the state and its population needed a vaster academic domain. In addition, the historicization of Zionism manifested the collective awareness that Israel had already become a fait accompli, which permitted a scholarly debate without compromising the country's sociopolitical and cultural foundations, hence, keeping both survival unit and habitus "intact".

A different scientific path, though equally historiographical, was taken by the peer-reviewed quarterly *Cathedra*: formally קָתֶדְרָה לְתוֹלְדוֹת אֶרֶץ יִשְׂרָאֵל וְיִישׁוּב (lit. *Cathedra: For the History of Eretz Israel and Its Yishuv*). Its main endeavour concerned the knowledge of the land of Israel. The journal was founded in 1976 (first issue, published in September 1976). It was initiated by Yehuda Ben-Porat (director-general of Yad Ben-Zvi Institute) (The institution was named after the second and the longest serving Israeli President, Yitzhak Ben-Zvi [1884–1963], who was active historian, specialized in the ancient history of Jewish communities and sects in Asia and Africa.) The journal's aim was to disseminate research in the field of *Eretz Israel*. Some of the issues regarding *Eretz yisraeli* history (the Hebrew adjective) had been dealt by several scholars on previous occasions, including the three proto-editions of *Cathedra*, published as bulletins and collections of lectures titled: "On the Cathedra: A Stage for Researchers of Eretz Israel and Yishuv Questions" by the same Ben-Porat.[20] The scientific interest was to set a distinct and autonomous scholarly platform vis-à-vis the two existent academic Jewish history and culture-related reviews *Zion* and *Tarbitz*.[21] Notwithstanding, the idea to establish a new

---

[20] See "Introduction", *Cathedra*, N. 1, September 1976; and Shavit Y. (2001). "*Avnei Yessod*" (lit. "Cornerstones"), *Cathedra*, N. 100, August 2001, p. 15–20.

[21] The quarterly *Tarbitz* (lit. "place of study") was inaugurated in 1929 at the Institute of Jewish Studies, Hebrew University of Jerusalem. It has been an intellectual platform and exchange of academic works concerning Judaism, biblical and Talmudic exegesis, Kabbalah and Jewish mysticism, Hebrew religious bibliography etc. Amongst its contributors: Jacob Nahum Epstein (1878–1952, founder of the Institute of Jewish Studies and first editor-in-chief of the quarterly), Gershom Gerhard Scholem (1897–1982), Saul Lieberman (1898–1983, second editor), Simcha Assaf (1889–1953; rabbi, historian of Jewish thought and rector of the Hebrew University [1948–1950], and judge of the Supreme Court of Israel [1948–1953]), etc.

scientific journal had already been piloted without the formal support of any academic committee. Despite initial worries concerning the lack of interest, economic resources and the potential consequences of a further subdivision of the historiographical field (criticized as journalistic), Ben-Zvi's widow, Rachel Yanait (1886–1979), who was an educator and head-figure of labour Zionism, and archaeologist Benjamin Mazar (1906–1995), brother-in-law of the President Ben-Zvi, supported the establishment of the scientific publication which would commemorate the president's own personality and versatile scientific interest (which also explains the inaugu-ration of the thematic journal *Pe'amim* in 1979).

As a result, *Cathedra* was entrusted to the Institute for the History of Eretz Israel and the Yishuv at Yad Ben-Zvi, where it is still considered the "flagship" of the institute. According to the journal's first editor-in-chief, Yaacov Shavit (2001), the first publication of *Cathedra* was to be linked to the events of the time, which went beyond the autonomous development of the historiographical research. It was claimed that its publication was a scholarly consequence of the Six-Day War (1967), which had strengthened the interest in the history of Eretz Israel, in general, and of the Jewish Yishuv, in particular. This historiographical stand was based upon the more or less conscious attempt to (re)write the history of *Eretz Israel* in light of the victorious national momentum. However, Shavit asserted that "its pub-lication was innocent of any ideological consideration".[22] That said, the journal was depicted as an instrument at the service of historical writing, some would argue revision, guided by political stands and interests. The connection between historical events and the publication of the journal was probably inevitable, due to the seemingly transversal and loud public echo, linked to the Zeitgeist (radically changed in the aftermath of the 1973 War).

The politicization around *Cathedra*, however, did not obstruct the quarterly's interdisciplinarity, as well as its intellectual openness, inspired by the literary journal *Keshet* (lit. "Arch", 1958–2008, which was edited by Israeli translator and poet, Aharon Amir [1923–2008] between the years 1958 and 1977). Till today, the journal's editorial line fosters four

---

[22] "[…] there is no doubt that the interest in research of Eretz Israel was in part the fruit of the development of a *national-territorial conscience*, yet it was equally the fruit of the *self-evident interest in research for the land where a community of scholars live* and *the availability of materials*. The interest of researchers combined with the general public interest for these subject-matters; thus, it led to have a public of thousands of readers from the first issue of the quarterly". Shavit, Y. (2001). "Avnei Yessod" (lit. "Cornerstones"), Cathedra, N. 100, August 2001, pp. 15–20 (cit. pp. 15, 18–19; my translation).

focal fields that share scientific interest in "Eretz Israel", namely the study of biblical exegesis (*Miqra*), combined with literary and archaeological and geographical discoveries (such as, the so-called Dead Sea Scrolls, the Second Temple period, Mishnah and Talmudic literature as well as early medieval Jewish history), the study of Christian and Islamic history of Palestine, and the history of Israel's early statehood. Not only did *Cathedra* formalize a scientific exchange about the land of Israel, but it also contributed to "establish and enlarge the study and teaching of the History of Eretz Israel at ad hoc academic departments, dedicated to history of the land, first at the University of Haifa in 1974, soon followed by Bar-Ilan University and Tel-Aviv University" (Shavit 2001, 19).

Despite the thematic interconnectedness and interdisciplinarity of both journals (aimed to increase their academic prestige), one element seems to have determined the different emphasis and prioritization of scholarly content, as promoted by the two journals: the weight of the two concurrent components of Israeli national habitus—the land and the state. Though the interest in the history of Zionism and the history of the land was complementary in the construction of Israeli statehood, the positional and situational identification with one of the two elements, namely the geographical setting and the ideological raison d'être of statehood, imply different sensibilities in terms of collective sense of belonging. The territorial "Promised Land", that is, the imaginative, singular, idealized and somewhat eschatological survival unit, makes the profound interest towards *Eretz Israel* a vehicle for a societal order based upon a rediscovered "heartland" that easily engenders national populistic interpretations (Taggart 2000).

Yet this utopian and idyllic source of identification, though already nationalized, situates local history and culture on a scale where the stratification of the place also entails hybridization and contamination between natives and new settlers within a structural colonial process through which different civilizations interact, either peacefully or, more often, violently, while producing a Hegelian synthesis, such as the cultural assimilation of the rightist cultural movement "the Canaanites" (or "young Hebrews"), in the 1940s, who advocated a bond between the peoples who lived in the ancient Land of Canaan/Palestine/Israel, while breaking away from the Jewish tradition, as developed in Diaspora. Hence, *Cathedra* sought after the stratification of *Eretz Israel*, by delineating a historical continuum. The diverse and evocative manifestations of local history and culture were and have been the main goal of the scientific journal. Therefore, one may argue that this scholarly framework converges with the more primordial and symbolic interpretation of national identity (Connor 1990, 1994; Smith 1986, 1991).

Very different was the rationale of *HaTzionut* and its "descendants"[23] that centred on the historical specificity of the Zionist state and the uniqueness of its genesis. The intellectual emphasis placed Jewish statehood not in the geographical territory per se but rather in the process of a national revival (Hebrew: *Komemyiut*, lit. "awakening"). That is not to say that the construction of the national survival unit was less idealized. Nothing of the sort. The journal posited its academic interest on the historical rupture vis-à-vis the past, while establishing that Zionism had been the ideological driving force for the Jews to finally take their destiny in their own hands and achieve the national goal they had longed for. Yet, the focus on the Zionist state-building process as an instrumental project to provide a safe haven for Jews' survival was chiefly linked to the ideological and normative dispositions of *Mamlakhtiyut*. The latter's ethical and cultural principles stemmed from a secularized, functional and civic conception of state apparatus, easy to be defined as a paternalistic and patriotic for of statism. Political Zionism was, after all, the result of a pragmatic compromise amongst different ideological currents, such as in the case of the 1948 Declaration of Independence, and not the enchanted fruit of utopianism.[24]

The not-so-subtle difference may thus raise questions regarding the barometer of the historiographical vantage point, and consequently of the

---

[23] We refer to the already mentioned *Israel: Studies in Zionism and the State of Israel— History, Society, Culture* (2002), which appears in Hebrew, as well as to the biannual *Journal of Israeli History: Politics, Society, Culture* in the English language (until 1994 named *Studies in Zionism*), which is published by Taylor & Francis Group in the UK.

[24] As observed elsewhere, the interrelational power-ratios between the different parts (and parties) comprising Israeli identity are fluid. They stem from dynamic negotiations that result in compromises and concessions among and within the represented communities (may such representation be strictly political, social or economic). See Helled, A. (2022). "A complex people-building: Israeli society as a precondition for the populist syndrome?" In Rotman, L., Gheorghe D. [ed.s], *Challenges of Modern Israel. Socio-Political Reality: Academic Perspectives*, "Theodor Herzl" Center for Israeli Studies, The National University for Political Studies and Public Administration (SNSPA), Bucharest, Editura Comunicare.ro (online volume), pp. 263–292; and Helled, A. (2023): *Sovereignty and (De)Civilizing Processes in the Israeli habitus between revolution and counterrevolution: A three-act story?*, in Historical Social Research/Historische Sozialforschung, special issue on "Law and (De)Civilisation" (in publication).

entire academic field, from both editorial and ideological perspective. Nevertheless, these apparently divergent historiographical alignments are rather complementary. Both *Catherdra* and *HaTzionut* have placed the Israeli national habitus within the long sequence of history. While one took off from the radical change of the ideologization of national independence, due to misfortunes of the long history of exile, the other assumed that the result of the same rupture, namely national statehood, related to the past of its territorial genesis, insofar as sociocultural revival. In addition, the two worldviews have perceived the Jewish *people* as a collectivity endowed with specific resilient *Volksgeist* (or *Volksseele*), to historicize the "spirit of the People". Either way, the scholarly interest met the national *mamlakhti* interest in nurturing profound cultural sentiments, aimed at celebrating state sovereignty after the millennial precariousness of Diaspora. In other words, the combination of the land-based disposition and the state-based disposition reflected the two faces of the Jewish national (and spiritual) redemption (Hebrew: *Geula*), as they had been stratified into the collectivization of the Israeli (Jewish) habitus.

THE DISCIPLINARY CORNERSTONES
OF ISRAELI HISTORIOGRAPHY

As Israel was establishing its autonomous identity away from diasporic Judaism, it began to address the years of *Komemyiut*, as in the case of *HaTzionut*. While the Hebrew University was losing its absolute academic monopoly with the opening of new Israeli universities (especially that of Tel-Aviv in 1956), it succeeded in "exporting" the academic division between general and Jewish history to the nascent academic establishments. The solid intellectual model of the "Hebrew University historiographical school" remained basically the same (centred upon Jewish Diaspora). Yet, the scientific interest encountered an exception.

Historian Israel Kolatt (1927–2007) came from a socialist Zionist background. Immigrated in Palestine with his family in 1935, he grew up in Tel-Aviv. He then attended the Hebrew University, where he studied both general and Jewish history. He earned a master's degree in 1955, and was awarded a PhD in Jewish history, under the supervision of professor Jacob Talmon (1964), having written a thesis titled: "Ideology and Reality in the Labour Movement in Eretz Israel: 1905–1919". As the US was becoming an important intellectual centre for Israeli academe to follow, he was sent to be trained as a postdoctoral researcher in Harvard University (academic year 1964–1965). Once he returned to Israel, he joined the Faculty of Humanities in the Hebrew University and was appointed a professor at the Harman Institute of Contemporary Jewry (amongst his students: historians Yaakov Goldstein [1935, Haifa University], Dr Aryeh Morgenstern [1937, The Shalem Center], Israeli civil servant and jurist Elyakim Rubinstein [1947, former Attorney General and Vice-President of the Supreme Court of Israel]).

As a professor, who had been socialized in the Mapainik milieu of labour Zionism, Kolatt formalized the new academic interest for the founding fathers of Israel, especially though connected to his own ideological stands (e.g., Berl Katznelson, Arthur Ruppin, Menachem Ussishkin and Ben-Gurion). By doing so, he set in motion the autonomization of the academic field of Zionist historiography, and consequently that of Israel, situated as a subfield within Jewish history which soon reached focal interest in teaching and research throughout Israeli academe. Yet, as any process, this new historiographical trend was free of issues. On the pages of the issue of *Cathedra* (September 1976),[25] Kolatt laid the foundations of the new historiographical topic. He exemplified the problematic engagement by (self-)reflecting the fact that, on the one hand, the same Israeli academic institutions (the Hebrew University to begin with) were the realization of the Zionist ideology, hence linked to and conditioned by national politics. On the other hand, he asserted that it was Zionism which had sought the liberation and acculturation of the Jewish people enabling secure and independent research.

Since the realization of *Mamlakhtiyut* meant the institutional expropriation of party-based mechanisms in favour of the general public frame of statehood, the production of knowledge and the local intelligentsia responsible for it were freed from factious obligations (similar to the

---

[25] Kolatt, I. (1976). "On the Research and Researcher of the History of the Yishuv and Zionism", *Cathedra: For the History of Eretz-Israel*, Jerusalem, Yad Ben-Zvi, Vol. 1, pp. 3–35 (in Hebrew; my translation). The article is divided in two independent parts: the first part deals with the profile of the young historian and historiographical mastery (p. 3–22); the second comments on the study of Zionism and the Yishuv (p. 22–35). Whereas the first part was written and published for the first time on *Cathedra*, the second had already been published in December 1972 by *Ha-Universita* (lit. "The University"), a journal of the Hebrew University of Jerusalem.

hegemony-inspired Gramscian organic intellectuals[26]). According to Kolatt (1976, 4), there was need for change, considering that "the uniqueness of every national history is put in doubt; yet not less difficult is the creation of historical units which are different from that of national history; and perhaps this cannot be the doing of the historian but of history-makers themselves". Nonetheless, it is the historian's deepest intent not to "be handed over the loyalties and values of the preceding generation but to examine their content, to see them in the light of the background of the historical period in which they were engendered [that is, through their context] and to evaluate their validity for the time he himself live in [...]" (ibid., p. 8), while he comes to terms with the fact that history itself "is not unequivocal. It depends, not to a slight extent, on explanation provided by values establishing its frame. The prudent and careful approach vis-à-vis the discovery of a trend evolving on the long-term did not bring historians to a singular fact as a sole certainty" (ibid., p. 10).

Noteworthy is the fact that Kolatt wrote and published his intellectual and methodological manifesto in the aftermath of the traumatic 1973 War, in order to distance historiographical research from politics, differently from the sociogenetic interdependence which stood at the heart of Zionism. In general terms, Kolatt envisaged that the outburst of the Six-Day War and its consequences brought about a new assessment of Zionism, starting from its geopolitical and spiritual status, which jeopardized its fundamental tenets. This ideological crisis, which increasingly characterized the post-1973 years in Israel, resulted from geopolitical Arab pressure and judgements against the authenticity of Zionist anti-colonial stand, as well as its aggressiveness. This criticism would mature into overt protest only in the 1980s, on the occasion of the 1982 Lebanon War. Kolatt's approach meant that the Zionist enterprise, once accomplished its national

---

[26] Gramsci's conceptualization was considered polemic. He viewed the imaginative importance that intellectuals attribute to themselves as false and self-referential because "[T]here is no human activity from which every form of intellectual participation can be excluded: *homo faber* cannot be separated from *homo sapiens*" (Gramsci, A. (1975). *Quaderni del Carcere*, Torino, Giulio Einaudi Editore, vol. III, pp. 1550–1551). Nonetheless, intellectuals "represent the entire cultural tradition of a people, seeking to resume and synthesize all of its history" in Gramsci (1978). *Selections from Political Writings (1921–1926)* [with additional texts by other Italian Communist leaders translated and edited by Hoare], London, Lawrence and Wishart (citation taken from page 462). See Gramsci (2007). *Nel mondo grande e terribile: Antologia degli scritti 1914–1935*, Giulio Einaudi Editore, Torino: "Gli Intellettuali", pp. 258–275.

cause, became susceptible to changes in the Western world, as well as other states belonging to the so-called free world vis-à-vis the communist bloc (and in domestic terms, chiefly in relation to the rise of the "new left"). The latter posed Israelis with dilemmas concerning the interpretative political value of their historical identity in light of the sociogenetic inheritance of early Zionism, whose ideological quintessence was freeing the Jewish people actively from the millennial subjugation in Diaspora.

Kolatt was sensitive to these transformations, as he wrote: "[T]he inner crisis in the Israeli party-system and the shift in leadership after the Yom Kippur War made the interest in domestic history of the Yishuv [a sort of] current affair" (ibid., p. 23). That said, the zeitgeist of the time was neither ideal nor politically balanced. Therefore, any reformulation of historical research seemed to be ideologically led, superficial and erroneous. The risk, in the eyes of Kolatt, was to present historical facts as either too unequivocal or a totalizing subordination of individuals' identity to historical inevitability (as in those days' communist regimes and "third-world" countries). Notwithstanding, criticism against the Zionist Jewish state was labelled as destructive, not to say a threat to common perceptions and founding myths. Another concern was the methodological criteria which had been established by the previous generation of historians (namely, the "Jerusalem School"). Hence, Kolatt proposed a revision of the discipline against accusations of scientific fallacy. He emphasized the imperative to take a step back from the common institutional manner of examining Jewish history, which had become canonical under the aegis of the "Jerusalem School", and disrobe the historiographical enquiry from the Zionist and somewhat apologetic ideological viewpoint. This did not mean to avoid recent national history or discussing it *ex-cathedra* (as some of Kolatt's colleagues at the Hebrew University had done), but rather to be more aware of the ideological component in history and to pay heed to the distinction between the political and the intellectual.

The aim was to research Zionism not in order to demonstrate an ideological stand but to contribute to free human knowledge. Moreover, and regardless of any ideological position, Kolatt was aware of the new methods and approaches, such as structural history, quantitative history, psycho-history etc., which slowly penetrated Israeli academe via international scientific exchanges, aimed to better reconstruct historiographical raw materials. While pondering the methodological use of newspapers, archival records and theories adapted from social, political and psychological sciences, Kolatt sought after the understanding of history through the specific contextualization of facts and events, and not through the universal principles of human nature. He thus put any general analytical theory in second order. He stated that "[T]he special history of the Jewish Yishuv is, indeed, easier to understand by particularistic and not universal approach" (Kolatt 1976, 17). Both the ideological and methodological concerns originated from the same general uncertainly around the state of Zionism and its history-writing (Tzahor 2001). The latter stemmed from a complicated historiographical situation regarding the availability of documents.

Kolatt's detailed manifesto listed the "historical buildings" in Israeli Zionist historiography. It emphasized the process of the Zionist nation-state, which was, indeed, a central unit of enquiry but not the only one to be tackled. Topics such as the political history of the Zionist movement, the Yishuv and the British Mandate (considered the availability of Zionist and British archives), Zionism and Jewish life (in Israel and in Diaspora), the Jewish settlement in the land of Israel, the intellectual-political history of the Zionism (including that of political parties, seemingly the most complicated subject-matter) and the [Jewish] "ethnical problem" seem to be rather trivial. However, Kolatt also mentioned Jewish-Arab relations as part of the issues historians must enquire, with emphasis on Jewish, Arab and British sources to be combined.

In this regard, noteworthy is the fact that since the early 1960s, historians who wished to study the history of the Yishuv and Zionism faced a substantial lack of literature and archival resources. This was due to the military censorship that had normed the up to 50 years state-secret closure period for any document related to military operation and event, as well as to the severe regulations and measures taken by the Israel State Archives (formally established by law in 1955). The latter already housed an extensive collection of institutional documents dating from the pre-Independence period, alongside documentation of previous governments in the land of Israel, namely the Ottoman rule (1815–1917), the British Mandate (1917–1948) as well as collections originating from the institutions of the Arab community in Palestine during these decades (nowadays collection numbers circa 400 million documents, maps, stamps, audio tapes, video registrations, photographs and special publications). Without the availability of archival materials, the research field of Zionist and Yishuv historiography could not make progress. Not only does the state-based ownership of those materials exemplify the *mamlakhti* monopolization of identity-building processes, anchored to Jewish state-building and its foundational ideology, that is, Zionism, but it also illustrates the sociopolitical interest in guarding unilaterally documents that belong to the antagonistic "other" of the Jewish survival unit, that is, Palestinian Arabs. This monopolization of archival materials echoes the aphorism, strongly associated with Winston Churchill, which states that "history is written by the victors".[27]

In the same issue of *Cathedra*, in which Kolatt introduced his historiographical creed, the meaningful point on the topicality and availability of materials received further attention. These themes are addressed in two discussion sections (transcribed from the oral source), published only a few pages after Kolatt's essay. The first (p. 61–97), titled "The Problem of the Historiography of the Independence War", consisted in an open debate (held before the Yom Kippur War [footnote, p. 70]) amongst several contributors, namely *Haganah* members with either formal or self-taught experience in history-writing. This social cohort of former 1948 fighters, all extra-academic historians of their own generation, became holders of public and/or political positions. The group included high-profile public figures, mostly civil servants and military experts, namely Nathanael Lorch (1925–1997) who had been a teacher and a Hebrew University-trained historian (graduated in 1951, obtained PhD in 1985), and was also a diplomat (head of the African Unit of the Israeli Ministry of Foreign Affairs) and the third secretary general of the Knesset (7–10, 1972–1983); Gershon Rivlin (1914–1994), member of *Haganah*, first editor of the military journal *Ma'arahot* (lit. "battles") and a military history expert of pre-Israel Jewish paramilitary groups, though never professionally trained as a historian;[28] Meir (Meir'ke) Pa'il (1926–2015), also a member of *Haganah* and Palmach (deputy commander of the Negev Brigade, 1943–1948), former colonel in the Israel Defense Forces, an Israeli politician and trained military historian, who had studied general history and Middle Eastern studies at Tel-Aviv University (he was awarded an MA in 1970 and a PhD in 1973); Elazar Galili (1903–1988), the

---

[27] This fact has made the construction of Palestinian collective memory a complicated task. As demonstrated by Yifat Gutman (2017), the demolition of Palestinian villages and the lack of materials could only be addressed by somewhat militant (and imaginative) activism that seeks mutual recognition between Jews and Arabs in Israel/Palestine. See Gutman, Y. (2017). *Memory Activism: Reimagining the Past for the Future in Israel-Palestine*, Nashville: Vanderbilt University Press.

[28] Gershon Rivlin co-authored the *Book of the History of the Haganah*, which was edited by Ben-Zion Dinur. The work consisted of three parts, divided in 8 volumes published between 1954 and 1972.

founder of the so-called Hebrew Military Thought; and Joseph "Yosefle" Tabenkin (1921–1987), a commander of the Fourth Battalion of the Palmach's Harel Brigade whose intervention is followed by the rather short commentaries of Elhanan Oren (1924–2007), a military historian, writer and translator.

Their debate, published by *Cathedra*, concerned the problems of studying and making a history out of the 1948 events. They discussed and commented on the denomination and classification of the war; the chronological, its geographical and political aspects; the methodology and availability of sources (also Arab ones); the issue of state secrecy vis-à-vis public and intellectual interest; etc. The overt discussion amongst those who had been directly involved in the war received supplementary attention and contextualization in another article (p. 98–101), titled "On the Arab Sources for the Research of the War of Independence", by Joseph Nevo (1942–2016), a historian of the Middle East who would become a professor at Haifa University (he had joined the faculty as a lecturer in 1975) and was also one of the first specialists in the history of the Kingdoms of Jordan and Saudi Arabia, and later in the Israeli-Palestinian conflict, Palestinian society and its historiography. In the article, Nevo analysed the different types of sources in the Arab world, namely official documents, biographies and memoirs, the so-called lesson-teaching literature (centred around the reasons for the shameful defeat of the Arab armies) and formal/semi-formal publications such as reports and memoranda.

Furthermore, he declared the shortage or total lack of national institutional history books dedicated to the war, as well as of ad hoc memoirs by leading Arab politicians (whose primary authenticity ought to be evaluated). Like Klatt, Nevo also stressed the impossibility for researchers to gain access to archival sources: "neither Israeli—and as far as it is known—nor western, nor Arab" (Nevo 1976, 101), thus reflecting the scarce availability in Israeli and in ex-Jordanian archives (namely, the Palestinian territories occupied by Israel in 1967). Despite the explicit interest, as demonstrated by *Cathedra's* first issue, it is noteworthy that giving a floor to politically sensitive topics (including Kolatt's call for historiographical revision) could only be addressed, though very generically at the time, by and within the limited group of scholars and senior civil servants.

That said, it seems that Kolatt's observations and teachings were assimilated and carried out, contemporaneously, by historians such as Yosef Gorny (1933), a former student at the Hebrew University and a Tel-Aviv University graduate student (later a professor at Tel-Aviv University), and

Tel-Aviv University student Anita Shapira (1940), who would become the
dean of the Faculty of Humanities at Tel-Aviv University (1990–1995)
and an Israel Prize Laureate in 2008 for her historical research, among
many other awards and honours for her specialization in political biographies.[29] The two were born in Warsaw, Poland, and lived through the
dramatic events of WWII. Moreover, both had been officially trained in
"general history" yet combined it with Jewish studies. They were the first
ones to establish "Israel Studies" within the historiographic landscape of
until then prevalent field of ancient *Eretz Israel* studies (based on face-to-
face/story-telling interviews held with prof Shapira (26/05/2016) and
prof Gorny (05/06/2016)).

The academic careers of the two had been preceded by teaching jobs in
municipal high schools, some years before their recruitment by Tel-Aviv
University. Their personal and professional careers determined the appropriation by this university of the nascent field of Israel's national historiography vis-à-vis the Hebrew University of Jerusalem. The inauguration of
the new field brought to the two the consequential academic prestige and
greater public visibility in comparison to some of their fellow-colleagues
and peers (such as Yehuda Nini [1930–2020], scholar of Yemenite and
Egyptian Jewry at Tel-Aviv University and 2008 Ben-Gurion Prize
Laureate; Yaacov Goldstein (1933), founder of *Eretz Israel* studies at
University of Haifa; Yosef Shalmon (1939), an expert on religion and
nationalism who headed the Jewish studies department at Ben-Gurion
University (1973–1975) and others). Their interest in local and

---

[29] Anita Shapira received numerous prizes and awards. She was awarded the 1977 Ben-Zvi
Prize for her book *The Futile Struggle: Hebrew Labour 1929–1939*, Tel-Aviv, Tel-Aviv
University: Am Oved Publishing (1977) [based on her PhD dissertation]; the 1992 Am
Oved Prize, for the best non-fiction book, on the occasion of its 50th anniversary of the
publishing house: (1992) *Herev Hayona: HaTzionut ve'Hakoah, 1881–1948*, Tel-Aviv, Am
Oved [English title: *Land and Power: The Zionist Resort to Force, 1881–1948* (Studies in
Jewish History) [translated by William Templer], Oxford [etc.], Oxford University Press
received the National Jewish Book Award in 1993 in the category "Israel"; in 2004 she was
awarded the Shazar Prize in Jewish history for her biography of Yigal Allon published the
same year, that is, *Yigal Aloon: Aviv Kheldo*, Tel-Aviv, Hakibbutz Hameuchad Publishing
House (in Hebrew)—published in English as *Yigal Allon, Native Son: A Biography* [trans-
lated by Evelyn Abel], Philadelphia, University of Pennsylvania Press, 2008; she was awarded
the 2005 Herzl Prize for her contribution to the research of Zionism; she was also awarded
the 2008 Israel Prize for Jewish history. More recently, she received both the 2012 National
Jewish Book Award and the 2014 Azrieli Award for Best Book in Israel studies in English or
French for her book *Israel: A History*, Waltham, Brandeis University Press (2012).

contemporary Zionist and Israeli history was soon shared by younger "Sabra" historians such as Zeev Tzahor (1941–2017), Yoav Gelber (1943), Yaacov Shavit (1944), Yisrael Bartal (1946),[30] Aviva Halamish (1946) and Yosef Goldstein (1947). Most of them can be labelled as "late bloomers", given their gradual entry into academe. This confirms the often-non-linear career trajectories, conditioned by personal constraints (the need of safe employment) in relation to the structural precarity in academe, particularly before one attains tenure, as well as by the slow development of the historiographical field.

This second generation of young historians, more or less of the same age, was socialized around, though, and by Israeli independence and the construction of *Mamlakhtiyut*. Either directly or indirectly, they followed Kolatt's footsteps. As a result, it is easier to categorize this historiographical generation as an established academic and epistemic community whose scholarly field is institutionally supported in relation to the previous one. There are several reasons for that. Firstly, their pioneering academic research was not stratified in a void. They entered an already structured academic milieu supported by the state with its centralized apparatus of ministries and public budget planification. Moreover, since the state developed and accumulated its public capacity, this generation of historians was facilitated in obtaining structural recognition. Yet, unlike the historiographical layer of "first generation historians", identified with the "Jerusalem School", second-generation historians could rethink the somewhat Palestinocentric continuation of the German Jewish historiography (the influential Wissenschaft des Judentums, adopted in Jerusalem), given that national identity had found its expression in the collective habitus, as provided by the unifying nation-state model.

Secondly, the expansion of Israeli academe and its inner bureaucratization also facilitated their recruitment. Historians could be professionally distributed between different academic institutions (all public and financed by the state), especially in the cases of Haifa University and Ben-Gurion University of the Negev which had been projected with the aim to facilitate and improve the conditions in Israel's periphery by providing higher education, following *mamlakhti* principles of governance. The process of institutionalization of the university system as well as that of research

---

[30] Yisrael Bartal seems to be the last "organic" successor of the "Jerusalem School", considering his academic career within the walls of the Jerusalem-based university was rooted in the teachings of Dinur and Ettinger.

institutes was reaching its peak. Public funds were engaged in specific research sectors, such as in the cases of Yad Vashem (1953) for the study of the Holocaust, the Ben-Zvi Institute (1964) for the research and study of the history of the land of Israel, Jerusalem and Jewish communities under Muslim rule and the Shazar Center (1973) founded by the Israel Historical Society and the Government of Israel in honour of Israel's third President Zalman Shazer, with the objective to promote research, teaching and dissemination of knowledge in the field of history of the "[Jewish] people of Israel" for historians, students and the general public. The inauguration of such public establishments reveals the rather direct connection between academe and politics. The professional habitus and ethics which crossed historians' careers had, consequently, much to do with the state and its agenda.

The intercross between historians and the public sphere discloses the former's relevance as experts and administrators of knowledge at the state's service. Some examples are in order. The Council for Higher Education of Israel (headed by the Israeli Minister of Education and whose members are nominated by the president via recommendation of the Israeli prime minister) set funding and teaching programmes for each and every academic sector. Furthermore, though not being "scientific strategists" par excellence, historians were co-opted to take part in ministerial committees on history education in Israeli schools. Such institutions and encounters (have) provided public visibility to politicians and scholars alike, and may be forums for accumulation of social and political capital, while reaching the status of "public intellectual" (the selection itself is, of course, a direct result of someone's reputation). This remains the general frame in which Israeli historians operate. Their interdependency with the Ministry of Education and the interlinked publics organs demonstrate the intertwined relations between scholarly professions and politics, while public prestige and state-related awards (chiefly the Israel Prize) exemplify such interconnections that might be as controversial as symbiotic but always instrumental (Ben-Amos 2004). Many of them are therefore considered members of the Israeli "Ivory Tower", an intellectual cohort shaped by and intertwined to the state.

The numeric increase in historians specializing in (mostly pre-Independence) Israeli history engendered variations in topics of research which became part of the discipline, namely military history, Jewish immigration, ideological movements etc. Nonetheless, most of the "second generation" historians dedicated their research to Mandate Palestine and labour Zionism. Key Zionist ideologues such as Brenner, Katznelson and Ben-Gurion were gradually "historicised" into biographies (a genre still highly appreciated and practiced in Israeli historiography[31]). The historiographical genre has always been based upon the positivistic interpretation of archival materials (methodological conservatism centred on "historical veracity"), which is no different from that implemented by "new historian" Benny Morris (see the next chapter). In this sense, the seemingly monolithic historiography of the 1970s, which was identified with and fostered by various political parties and organizations, broke down into different sub-groups (for instance, Anita Shapira who was identified with the heritage of Mapam-Oriented Palmah and Yoav Gelber who placed himself with a somewhat Ben-Gurionist line etc.): a scholarly division which totally refuted any thesis about left-wing Zionist intellectuals being forced to observe "party-discipline".

Consequently, many historians, heretofore mentioned, were and have been socially and politically identified with the Israeli left, though they rarely participate in explicit political initiatives. That is not to say that all these historians were to produce the same kind of historiography. Each of them sharpened and critically developed his/her own way, following personal preferences and availability of resources (as traced by Kolatt in 1976). Nonetheless, their works offer a common thread running through their contribution to Israeli historiography, namely the particularity of Zionism as a "virtually unparalleled" endeavour whose success is embodied by the establishment of an independent democratic Jewish state in *Eretz Israel* against tremendous geopolitical odds. The intimate identification with the state's *Mamlakhtiyut*, as the product of Zionist "utopic realistic" resolve concretized into life-changing ideological action, collectivizes these historians as both bearers and producers of the Israeli national habitus (Shapira and Reinhartz 1996; Gorny 2015).

---

[31] It is true that traditional historiography paid much attention to memoirs and chronicles. One should only think of the prominent career of prof Anita Shapira whose scientific production has consisted in numerous biographies (e.g., *Berl: The Biography of a Socialist Zionist, Berl Katznelson, 1887–1944*, translated by Haya Galai. Cambridge University Press, 1984; *Yigal Allon, Native Son: A Biography*, translated by Evelyn Abel. University of Pennsylvania Press, 2008; *Yosef Haim Brenner: A Life*, Stanford University Press, 2014; *Ben-Gurion: Father of Modern Israel*, Yale University Press, 2014). Shapira also published her own autobiography in 2022 (in Hebrew). See Shapira (2022). *Kakha ze Haya. Sipur Khayim* (lit. "This was That Way: A Life Story"), Tel-Aviv, Am Oved, Sifriyat Ofakim.

In spite of the apparent generational homogeneity in espousing Israeli statehood, this stratification does not necessarily mean automatism or intellectual one-sidedness. Neither does it take possession—once and for all—of the major changes and different issues that Israeli society has faced. Even the first impression of a monolithic interest in left-wing Zionism is not a sure thing. The supposedly symbiotic relationship between the academic and political fields had already begun changing in the 1960s, followed by the ideological shifts and ruptures of the 1970s (namely, the 1973 Kippur War and the 1977 political upheaval). Was the structural and formalistic *Mamlakhtiyut* able to keep producing a lasting nationwide ethos? Was the latter strong enough to preserve the inherited habitus and the identification with the state deriving from it?

The Israeli, Zionist and Jewish survival unit, hence the bearer of the once predominant Mapainik (socialist and lay) spirit and the forger of the Sabra-based model of Israeliness, soon commenced to perpetuate a novel kind of processual politicization. The nation-state, its structures and the collective habitus it handed down remained a product of inner partition and sectorialization of power. Though civic and republican in its pragmatism, the compactness of the survival unit began to wane. The political establishment took no concrete measures to solve the dichotomous social cleavages between Ashkenazi and Mizrahi-descent Israelis, urban centres and periphery, lay and religious, Jews and Arabs. The nation-state ingathered the Jewish "exiles"; however, it did not fuse them. Many *olim* (and their descendants), for instance, felt estrangement and rootlessness in the *mamlakhti* framework, despite melting-pot policies. The nation-state-based national survival unit fortified itself in an existent status quo, ignoring societal processes that concerned shifts towards greater individualism, inspired by neoliberalism and post-modernism. The Eliasian figurational integration of socialized individuals into tight interdependencies had not been completed, thus, leaving structural fragilities which could generate disintegrational trends, if not decivilizing regression.

The Zionist communion that had once stood strong against threats of elimination on the geopolitical level, which legitimated the shared form of civic duty (the military service) and the strong identification with the collective, was gradually emptied from its original voluntaristic pioneering fervour of the nation-building years (one can generalize the sociocultural contrast between the utopistic pre-state Zionist pioneering and the organizational centralism constituted by *Mamlakhtiyut*). The routinization of Israeliness, as product of the state, became merely a ritual automatism and could not satisfy the demands for a more critical, less ideological, pluralistic and individualistic society. Despite structural robustness, the growing acquisition of Zionist and Israeli historiography contemporaneously moulded and accompanied the national *mamlakhti* habitus. It had to come to terms with the routinized reproduction of the state. It was precisely the tangible trivialization of the Israeli nation-state, that is to say, the habitualization of its formal existence, which set the foundations of the historical revision in the early 1990s. The latter was initiated by members of the next generation of Israeli historians, whose intellectual efforts cracked old paradigms and revealed the deficiencies of what had seemed to be a hermetically sealed field. This generation of historians wished to revitalize national historiography and place it in relation with the other national history of Land, that of the Palestinian people. Born into the *mamlakhti* national habitus, these historians embodied a new phase in Israel's contemporary sociopolitical reality, that characterized by *Artziyut*. This historiographical generation is discussed in the next chapter.

References

Alroey, G. (2014). *An Unpromising Land. Jewish Migration to Palestine in the Early Twentieth Century*, Stanford, Stanford University Press.

Bareli, A. (2007a). *Mapai in Israel's Early Independence: 1948–1953*, Jerusalem, Yad Ben Zvi Press (in Hebrew).

Bareli, A. (2007b): "Mamlakhtiyut, Capitalism and Socialism during the 1950s in Israel", *Journal of Israeli History*, Vol. 26, N. 2, pp. 201–227.

Bareli, A. (2009). "Mapai and the Oriental Jewish Question in the Early Years of the State", *Jewish Social Studies: History, Culture, Society*, Vol. 16, no. 1 (Fall 2009), pp. 54–84.

Bareli, A. (2017). "Hierarchy, Representation, and Inclusion in a Reflective Democratic Culture: Conflicting Perspectives in Israel's Nascent Years", *Israel Studies*, Vol. 22, N. 1, Spring 2017, p. 139–164.

Bareli, A., Cohen, U. (2008a). "Distributive Justice and a Rising Middle Class: Conflict between MAPAI and White-collar Professionals before the 1955 General Elections in Israel", *Israel Affairs*, Vol. 14, N. 2 (Apr. 2008), pp. 255–76.

Bareli, A., Cohen, U. (2008b). "The Middle Class versus the Ruling Party during the 1950s in Israel: The 'Engine-Coach Car' Dilemma", *Middle Eastern Studies*, Vol. 44, N. 3 (May 2008), pp. 489–510.

Bareli, A., Cohen, U. (2012). "The Strike of Professionals in 1956", *Cathedra: For the History of Eretz Israel and its Yishuv*, N. 143, April 2012, pp. 153–184 (in Hebrew).

Bauer, Y. (2002). *Rethinking the Holocaust*, New Haven, Yale University Press.

Ben-Amos, A. (2004). "Le Prix Israël (1953–2003). Entre Controverse et Instrumentalisation", *Genèses* 2004/2 (no. 55), pp. 62–83.

Bourdieu, P. (1990). *The Logic of Practice*, Stanford, Stanford University Press.

Bourdieu, P. (1998). *Practical Reason: On the Theory of Action*, Stanford, Stanford University Press.

Canetti, E. (1962). *Crowds and Power* (translated from the German (1960) by Carol Stewart), New York, Continuum.

Cohen, U. (2001). "The Hebrew University of Jerusalem from Yishuv to State: initial Perspectives on the Development of the Credential Society in Israel", *HaTzionut*, N. 23, pp. 297–329.

Cohen, U. (2014). *Academia in Tel-Aviv: The Making of a University*, Jerusalem, The Hebrew University Magnes Press (in Hebrew).

Collins, R. (1979). *The Credential Society: An Historical Sociology of Education and Stratification*, New York, Academic Press.

Connor, W. (1990). "When is a Nation?", *Ethnic and Racial Studies*, Vol. 13(1): 92–103.

Connor, W. (1994). *Ethnonationalism. The Quest for Understanding*, Princeton: Princeton University Press.

Gardos, Y., Nevo, I. [eds.] (2014). *Science and Scholarship in the Negev: The Story of Ben-Gurion University in the Negev*, Vol 1: "The Founders" [Mada u'Ruakh ba'Negev: Universitat Ben-Gurion ve'Toldotea be'Reyi ha'Mekhkar], Beer-Sheva, Ben-Gurion University Press.

Gorny, Y. (1997). "The Decade of Wonder: Reflections on the First Decade of the State in the Jubilee Year" in Zameret, Z., Yablonka [ed.s] (1997). *The First Decade: 1948–1958*, Jerusalem, Yad Izhak Ben Zvi Publications.

Gorny, Y. (2015). *Men of Here and Now: The Utopic Realism the Shapers of the New Jewish Society in Eretz Israel*, Sde-Boker: Beer-Sheva, Ben-Gurion University: Ben-Gurion Institute (in Hebrew).

Gramsci, A. (1975). *Quaderni del Carcere*, Torino, Giulio Einaudi Editore.

Gramsci, A. (1978). *Selections from Political Writings (1921–1926)* [with additional texts by other Italian Communist leaders translated and edited by Hoare, Q., London, Lawrence and Wishart

Gramsci, A. (2007). *Nel mondo grande e terribile: Antologia degli scritti 1914–1935*, Giulio Einaudi Editore, Torino.

Gutman, Y. (2017). *Memory Activism: Reimagining the Past for the Future in Israel-Palestine*, Nashville: Vanderbilt University Press.

Hacohen, D. (2010). "*The 1953 State Education Law: A Missed Decision?*" in Hacohen, Lissak [ed.s] (2010). *Decisional Crossroads and Key Matters in Israel*, Ḳiryat Sedeh-Boḳer, Ben-Gurion Institute: Ben-Gurion University Press (in Hebrew: "*Tsomte hakhra'ot u-farshiyot mafteaḥ be-Yiśra'el*").

Hadari, Z., Tal, H. (1984). *Chapters in The History of the University* [Prakim be'Toldot ha'Universita], Beer-Sheva, Ben-Gurion University Press.

Helled, A. (2022). "A complex people-building: Israeli society as a precondition for the populist syndrome?" In Rotman, L., Gheorghe D. [ed.s], *Challenges of Modern Israel. Socio-Political Reality: Academic Perspectives*, "Theodor Herzl" Center for Israeli Studies, The National University for Political Studies and Public Administration (SNSPA), Bucharest, Editura Comunicare.ro (online volume).

Helled, A. (2023). "Sovereignty and (De)Civilizing Processes in the Israeli habitus between revolution and counterrevolution: A three-act story?", *Historical Social Research/Historische Sozialforschung*, special issue: "Law and (De) Civilisation" (in publication).

Iram, Y., Friedlander, Y., Ohaion, S. (2013) [ed.s]. *The Mission of a Religious University* [Yiuda Shel Universita Datit], Ramat-Gan, Bar-Ilan University Press.

Kabalo, P. (2009). "Pioneering Discourse and the Shaping of an Israeli Citizen in the 1950s", *Jewish Social Studies*, Vol. 15, No. 2 (Winter 2009), pp. 82–110.

Kedar, N. (2002). "Ben-Gurion's Mamlakhtiyut: Etymological and Theoretical Roots", *Israel Studies*, Vol. 7, No. 3 (Fall, 2002), pp. 117–133.

Kedar, N. (2007a). "Law, Culture and Civil Codification in a Mixed Legal System", *Canadian Journal of Law and Society*, Vol. 22, N. 2, 2007, pp. 177–195.

Kedar, N. (2007b). "Jewish Republicanism", *Journal of Israeli History*, Vol. 26, N. 2, pp. 179–199.

Kedar, N. (2008): "A Civilian Commander in Chief: Ben-Gurion's Mamlakhtiyut, the Army and the Law", *Israel Affairs*, Vol. 14, N. 2, p. 202–217.

Kedar, N. (2013). "Ben-Gurion's view of the place of Judaism in Israel", *Journal of Israeli History*, Vol. 32, N. 2, p. 157–174.

Klein, M. (1997). *Bar-Ilan: Academy, Religion and Politics* [Bar-Ilan: Academia, Dat u'Politica], Jerusalem, Hebrew University Magnes Press.

Kolatt, I. (1976). "On the Research and Researcher of the History of the Yishuv and Zionism", *Cathedra: For the History of Eretz-Israel*, Jerusalem, Yad Ben-Zvi, Vol. 1, pp. 3–35.

Lissak, M., Cohen, U. (2010). "The Scientific Strategists in the Period of Mamlakhtiyut: The Symbiotic Relations between the Academic Community and the Centers of Power", *Iyunim Bitkumat Israel*, Vol. 20, pp. 1–27 (in Hebrew).

Lissak, M., Cohen, U. (2011). "Scientific strategists in the period of Mamlakhtiyut: Interaction between the academic community and political power centers", *The Journal of Israeli History*, Vol. 30, No. 2, September 2011, pp. 189–210.

Malešević, S. (2019). *Grounded Nationalisms: A Sociological Analysis*. Cambridge: Cambridge University Press.

Mautner, M. (2011). *Law and the Culture of Israel*, Oxford: New York, Oxford University Press.

Neumann, B. (2009). *Teshikat a'Halutzim* ("The Passion of Pioneers"), Tel-Aviv, Sapir: Am Oved.

Nevo, J. (1976). "The Arab Sources for a Study of the War of Liberation/". על המקורות הערבים לחקר מלחמת העצמאות *Cathedra: For the History of Eretz Israel and Its Yishuv*/ קתדרה: לתולדות ארץ ישראל ויישובה, no. 1 (1976), pp. 98–101.

Schwartz, D. [ed.] (2006). *Bar-Ilan University: From Idea to Action* [Universitat Bar-Ilan: MeRah'aion le'Maas], 2 volumes, Ramat-Gan, Bar-Ilan University Press.

Shapira, A., Reinhartz, J. [eds.] (1996). *Essential Papers On Zionism*, New York: London, New York University Press.

Shapira, A. (2022). *Kakha ze Haya. Sipur Khayim* (lit. "This was That Way: A Life Story"), Tel-Aviv, Am Oved, Sifriyat Ofakim (in Hebrew).

Shavit, Y. (1992). "Messianism, Utopia and Pessimism in the 1950s: A Critique on the 'Ben-Gurionian State'", Iyunim Bitkumat Israel, Vol. 2, 1992, pp. 56–78 (in Hebrew).

Shavit Y. (2001). "Avnei Yessod" (lit. "Cornerstones"), *Cathedra*, N. 100, August 2001, pp. 15–20.

Smith, A.D. (1986). *The Ethnic Origins of Nations*. Oxford: Blackwell.

Smith, A.D. (1991). *National Identity*. London: Penguin Books.

Tadmor-Shimoni, T. (2010): *A Homeland Lesson: National Education and State-Building 1954–1966*, Kiryat Sedeh Boker, Ben-Gurion Institute: Ben-Gurion University Press.

Taggart, P. (2000). *Populism*, Buckingham, Open University Press.

Tsur, Y (1997). "Aliyah from the Islamic Countries", pp. 57–82 in Zameret, Z., and Yablonka, H. [ed.s] (1997): *The First Decade: 1948–1958*, Jerusalem, Yad Izhak Ben Zvi Publications.

Tzahor, Z. (2001). "The History of the State of Israel: Academe and Politics" (Toldot Medinat Israel: Academia ve'Politica: in Hebrew), *Cathedra*, N. 100, August 2001, Yad Ben Zvi Press, pp. 377–394.

Yablonka, H. (1999). *Survivors of the Holocaust*, Basingstoke: London, Macmillan Press [first published in Hebrew as "Foreign Brethren: Holocaust Survivors in the State of Israel, 1948–1952", Yad Izhak Ben-Zvi Press: Ben-Gurion University of the Negev Press (1994)].

Zameret, Z. (2002). *The Melting Pot in Israel: The Commission of Inquiry Concerning Education in the Immigrant Camp during the Early Years of the State*, Albany, State University of New York Press.

Zameret, Z. (2003). *The Education in the First Decade*, Tel-Aviv, Open University Press (in Hebrew).

Artziyut: No Country Other and the Double-Edged Banalization of Israeli National Habitus in Israeli Historiography

I Have No Country Other
Lyrics: Ehud Manor
Music: Corinne Elal

I have no country other
Though my land's been torn asunder.
Just a word in my native tongue delves
In my veins, and in my soul …
Half torn apart, with hungry heart
Here is my home.

Can't keep silent in light of
How my country's changed her guise.
Won't quit trying to remind her
In her ears I'll sing my cries,
Until she opens her eyes.

I have no country other …

Can't keep silent in light of …

I have no country other
'Til her old'n days are reprised,
Until she opens her eyes.

A. Helled, *Israel's National Historiography*, Palgrave Studies on Norbert Elias, https://doi.org/10.1007/978-3-031-62795-8_5

This tear-dropping poem was written in 1982 by Israeli lyricist Ehud Manor in memory of his brother who had fallen in battle during the War of Attrition (1967–1970). Over the years the song became an artistic (and symbolic) part of Israeli culture. It is one of the most popular songs in the genre of "Homeland songs". It is sung on the Memorial Day for the Fallen Soldiers of Israel and Victims of Terrorism (*Yom Hazikaron*) but also at manifestations of political protest (it has been "adopted", as adapted, by the entire political spectrum in Israel). As such it fairly represents the national habitus, expressed by the emotional attachment of (Jewish) Israelis, to their homeland, their difficult yet only survival unit. It is neither trivial nor banal that the song encompasses the various animas of Israeliness. It does not "speak out" by itself from a definable political perspective. It provides no ideological specificities. It only portrays the worries of citizenry vis-à-vis the hardships and sacrifices which have been affronted. There is neither indifference to the price Israeli society pays nor acceptance of it. Love and hope, accompanied altogether by resilience and stubbornness, are the combination which Israeli national habitus is made of. One can be as much as disappointed in and anguished by the country he/she considers so dear. The reality of sufferings, frustrations and uncertainties does not necessarily lead to such a sentimental patriotism. Inasmuch as the connection of Jewish Israelis to the state is complex and changeable, especially in the case of the different Jewish "publics", namely the discriminated Mizrahim and the non-Zionist ultra-orthodox, the national habitus sets a unique figurational "state of mind" of Israeliness. The latter entails often contradictory and antagonistic reactions. The figuration of the nation-state, as the survival unit, is effective insofar as it constructs the all-embracing monolithic sense of belonging, codified into national identity. Once the inner integrity and solidity of the survival unit experiences decivilizing fragmentation, namely, the enfeeblement of interdependencies between citizenry and state, the national habitus changes, though not immediately. Self-preserving coherence and institutionalized uniformity resist initial change, while the sociopolitical fabric vehicles more than one mode of perception and action.

In this reading, the plurality of states of mind is no other than a substructural corpus of modes, attitudes and mental pictures through which reality is constructed by different people. Whereas the national habitus remains stably collectivized and formalized by the nation-state, different states of mind coexist, as temporary and transitory sentiments in relation to the survival unit and habitus it socializes into (Lindblom 1982; Rielly 1987; Morgan 2000). They are, therefore, more ephemeral than the habitus, since they have less dispositional capacity to stratify collectivity. The national identity is institutionally established; however, this does not mean that alternative modes and attitudes cannot occupy the social space and interact within its boundaries. Hence, the dynamic processes of nation-building and the construction of national identity also contain states of minds of "infatuation" with nationalism as well ones which are lesser monochromatic in relation to national features.

Furthermore, given the age of contemporary globalization, nation-states undergo continuous processes which present challenges to their collective habitus. The fast exchange of information, geopolitical stakes and sociocultural fashions cross society rapidly, and thus uncover the nation's vulnerabilities. There are cracks in the solemnity of the nation-state. Once considered as the universally accepted survival unit, its traditional monopoly has undergone processes of banalization, misuse, trivialization and superficialization of national cohesiveness as a result of the processual so-called waning state vis-à-vis the capitalist marketization of democracies, which entails "the detachment of sovereignty from the nation-state" (Brown 2010, 24).

In the Israeli context, this ongoing relativizing temporality may be called the phase of *Artziyut*. The Hebrew word denotes materiality, worldliness, tangibility and corporeality in opposition to spirituality, meaning the sacredness of the nation-state in our case. There is by no means a singularity of Israeli nationhood. As the national habitus socializes citizens into the nation-state figuration as the only possible survival unit, it reproduces and preserves the same institutional framework and conditions in power-ratios between state and citizenry. The mundane routinization of the latter, once "cold", "colder", "hot" and "hotter", are all different degrees in the banalization of nationalism, usually taken for granted, almost unobserved (Billig 1995).

Israeli *Artziyut* is the Israeli variation of this endemic sociopolitical reproduction of national identity (Jewish and Zionist). It entails osmotic relations between the social and the political fields. The normalization, reproduction and stratification of the national habitus and the *mamlakhti* societal order amongst Israeli citizenry would not have been possible without Israeli historians writing national history. Set by first-generation historians (the "Jerusalem School") and accumulated by second-generation historians, Israeli national history had been placed as expressive evidence of the processual link between people and land for Jewish nation-state building to be possible. Alongside national symbols, the Hebrew language and *mamlakhti* public rites, namely the days of remembrance for the Shoah and the one for fallen soldiers, and national historiography contributed to the Israeli state for it to become "an unreflexive presence in [our] daily lives, a powerful register that shapes the ways people think of and act in the world" (Skey and Antonsich 2017, 2). Moreover, by producing national-Zionist history, the repeated discreet omnipresence of the nation-state as the processual finality of *Komemiyut* (see the specific chapter), Israeli historiography implied "a complex dialectic of remembering and forgetting" (Billig 1995, 37), which entailed objective lacunae in historical memory (islands of historical amnesia), "used in time present to control the future" (Douglas 1995, 23).[1] This became increasingly evident in the lack of history-writing that comprised documentation regarding the Palestinians and the relationship between Jews and Arabs in pre-1948 Palestine/land of Israel. This issue remained underattended, despite Kolatt's 1976 historiographical manifesto. Even in the scholarly disciplines specialized in the Arab world and the Middle East, "Arabists" and "orientalists" did not produce significant works on the Palestinian population.

In this sense, Israeli historiography was not structurally ready to open itself to demolish the dichotomic walls between the established Zionist Israeli Jew and the Arab Palestinian outsider, detached from Israeliness (Elias and Scotson 2008). Their respective (hi)stories had to remain separate; as if historiography were a fortress protecting the survival unit of the Jewish nation, similarly to the securitarian-driven policies that have made Israel a besieged society (Del Sarto 2017). This had been a distinctive feature of an ethno-religious and sociocultural compartmentalization between Jews and non-Jews in Palestine, reflected by Israeli academe (De Swaan 2015). Given the thematic selectiveness, historical studies made very little progress in widening research. I did not pose a threat to nationality, inasmuch as history enquiry had largely remained not only

[1] Douglas, M. (1995). "Forgotten Knowledge" in Marilyn Strathern (series editor) "*Shifting Contexts: Transformations in Anthropological Knowledge*", London: New York, Routledge, 1995 [first edition]; see pp. 13–29 (citation p. 23).

Zionist-based but also Zionist-centred. As asserted by Renan, already in 1882, no one wanted to "throw[s] light on the violent acts that have taken place at the origin of every political formation, even those that have been the most benevolent in their consequences".[2] Israeli history and collective memory were unmovable, fixed to the top-down principles of Mamlakhtiyut. In this "established and outsides" figuration, two interrelational tendencies among Israeli Palestinians were engendered. The first one was the creation of an almost exogenous citizenry and inner national sentiments for another polity (the Palestinian Occupied Territories). The second one was a militant sentiment of hostility towards Israel as a Jewish State, while supporting a binational democratic state as a political solution (with no Jewish character, whatsoever) to replace Israel.

All these dialectics were conducive to the national habitus and the model of citizenry it aimed to shape and eternalize. Yet, in terms of national banalization, following Billig (1995), Israel presents, perhaps more polemically than in other societies, a double-edged nature of national banality. On the one hand, the Israeli nation-state began to be taken for granted as a consolidated survival unit, after the 1973 War which had been a national trauma to be slowly overcome with educative slogans such as "All Israel are responsible for each other" (Hebrew: כל ישראל עֲרֵבִים זה בזה), a Jewish proverb, which implies mutual self-reliance amongst Jews. On the other, this value, much endorsed by the mandatory military service, marginalized and counterbalanced values of pluralism, causing a routinized "military-cultural complex" (Kimmerling 2001). In other words, the civic republicanism fostered by the *mamlakhti* habitus did not cultivate universal ethics but monolithically legitimated intra-Jewish solidarity. Yet, the privatization of economy in the 1980s, under the centre-right governments headed by Menachem Begin, brought about a decrease in the states' ideological strength. The individual began its ascent vis-à-vis collectivity. This was not an Israeli peculiarity.

Israeli sociopolitical and economic public policies were inspired (even emulated) by Reaganian neoliberalism in the US, and to lesser extent, by British Thatcherism. With Mamlakhtiyut receding from its social engagement (as structured by socialist Zionism until Begin's victory in 1977),

---

[2] Renan, E. "What is a Nation?" text of a conference delivered at the Sorbonne on 11 March 1882 (original title: "*Qu'est-ce qu'une nation?*"), Paris, Presses-Pocket, 1992 (translated by Ethan Rundell).

forms of demagoguery, populism and fanaticism took root, as social malaise increased. This assertion is not a stretch and cannot be underestimated. Neither should it be used to rewrite a genealogy of absolute values dating back to the ancient zealots (66–73 CE) nor should it be reduced to simple individual psychology. According to writer Amos Oz (2018), such phenomena in Israeli society derived from European Jewry whose revolutionary zealousness had engendered Zionist pioneering and the myth of the "new Jew", that is, the nativized "Sabra", a unique synergy between the virtues of the Jewish people and twentieth-century socialism in the land of Israel (Almog 2000; Kimmerling 2001).[3] Consequently, national zealousness with its altar of militarism and all kinds of hallucinations about imperialistic greatness came from Europe. This had also been the trajectory of Haredi Orthodoxy that closed itself within a fortified ghetto in order to defend its identity of external influences (in comparison to the coexistence and moderation of oriental Jewry that served in the IDF, and only marginally developed an ultra-orthodox lifestyle).

In addition, the withdrawal of Mamlakhtiyut from some of its constitutive values indirectly uncovered the "Sabra-model" as an elitist repetition of pretentious Eurocentrism in a land that had not been his, or at least had lost its spiritual centrality. This banalized and downgraded the nation-state from its pioneering pedestal. According to Leibowitz (1954), the triad of people-religion-state produced cynic secularism, either as a result of historical default (the material necessity of Jewish immigrants to escape annihilation in Europe during the Shoah) or because of Ben-Gurion's Mamlakhtiyut which strove to govern a secular state by using the theological notion of Jewish *Geula* (redemption). A pact which consisted, according to Leibowitz (1971), not only in blasphemy (*Hilul Hashem*), that is to say, the contempt for the Torah and the destruction of the Jewish religion, but also in the corruption of social life and profane political interests in humanistic terms. Given the falsehood and hypocrisy of the dual nature of Israel, the state manifested continuous crises of "atheist-clerical coalition", regardless of any geopolitical reality or uniqueness of Jewish life, and risked to become a meaningless "artificial synthesised creation", thus, a fictitious entity in the Middle East with no real content.

[3] The reference is of course to the founding myth of the Sabra and its role in creating a new Jewish society in Palestine. This sort of "nativization" by an élite group of youth who carried the standard of labour Zionism. Kimmerling (2001) and Almog (2000).

That said, there is no wonder that this *humus* of different and contradictory ingredients resulted in sociopolitical fragmentation (the so-called antagonistic sectorialization of Israeli society and the socioeconomic and ethno-cultural cleavages that remain unbridgeable).[4] From the emerging particularities and complexities of Israeli society, combined with the growing legitimization of individual stands, sprouted expressions of more critical and disenchanted states of mind vis-à-vis the institutional formalized national habitus. Some scholars, especially sociologists and historians, initiated a process of sociopolitical self-awakening by digging deep under the surface, aimed to uncover political inadequacy and structural fragilities in a society, once regarded as exemplary and idealistic. As we shall see, the historians who sought to exit the established historiography, and thus polemicize over Israeliness, were placed in-between the lines of scholarly work and political contention. Was an ideologico-historiographical revolution about to happen?

"Old" and "New" History? Or What the Post-Modern Fuss Is All About

There is no doubt that the intellectual field, being cosmopolite in its transnational exchanges, has often been quicker than general society in adopting external trends and experimenting new perspectives and tools. Israeli historiography, therefore, soon became an arena of confrontation with the rise of *Artziyut*. The demand for a revision of historical and sociological research began as a claim by some post-modernist, later labelled as "post-Zionist", scholars who accused "old generation" historians of having formed a tacit alliance with the political élite, namely the hegemonic Labour-Zionist establishment, and of serving it as "court intellectuals", whose only function was to provide "official versions" of Israeli collective

---

[4] The latter had already become visible in the 1971 protest of the Israeli "Black Panthers", a movement that consisted of second-generation Jewish immigrants from North Africa and Middle Eastern countries. It was one of the first organizations in Israel that called for social justice for Sephardi and Mizrahi Jews, while drawing inspiration from the African American Black Panthers.

memory.[5] This did not mean that this mechanism was acknowledged by historians whose positions were linked to the establishment.

As argued by Friling (2009, 140): "[P]olitics may have played with history, and present and future needs in shaping the past", even in the apparently most unifying study of the Shoah. That said, as all labels, "post-Zionism" per se revealed various characterizations and interpretations. Since it was not the result of self-attribution, it has been widely used in different contexts, namely political, cultural, academic etc. It was first attributed by Hillel Weiss, professor of literature at Bar-Ilan University, already in 1974, in an article about the absence of heroic figures in contemporary Hebrew literature (the article was published in the Religious Kibbutz Movement's periodical *Amudim*). An interesting conceptualization of the label is offered by Gorny (1996), a historian of Zionism member of Israeli "old historians".[6] Gorny divided post-Zionism into two types: (1) rejecting post-Zionism and (2) binding post-Zionism. The first refers to the traditional anti-Zionist worldview (such as the equally moralistic and ideological stands of the ultra-Orthodox opposition or the communist one), which spread via radical post-modernistic relativism.

The second type is more recent, pragmatic and realistic in political and psychological terms, inasmuch as it does not denounce the Zionism but perceives it as an ideological fait accompli, having achieved its historical mission. This modernist perspective seeks to dialectically overcome the Jewish Zionist nation-state (the national habitus), and transform the existing polity into a binational state in order to put an end to the conflict with the Palestinians and Arab world. In addition, it is noteworthy to mention the polar antonym of post-Zionism, which is not Zionism but rather "neo-Zionism", namely "the admixture of Zionist and Jewish ingredients [...]

[5] The mechanism is acknowledged by those historians whose positions are linked to the establishment: "Politics may have played with history, and present and future needs in shaping the past"; see Friling, T. (2009, 140). Nonetheless, the impression most "established" historians gave during interviews was that they have had much lesser impact on sociopolitical salience within Israeli society than "first generation" historians (with Ben-Zion Dinur as the emblem of such influence).

[6] See Gorny, Y. (1996). "From Post-Zionism to the Renewal of Zionism" in "Zionut: Pulmus Ben Zmanenu" [Zionism Controversy], *Iyunim Bitkumat Israel*, 1996 (thematic issue edited by Bareli and Ginossar), p. 514–530.

an exclusionary, nationalist and even racist, and anti-democratic political-cultural trend" (Ram 1999, 333[7]). Yet, neither post-Zionism nor anti-Zionism, which is often erroneously used as a synonym of the first, is necessarily anchored to relativist positions. Nevertheless, both are based on a critique of Zionism as having violated human rights. Even the somewhat marginal idea of a binational state does not automatically espouse post-modern, orthodox or communist worldviews. Therefore, the intellectual struggle to autonomize the academic field from politics found more room for manoeuvre in the self-attributed "critical sociology", where theories of cultural hegemony and domination had already been studied in the 1970s.[8] Their demand was based on sociopolitical and sociocultural circumstances.

On the academic level, post-modern critical theory was becoming in vogue worldwide and was gradually imported and adopted in Israeli academia, thus showing an increasing degree of scientific internationalization and contamination. This sociological novelty overtly endorsed a political engagement against established sociology, as embodied by Shmuel N. Eisenstadt (1923–2010) who had brought and hegemonically championed Parsonian structural functionalism. The "rupture" brought Israeli social scholars such as Yonathan Shapiro (1929–1997), the precursor of elitist social theory; Sammy Smooha (1941), pioneer of ethnic democracy theories; and Haifa University Marxist sociologists, namely Shlomo Swirski, Deborah Bernstein, Shulamit and Henry Rosenfeld and others, to enrich social sciences with feminist theory and post-colonial studies from

---

[7] Ram, U. (1999). "The State of the Nation: Contemporary Challenges to Zionism in Israel", Constellations, Vol. 6, No. 3, Blackwell Publishers Ltd, p. 325–338. The same words are used by Ram (2001, 58) in his article "Historiographical Foundations of the Historical Strife in Israel", *Journal of Israeli History*, Vol. 20: 2–3, p. 43–61; where the sociologist juxtaposes ethnic neo-national/neo-Zionist historiography to civic post-national/post-Zionist historiography.

[8] Ram, U. (1995). *"The Changing Agenda of Israeli Sociology: Theory, Ideology, and Identity"*, Albany [NY], State University of New York Press; (the latter is an extended version of a chapter entitled "Society and Social Science: Institutional Sociology and Critical Sociology in Israel" (p. 7–39) in the 1993 volume (edited by the same Ram): "Israeli Society: Critical Aspects" [in Hebrew]). An exhaustive discussion from the "established-side" of Israeli sociology was made by Lissak (1996): *"'Critical' Sociologists and 'Institutional' Sociologists in the Israeli Academic Community: Ideological Struggles or an Academic Matter-of-Fact Discussion"* (in Hebrew), in *"Tzionut: Pulmus Ben Zmanenu"* [Zionism: A Contemporary Controversy], *Iyunim Bitkumat Israel*, 1996, p. 60–98.

the mid-1980s onwards. The former sought better understanding of social problems through different relations of hegemony, micro-social and cultural analysis. The group was gradually followed by hordes of others. Almost needless to say that this group evoked considerable attention.

The politicization of social issues in Israel, namely the Mizrahim's under-representation in politics and their social protests (linked to difficulties in migration and integration, given the policy of settling them in refugee absorption camps upon arrival, in immigrant camps—the so-called *Ma'abarot*—and in peripheral "development towns"), the memory of the Shoah and its influence on Israeli society and the post-trauma of the 1973 War etc., provided fertile grounds to test critical theories on Israeli society. In this intellectual exchange the 1982 Lebanon War (dubbed "Operation Peace for Galilea") was a turning point. The war engendered turmoil in terms of national consensus with street demonstrations (chiefly the pacifist "Peace Now" movement, already established in 1978), and the growing phenomenon of conscientious objectors (the so-called refusniks). Consequently, post-modern theories made social scientists a new avant-garde of scholars bearing the torch of new intellectualism in the fields of culture, education, literature, arts, gender studies and law. The latter rediscovered both domestic and external types of otherness and social exclusion (the first: the *Mizrahim*, the second: the Palestinians), and emphasized the mechanisms of sociopolitical and economic oppression pertaining to the formative years of the state. Historiography was no exception.

THE CHRONICLES OF ISRAELI NEW HISTORIOGRAPHY

History as a discipline gained new ground at the end of the 1980s in the form of the so-called New History. In its first decade (1988–1998), "new historians" spread their influence beyond the narrow confines of academia and generated intense public debate within the Israeli society. Four intellectuals pioneered the historiographical debate. The first was Simha Flapan (1911–1987), a journalist and a radical-left activist, who had published two influential books: *Zionism and the Palestinians*, London, Croom and Helm (1979); and *The Birth of Israel. Myths and Realities*, New York, Pantheon Books (1987). Whereas Flapan had no academic position in Israel and belonged to the political field than to that of university and research, two historians Benny Morris (1948) and Ilan Pappé (1954) dedicated their research to the 1948 War. In addition to these three, one may also mention Israeli-British historian Avi Shlaim (1945), though never a member of Israeli academe, who was working at the time on his book *Collusion Across the Jordan: King Abdullah, the Zionist Movement and the Partition of Palestine* (1988). While Flapan initiated the process of re-examining the policies of Israel's first Prime Minister David Ben-Gurion, Morris coined the label "New History" versus "Old History" (1988).[9]

The historiographical divide was based on generational and professional criteria, such as age, position and methods of research. This positioning entailed a contrast between the new "outsiders", hence historians who were not on tenure track at the time, and "established" scholars such as Itamar Rabinovich (former dean of humanities and rector of Tel-Aviv University, Israeli ambassador to the UN at the time [1993–1996] and later 6th president of Tel-Aviv University, 1998–2007) and Anita Shapira, who were doing, according to Morris, "the same old history" as their masters had done. Thus, seniority and public profile were also criteria in labelling Israeli historians as either "old" or "new". Ilan Pappé, however, adopted Morris's label but dichotomized it further, as he categorized the two groups via their historiographical approach: historical positivism versus historical relativism (which later on excluded Morris after professing both Zionism and positivist approach to history). Consequently, no accurate analysis can truly aggregate "new historians" under the same category. Moreover, new historiography has never formed a school, which makes it difficult for any social aggregative analysis.

Nevertheless, 'New Historiography' deconstructed the "official historical version" of the 1948 War, which had been articulated around Arabs' intransigence vis-à-vis the UN partition plan (Resolution 181 II), their aggression against the nascent Jewish state and the general British ambiguity, even disfavour, to the Zionist enterprise (as manifested by the United Kingdom's vote of abstention at the UN General Assembly vote on the abovementioned Resolution 181, on 29 November, 1947). The new version of historical events broke the common belief that the Jews were numerically inferior to the armies of the Arab League (a belief rooted in the rereading of the biblical fight of young David against Goliath in modern terms). Moreover, a new generation of historians asserted that

[9] Morris, B. (1988). "The New Historiography: Israel Confronts it's Past", *Tikkun* 3/6 (1988), p. 19–23, 99–102 (republished various times). *Tikkun*, founded in 1986, is a quarterly interfaith Jewish left-progressive magazine, published in the US. It mainly analyses American and Israeli culture, politics, religion and history in the English language.

Israel had blurred its responsibility for the Palestinian *Nakba* during which approx. 700,000 Palestinians were actively expelled from their towns and villages, consequently depopulated and destroyed by the nascent Israeli army (only a minority remained, while some fled their homes with the false hope to be able to return one day): Israeli historian Benny Morris (1948), with the publication of his book *The Birth of the Palestinian Refugee Problem, 1947–1949*, Cambridge University Press (1988; published in the Hebrew only in 1991), and later Ilan Pappé (1954) accused the Jewish state of premeditated military actions, even mass murder and ethnic cleansing.[10]

The questioning of the purity of arms (Hebrew: *Tohar Haneshek*), in a society in which almost every citizen was, is, has been and will be a soldier, caused a scandal. Yet, the formal ethical military document "The Spirit of the Israeli Defense Forces" was only codified in 1994. Not only was this criticism aimed at the Israel of the past, but it also asserted and morally condemned the cynical use of Holocaust survivors by Labour-Zionist élite (the founding political class of Israeli Mamlakhtiyut) in order to legitimize Jewish aggression, given that circa 20,000 of Shoah survivors fought the 1948 War, alongside Sabra fighters (approx. 68,000).[11] According to Ram (2009, 367), the Jewish-Arab conflict generated a rigid dichotomy, wherein each side "musters the best sources it can to construct the material and symbolic edifice which buttresses 'our' identity and 'our' rights, as against 'theirs'", while "narrated forgetting" (self-censorship), "material forgetting" (physical annihilation) and "symbolic forgetting" (recreation and substitution) take place. The accusatory stand of "new historians" was

[10] Ilan Pappé is, perhaps, the most vocal promoter of this thesis. Pappé, I. "The 1948 Ethnic Cleansing of Palestine", *Journal of Palestine Studies*, Vol. 36 No. 1, autumn 2006; (pp. 6–20), which anticipated the book by a similar title: *The Ethnic Cleansing of Palestine* (2006), Oxford, Oneworld Publications. Pappé believes that an ethnic cleansing was deliberately implemented by Jewish armed forces (the so-called Plan Dalet, approved by Ben-Gurion on 10 March 1948). At any rate, these accusations were especially addressed to Ben-Gurion. The latter were systematically rebutted in 1989 on the pages of *Haaretz* by Shabtai Teveth (1925–2014), an Israeli historian and an anti-revisionist author, who published, since 1977, several biographies on Ben-Gurion (four chronological volumes and five thematic ones).

[11] Yablonka, H. (1999). *"Survivors of the Holocaust"*, Basingstoke: London, Macmillan Press [first published in Hebrew as "Foreign Brethren: Holocaust Survivors in the State of Israel, 1948–1952", by Yad Izhak Ben-Zvi Press and Ben-Gurion University of the Negev Press (1994)].

the construction of a victimizing collective memory which situated Israel in a perennial hostile environment and thus justified the country's security imperative and consequential aggressiveness versus the Palestinians. However, this element has never been one-dimensional. Zerubavel (1995, 2002) demonstrated the political interplay in Israel between "decline narratives" and "progress narratives", involving history, literature and folklore which transform past events into mythopoeic moments, beyond the 1948 War (the author numbers two ancient episodes, namely the fall of Masada [73 CE] and the Bar Kokhba Revolt against the Romans [ca. 132–135 CE] and the pre-state battle of Tel-Hai on 1 March 1920).

With regard to the historical deconstruction of the 1948 War, criticism started from fellow historians, former officials and retired commanders. All rebuked new historians to have presented a politically driven history and to have distorted and misread archival materials. A noteworthy example of the vocal critique was the one expressed by Israeli-British historian Efraim Karsh (1953), a former major and research analyst for the Israel Defense Forces, who had been trained in Arabic and Modern Middle Eastern history in both the Hebrew University and Tel-Aviv University. In 1996, Karsh published an article titled "Rewriting Israel's History" in *Middle East Quarterly* (Vol. 3: N. 2, June 1996, p. 19–29) that aroused immediate reactions and objections by most "new historians". Shlaim responded in "A Totalitarian Concept of History", (1996) p. 52–55, and Pappé in "My Non-Zionist Narrative", p. 51–52; both published by *Middle East Quarterly*, (Vol. III, 1996, n. 3).

In light of Karsh's position, Benny Morris simply wrote: "Efraim Karsh's article on the new Israeli historiography is a mélange of distortions, half-truths, and plain lies that vividly demonstrates his profound ignorance of both the source material (his piece contains more than fifty footnotes but is based almost entirely on references to and quotations from secondary works, many of them of dubious value) and the history of the Zionist-Arab conflict. It does not deserve serious attention or reply" (Morris, "Undeserving of a Reply", *Middle East Quarterly*, September 1996, p. 51). The scholarly, highly personalized quarrel, continued with Karsh's book (1997) *Fabricating Israeli History. The 'New Historians'* and Morris's article: "Refabricating 1948", published in *Journal of Palestine Studies* (XXVII (1998), n. 2, p. 81–95). As Karsh kept criticizing Israeli "new history" in "The Unbearable Lightness of My Critics", *Middle East Quarterly*, IX (2002), n. 3, p. 63–73, Morris kept answering back.

Not only did this historiographical quarrel sharpen the sensible edges of Israeli historiography as a scholarly debate, but it brought about concrete measures and academic professional circumstances. The well-known "Tantura-case" exemplified the practical repercussions of the "new" versus "old" historiographies. Yoav Gelber (1943), a military historian at Haifa University, who had served as the academic and military assistant to the Agranat National Commission of Inquiry (1973–1975), following the 1973 War, and who participated in the official inquiry into the 1933 political murder of labour-Zionist Haim Arlosoroff (1982) showed his opposition to the "new historians"[12] in a personal dual against his fellow colleague Ilan Pappé, around a master's degree thesis, submitted in 1998 by Theodore (Teddy) Katz, a Haifa University student attending a curriculum in History of the Middle East. The thesis claimed that Israeli troops had committed a massacre of 200–250 people in the Palestinian fishermen village of Tantura, located eight kilometres northwest of Zikhron Ya'akov (a Jewish town, founded as an agrarian settlement in 1882, on the Carmel Mountain range, south to Haifa), which was completely destroyed in May 1948 during the Israeli War of Independence. Katz based his research upon interviews with Arab villagers and with Israeli veterans of the operation (former Alexandroni Brigadiers of the *Haganah*).

In January 2000, the Israeli daily *Maariv* published Katz's findings and the case became public, intensified by reports and commentaries on Israeli dailies *Maariv* and *Haaretz*. In December 2000, Katz was sued for libel by veterans of the Alexandroni Brigade, headed by former commander Ben Zion Friedan (1917–2014), who argued that no such massacre had taken place but that around seventy men were killed in battle. Plaintiffs claimed that there were crucial discrepancies between the taped interviews Katz conducted and the content of his thesis. After the testimonies were heard, a compromise agreement was stipulated. It consisted in the revision of the thesis and a formal apology by Katz. Katz thus retracted his allegations

---

[12] His opposition has been expressed in various publications such as Gelber, Y. (2005). "*Why did the Palestinians Run Away in 1948?*", in "History News Network", 8 August 2005, (www.hnn.us); Gelber, Y. (2007a). "The History of Zionist Historiography. From Apologetics to Denial", in Morris, B. (2007). *Making Israel*, Ann Arbor, University of Michigan Press; and Gelber, Y. (2008). "*The New Post-Zionist Historians*", New York, American Jewish Committee, 2008; Gelber, Y. (2011). *Nation and History. Israeli Historiography Between Zionism and Post-Zionism*, London, Vallentine Mitchell.

about the massacre but retracted his own retraction 12 hours later. However, he was obligated to keep the agreement. He, consequently, revised his thesis and the university appointed a committee to re-examine it.

The assessment of the revised thesis was highly mixed and was eventually disqualified on the basis of insufficient empirical evidence and fundamental discrepancies in the forty oral testimonies Katz's had collected. Ilan Pappé, who was not Katz's supervisor (the supervisor of prof Kais M. Firro, an Israeli Druse), took Katz's defence and published an article titled "The Tantura Case in Israel: The Katz Research and the Trial", in *Journal of Palestine Studies* (XXX (2001), n. 3, pp. 19–39). Pappé insisted on the historiographical value and academic credibility of Katz's thesis and accused the committee of denying academic freedom, motivated by political interests. In addition, he denounced the Committee's behaviour to the American Historical Association. The case was then addressed by Tom Segev, a journalist and historian, in "His Colleagues Call Him a Traitor" (23 May, 2002, *Haaretz*), as well as by Benny Morris who published "The Tantura 'Massacre' Affair" (The Jerusalem Report, 9 February, 2004).[13] Pappé's position was heavily criticized by the abovementioned prof Gelber and other peers. The academic dispute within Haifa University led to a disciplinary action against Pappé (2002), and eventually to his expulsion/resignation from the university in 2007 (he consequently moved to the UK, where he found a position at the University of Exeter).

His accusations of deliberate ethnic cleansing against the nascent Israeli armed forces and his "interference" were, therefore, marginalized via institutional response. Yet, even his fellow new historian, Benny Morris, criticized Pappé's own historical thesis. He wrote (2004) as follows:

> In the case of Pappé and myself, there was always methodological discord. […] Pappé regarded history through the prism of contemporary politics and consciously wrote history with an eye to serving political ends. […] Unfortunately, much of what Pappé tries to sell his readers is complete fabrication. […] This truly is an appalling book. Anyone interested in the real

---

[13] In the meantime, Pappé published his "*A History of Modern Palestine: One Land, Two Peoples*", Cambridge, Cambridge University Press (2004); "*The Modern Middle East*", London: New York: Routledge (2005) and his both politically and historiographically controversial "*The Ethnic Cleansing of Palestine*", Oxford, Oneworld (2006).

history of Palestine/Israel and the Palestinian-Israeli conflict would do well
to run vigorously in the opposite direction.[14]

In his immediate response to Morris, Pappé underlined that

Benny Morris tells his readers in the New Republic that he and I walked a
stretch of road together as 'revisionist historians'. This is how an article begins
with a factual mistake; an article which is meant to show that my works are a
fabrication. This is a falsification of history as I could not be a partner to a
person, who had already in 1988 held views, I found morally unacceptable. I
was privy to the views he only aired later on, already in our first meeting back
in the late 1980s. I was fully aware—as he seemed to trust me—of his abomi-
nable racist views about the Arabs in general and the Palestinians in particular.
Unlike others, I did not feel that his good qualities as a chronologist which
came out in his most famous book, *The Birth of the Palestinian Refugee
Problem* (Cambridge 1987)—he was never a proper historian and especially
his invaluable contribution in aggregating data for us on the 1948 ethnic
cleansing—made up for his bigotry and narrow-mindedness.

Yet, the historiographical quarrel became even more personal as Benny
Morris's critique went further: "At best, Ilan Pappé must be one of the
world's sloppiest historians; at worst, one of the most dishonest. In truth,
he probably merits a place somewhere between the two" (Morris, "*The
Liar as Hero*", 17 March 2011, New Republic). It is noteworthy to
emphasize that the two "new historians" much differed in their examination of the Israeli leadership towards the Palestinian refugees. Whereas
Morris considered the 1948 to be a by-product of the 1948 war, Pappé
insisted on the deliberate and premeditated project of Zionism. Pappé
later published *Out of the Frame: The Struggle for Academic Freedom in
Israel*, London, Pluto Press. 2010. The latter was vehemently criticized by
Haifa University professor Yossi Ben-Artzi, a historian and geographer (as
well as former dean of the Faculty Humanities and the University rector).[15]

[14] Morris, B. *"Politics by other means"*, in "The New Republic", [post-date 03.17.04; Issue
date 03.22.04]. Ilan Pappé soon replied: "*Response to Benny Morris' 'Politics by other means'
in the New Republic*", The Electronic Intifada, 30 March 2004.
[15] Ben-Artzi, Y. (2011). "Out of (Academic) Focus: On Ilan Pappé, Out of the Frame: The
Struggle for Academic Freedom in Israel", *Israel Studies*, Vol. 16, No. 2 (Summer 2011),
p. 165–183. As Pappé himself did not want to address the matter during an interview held
on 6 July 2016, we cannot add to what has been already said and published.

Certainly, the "Tantura Case" provided evidence of the extent to which Israeli new historians were engaged in mutual criticism and replica that surpassed the national academic field and consequently placed the issue at the centre of international intellectual attention. In this regard, Israeli "new history" also showed that the supposedly inner-Israeli academic debate, in which Israeli historians were engaged, interested the study of the Middle Eastern conflict abroad. Their polemic covered the pages of internationally acclaimed scientific reviews, namely *Middle East Quarterly* and *Journal of Palestine Studies*, which supported the antagonistic dual between the two historiographic stands. Even newspapers such as *The Guardian*, *The Washington Post* and *The Jerusalem Post* (chiefly read by English speakers living in Israel or by diplomatic corps) contributed to the internationalization of the debate outside Israel. The "Tantura Case" was recently re-opened on the occasion of the 2022 docufilm "Tantura" by director Alon Schwartz, broadcasted on Israel' public Channel Kan 11, after having participated in Tel-Aviv's DocuFilm Festival.

The debate between "old historiography" and the "new" can also be explained in terms of "issue-ownership", a concept usually used in political communication, which delineates thematic centrality overtime and multi-dimensional competence (Walgrave et al. 2012). The institution-based "old historians", viewed as paladins of the established Zionist élite and identified with methodological conservatism (positivism), were juxtaposed with the "new historians", critical and rebellious and identifiable with post-Zionism, post-modernism and relativism. The divergence between the two groups consisted in a "competence" dimension and an "associative" dimension. This placed historians on a scale of emerging historical issues, namely the 1948 War, the Holocaust, etc. in their plurality of voices and narrations. While "new historians" claimed their ownership on topics relevant to the Israeli public sphere (for instance, the Palestinian refugee problem, the cynical use of the Holocaust and the victimization of Israel and other similar issues), they denounced the conservatism in which "old historians" had been fossilized into by the political establishment.

They built up a catchy category and a rebellious unsettling public image, anchored to the notions of novelty, originality, freshness and objectivity. The label, consequently, produced its own attractiveness and got identified with the freedom of the intellectual spirit, non-conformism and its full expression vis-à-vis the presumed bias of "old history". Nonetheless, no one can really measure or compare the two groups. It is no matter of preference or democratic choice (as it is in politics). Yet, it is plausible to assume that "new history" reflected some of the sociopolitical unrest of its genesis, while "old history" presented the solidity of the known, thus, further strengthening the national habitus. The latter enjoyed greater social capital, as well as a numerical advantage, combined with symbolic capital (accumulated public prestige). That said, the debate enjoyed visibility and keeps nurturing waves of both national and international polemics (generalizable to issues emerging in every changing society in the global era).

Beyond highly politicized and mutual personal accusations, Israel's new historiography rethought the past and placed Israel's collective memory on the historical continuum of contingencies, political choices and societal changes. Nevertheless, this intellectual preference was also a "slippery slope". As argued by an absolute outsider, Kumarswamy (2017), the progress of New History in Israel was severely undercut on the back by three factors: (a) the "deeply ingrained debate" inculcated in Jewish culture (the author cites the maxim "*Two Jews, three political parties!*" as a behavioural norm) which makes Jews more litigious and challenging than other ethnicities; (b) the internal divisions over the 1982 Lebanon War and the prolonged occupation of Palestinian territories (with the outbreak of the first Intifada in December 1987); (c) the politicization of historiography as an academic discipline which decreased its value. Furthermore, Kumarswamy ascribes the historiographical trend to be "a sign of maturity and self-reflection". Surely, the period coincided with the Middle Eastern peace process, which engendered at the time high hopes for reconciliation with the Palestinians and the Arab world, making "new historians" a channel of negotiation between two national histories. In this regard, the high point of "New History" was bringing out on the public stage a different national narrative with great vitality and visibility. The new label brought to those scholars worldwide fame, that of avant-garde "myth-breakers".

They flagged the Arab viewpoint on the 1948 War which was briefly introduced in the school curriculum for the *Bagrut* in history (the Israeli high-school matriculation examination) both in Jewish schools and in Arab Israeli ones, despite continuous debates. Attempts to introduce some Palestinian (and Arab) viewpoints had already been carried out as of 1984

with no real success (Ben-Amos 2002; Podeh 2002).[16] However, the
Israeli public was not ready to accept the 1948 Palestinian Nakba, as part
of the formation of the Jewish state. Political tensions reached their peak
with the assassination of Israeli Prime Minister Yitzhak Rabin on 4
November 1995. Around the political assassination, and consequently the
disintegration of the peace process, the historiographical trajectory promoted by Israeli "new historians" lost its momentum in terms of public
intellectualism. Rabin's assassination by a Jewish extremist violently shook
Israeli society. The dramatic episode uncovered the polarization and politicization within Israeliness. Israeli historiography did not escape this kind
of overt politicization which considerably robed its academic objectivity. It
worsened the personalization of academic and intellectual conflicts. The
political clash eclipsed any intellectual significance and "deactivated" the
efficiency of serious historiographical revision. In the long run, the latter
rendered bad service to the works of the "new historians", which became
a political tool in the hands of anti-Israeli activists who banalized their
academic research.

Though this sinister episode left hurtful scars within the intellectual
field, some elements must be considered. Firstly, the antagonistic relations
between fellow historians achieved high visibility (as commonly said: "any
publicity is good publicity") and thus provided a stage for well-established
historians to reaffirm their position in contrast with new historians who,
though receiving harsh criticism, were successful in occupying space in the
local intellectual field, whereas some earned international acclaim (as in
the case of Ilan Pappé). Secondly, although the intense quarrel short-lived
in terms of public debate, it turned the tide of the ground rules of Israeli
historiography. Post-modernism and post-Zionism prefixed the place of
history as competitive narratives and interpretive tools.

The dichotomous dialectic between "we" and "others", core of traditional national history, left room for multiple interpretations. The "new"

---

[16] The inclusion of the Arab/Palestinian viewpoint into high-school curricula goes beyond
the scope of this work. Yet, one example of such debates was the polemic over the inclusion
of Palestinian poetry by Mahmoud Darwish and Siham Daoud, into the literature curriculum, on voluntary basis of teaching (not in history) as declared on 1 March 2000 by then-
incumbent Israeli Minister of Education Yossi Sarid. See Ben-Amos, A. [ed.] (2002). *History,
Identity and Memory: Images of the Past in Israeli Education*; and on the 1948 War and the
way Israeli textbooks dealt with the event, Podeh, E. (2002). *The Arab-Israeli Conflict in
Israeli History Textbooks, 1948–2000*.

historiography did not fail in "flooding the system" and cleansing it from the over monochromatic interpretation of history anchored to conservative historiography. It became a source of enrichment and different historiographical sensibilities within Israeli public discourse. Noteworthy was the case of "new history" outside the purely academic field. The appeal for new historical interpretation inspired the 1998 TV documentary series *Tkumah: 50 Hashanim Ha'Rishonot* (lit. "Revival: The First 50 Years"). The latter, after "learning the lesson" of the Ashkenazi one-sidedness of *Amud Ha'Esh* (lit. "The Pillar of Fire", screened by state-owned Channel1 in 1981), as criticized by Mizrahi Israelis, showed greater openness to the plurality of backgrounds within Israeli society. Yet, it received accusations for its unbalanced pro-Palestinian narratives by rightist groups, which further exemplified its public significance. Some analytical compromises were, therefore, criticized as legitimating impressionistic falsehood, rather than historical truth.

There is a factor to the whole story that cannot be underestimated or considered as mere technicality. In the historiographical debate, which either anticipated or followed the genesis of "New History", the usefulness of state papers, such as office records of governmental institutions, was now available to researchers by Israel State Archives at the end of the 30-year rule of secrecy, due to the amendment of the Israel Archives Law in 1981 by Begin's right-wing government. Open archives meant the possibility to conduct research on once classified materials and, therefore, critically examine the 1948 War. Without this "revolutionary" technical change, no "new historian" could have seen the light. That said, one should also consider the socio-psychological aspects which guided new historians' academic interest. In general terms, the 1982 Lebanon War manifested two conflicting states of mind in Israeli society. On the one hand, a considerable part of the Israeli public opinion was against the war and condemned it; on the other, the war crystalized the fact that Israel was successful in taking offensive measures against external threats and had consolidated its regional primacy.

These two poles set the mental frame of reconstructing the genesis of the Israeli survival unit via historical research. Unlike previous historiographical generations, the historians who approached the archives in the 1980s belonged to a different generation. They were all born after the 1948 War. This socio-biographical aspect explains much of their interest. They ambitiously sought to provide new evidence to the geopolitical situation Israel found itself in. Moreover, their generational detachment became a criterion of objectivity, since they had no personal involvement with the history they were investigating. Nonetheless, the problem of first-hand source materials still could not present the whole picture, since the Israeli State Archives had only materials written by Israeli authorities. No Palestinian or other Arab materials could be analysed. In addition, no new historian had the language skills required to address sources in Arabic. This seemingly trivial fact cannot be overlooked, as it put in question the ability to enter a serious historiographical relation with Palestinian history. Consequently, there was no true reception of the Palestinian side. Neither Israeli intellectuals nor Palestinian intelligentsia established a dialogue aimed to mutually formalize the revision of this shared history. Hence, even the rebellious and critical new historiography was able to produce a partial (some would claim unilateral) history.[17]

NEW HISTORY: DEBATES OVER THE SHOAH

The contemporary era of *Artziyut* and the historiographic revisionist state of mind have also involved the history of the Holocaust. Since the latter is the worst act of dehumanization and violence against the Jewish people (and against any ethnic group), some question marks were raised, already in the 1980s, on whether Israel had fallen into a morbid trap of "Shoah worship": a cult which not only fetishized the Holocaust but perpetuated Jewish particularism, victimization and justification a priori, thus, a cynical and specious political tool. According to Friling (2012), the Holocaust and its counter-narrative re-opened the "court-case" against the Zionist Yishuv, based upon four interlinked issues: (1) the (un)predictability of the catastrophe; (2) the actions to save European Jewry; (3) its instrumental attitude/emotional and cultural alienation towards the survivors (so-called: *Sh'erit ha-Pletah*; Hebrew: שארית הפליטה, lit. "the surviving remnant"); (4) the incomprehension of the Holocaust's meaning for the

---

[17] Only the case of historian Hillel Cohen (1961) seems to truly exemplify an engagement in producing a "bilateral" historical enquiry by using Israeli and Arab sources (archival documentation and oral testimonies) in the study of the geopolitical conflict. In his book *Year Zero of the Arab-Israeli Conflict 1929* (published in Hebrew in 2013, English edition: 2015 English), Cohen provides the chronicles of one week in August 1929 through which he situates the genesis of the Jewish-Arab conflict in Palestine. Interestingly enough, Hillel overtly criticizes the "new historians", namely Ilan Pappé and Benny Morris, of having "used the 1929 riots not in order to understand them but as a tool to present their own stands", thus for misinterpretations and inaccuracies (Cohen 2013, p. 386–89; my translation).

entire Jewish people and the construction of memory.[18] All four elements have served as accusatory arguments in emphasizing the inherent "Palestinocentrism" of the Zionist movement that concentrated its efforts on building the "new Jew" and achieving political independence, rather than taking concrete measures to save European Jewry (the so-called negation of Diaspora).

The intellectual fundaments of this mainly post-Zionist critique have originated from two distinct sources. The first was Hannah Arendt's perception of the Holocaust as a crime against the entire humanity which posited the event alongside other genocides. The second has derived from the Zionist-led national "memory overdose" which keep eternalizing the "psycho-pathological" distinction of Jews vis-à-vis all other identities (Rose 2005). In Israeli "new" historiography one of the most important precursors of the universalistic significance of the Holocaust against any national particularistic interpretation is Idith Zertal (1945), historian and former journalist. Zertal published two fundamental books on the issue: *From Catastrophe to Power: The Holocaust Survivors and the Emergence of Israel*, Berkeley, University of California Press (1998), and *Israel's Holocaust and the Politics of Nationhood*, Cambridge: New York [etc.], Cambridge University Press (2005). Moreover, Zertal is the most prolific translator and editor of Hannah Arendt in Hebrew, namely of the latter's first major work *"The Origins of Totalitarianism"* (2010) as well as of her *"Jewish Writings"* (2011). She has long been identified with the political party *Meretz* which positioned her in the unrealistic place (86th) in the Israeli 2013 legislative elections.

As expressed by Israeli historian Daniel Gutwein (2009, 36): "[...] Holocaust memory has undergone several transformations corresponding to different phases of nation building that have been reflected in the remodeling of Israeli collective identity".[19] Whether a "divided

---

[18] The point is succinctly discussed in Friling, T. (2012). "Do not worry Chloe, Not everything is lost-At Least not for the Time Being", *Israel*, N. 20, 2012, p. 209–218 (especially p. 212 et seq.; in Hebrew).

[19] Gutwein, D (2009). "The Privatization of the Holocaust: Memory, Historiography, and Politics", *Israel Studies*, Vol. 14, No. 1, "Israelis and the Holocaust: Scars Cry out for Healing" (Spring, 2009), 36–64. The article is a shorter and translated version of an analogue article in Hebrew; *"Hafratat HaShoah: Politica, Zikaron ve'Historiografia"* which appeared on *Dapim LeKheker Tkofat HaShoha* ("Research Papers on the Period of the Holocaust"), Vol. 15, 1998, p. 7–52. The historian explores the privatization of the Holocaust memory by examining a number of texts which reflect the context and role played by post-Zionism during the 1980s and 1990s.

memory", prior to Israeli statehood, or a political institutionalized acquis of Mamlakhtiyut via national rituals and establishments (namely, Yad Vashem and the Remembrance Day for the Holocaust and Heroism), after which empathic identification with the victims reached its peak around the 1961 Eichmann Trial, the Shoah resists in terms of collectivization and keeps playing a significant role in the national habitus and its preservation, regardless of the historiographical trend or any state of mind.

Notwithstanding, the privatization of memory that started in the 1980s engendered a process of individualization from which geopolitical moral dilemmas emerged (the reference is the Sabra and Shatila massacre committed during the 1982 Lebanon War, with Israeli troops enabling Lebanese Christian Phalanges to kill between 460 and 3500 Palestinian civilians). As in the case of the debate around the 1948 War and the Nakba, the generation of Israeli historians faced their own society and its contingencies. In addition, as new historians had not fought the war they were historically deconstructing, Shoah scholars began facing the gradual demographic disappearance of first-age survivors and the increasing centrality of the impact of their experiences on their descendants (Shoah's second generation).

Gutwein entered in polemics with the abovementioned Tom Segev over the latter's relativist and post-Zionist stands, expressed in his book (2000) *The Seventh Million: Israelis and the Holocaust*, New York, Owl Books (already published in Hebrew in 1991, and which inspired a documentary series broadcasted on prime time on the state-owned television channel 1 during the summer of 1995). The latter had already been criticized by Holocaust historians, Yehuda Bauer and Tuvia Friling (1993), who judged Segev's work as partial and scarcely rigorous.[20] This critic led to Friling's book (collection of essays), *An Answer to a Post-Zionist Colleague*, Tel-Aviv, *Yedioth Ahronoth* (2003), which focuses on Israeli new historians, domestic shifts within Israeli society and the increasing

---

[20] Bauer, Y., Friling, T. (1993). "No Tom, No Segev: Joel Brand's Mission and the 'Seventh Million'", *Iton 77* (lit. "Newspaper" N. 77: an Israeli monthly literature and culture magazine, established in 1977), N. 160–161, May–June, pp. 24–28 [in Hebrew]. The latter reprised Friling's prior critique: "*The Seventh Million as the March of Folly and Evil of the Zionist Movement*", *Iyunim Bitkumat Israel* [studies in Israeli and modern Jewish society: a multidisciplinary journal founded in1991, published annually by the Ben-Gurion Research Institute for the Study of Israel and Zionism at the Ben-Gurion University of the Negev (Sede-Boker)], N. 2, 1992, p. 317–367.

dominance of post-modernism as a historiographical method. A similar critique was addressed to Segev's book (1999), *The Days of the Anemones: Eretz Israel During the British Mandate*, by Hebrew University historian Yehoshua Porath (1938–2019), an expert on Muslim countries and Palestinian nationalism (Porath 2000), Holocaust historian and political scientist Shlomo Aronson (1936–2020) and fellow new historian Benny Morris.[21]

Since the ideological debate on the media eclipsed the history of the Shoah, with reference to the pure academic study of documents related to the eventful tragedy, it became a tool to discredit the Zionist leadership in the *Komemyiut* and *Mamlakhtiyut* periods and undermine the legitimacy of the Zionist enterprise. The 1988 article "The Need to Forget" by professor Yehuda Elkana exemplifies this point. Elkana (1934–2012), a survivor of Auschwitz, was a philosopher of science and historian (former head of the Cohn Institute for the History and Philosophy of Science and Ideas at Tel-Aviv University and director of the Van Leer Institute in Jerusalem). In his article, published on the pages of *Haaretz* on 2 March 1988, Elkana denounced the attitude of the Israelis towards the Palestinians, at the outbreak of the First *Intifada*, in terms of "victimhood consciousness" justifying acts of violence.

According to Elkana, the lesson that had to be drawn from the dreadful tragedy of the Holocaust was that Nazi brutality had not been exclusively German and, therefore, could not be attributed to a specific nation or time in human history. More specifically, a similar violence could potentially emerge even from the Jewish people who had suffered such atrocities. Yet, he concluded: "[A]ny life lesson or life perception whose source is the Holocaust is a disaster. [...] Democracy is the cultivation of the present and the future; the cultivation of memory and the immersion in the past undermine the foundations of democracy". The Ben-Gurionist rhetoric of "the whole world is against us" (somewhat complementary with the

[21] Porath, Y. (2000). "The Dubious Mandate of Tom Segev", Azure (Tchelet), N. 9, 158–166 [in Hebrew]; Aronson, S. (2000). "Historia Meduma Le'Umat Historia Re'huya le'Shema ("Faked History in comparison to well-deserved history"), *Iyunim Bitkumat Israel*, Vol. 10, 2000, 678–687 (in Hebrew); and Morris, B. (2000). "Segev is negligent in diagnosing the facts" (p. 145) in *HaZman HaAdom* (The Red Time), *Israel*, N. 1, 2000, p. 143–148 (in Hebrew).

colloquial expression *um-shmum*),[22] which had penetrated Israeli political socialization, hence the national habitus and the logics of the Israeli survival unit, via educational travels to Auschwitz of high-school students and IDF soldiers, had begun in 1965 (suspended in 2020 due to the COVID-19 pandemic, yet resumed[23]). The "paralysis of remembering", asserted by Elkana, resulted in sociopolitical anomalies, such as the externalization of the culture of grief and the "militarized victimization" of Israeli Jewish society vis-à-vis perennial threats (Friling 2014).

The intellectual foundations of "New History" and its post-Zionist critique became a political manifestation, no less politics-grounded than the historiography it criticized. According to Shapira (1999):

> "In fact, the ideas advanced by Benny Morris, Avi Shlaim, and Ilan Pappé, the vanguard of the 'new historians', were nothing new. An anti-narrative of Zionism, counter-posed to the Zionist (and Israeli) narrative of Zionism, had existed since the very inception of the Zionist movement. Opponents of the movement, Jewish and non-Jewish, had created an entire literature explaining

[22] "Um-Shmum" (Hebrew: אֻ"ם שמום), where "um" is the Hebrew acronymic for U.N and the "shmum"-prefix signifies dismissal, contempt or irony. The phrase was coined by the Israeli Minister of Defense (and former Prime Minister) David Ben-Gurion on 29 March 1955 during a cabinet debate regarding his plan to take the Gaza Strip from Egypt in response to the increasing fedayeen terror attacks on Israel (as accounted by Prime Minister Sharett in his diary).

[23] The sanitary suspension was prolonged as a consequence of a diplomatic crisis between Israel and Poland. On 1 February 2018, the Polish Senate approved a bill prohibiting accusing Poles of involvement against Jews in the Holocaust. The law drew sharp criticism in Israel. The crisis further intensified after the Prime Minister of Poland, Mateusz Morawiecki, was asked about the law and replied that Jews collaborated with the Nazis just as the Poles did. In September 2019, Polish President Andrzej Duda claimed that Israel was "responsible" for the attacks on Jews and the increase in cases of anti-Semitism in Poland, after Israeli Foreign Minister Israel Katz had said that "the Poles will cleanse anti-Semitism from their mother's milk". In June 2021, mutual diplomatic reprimand talks were held, following the Polish legislation seeking to delete or stop pending property claims (by Polish-descent Israelis), which have not reached a decision in the last 30 years. In July, the Polish Senate approved the law. Knesset Speaker Miki Levy announced that he would not establish the inter-parliamentary friendship group between Poland and Israel. Consequently, diplomatic relations were suspended with both ambassadors' departure. Tensions gradually subsided. On 20 April 2023, Poland appointed Joanna Hoffman (former director of the Institute of Polish Culture in Israel) as Polish ambassador to Israel. This ended the crisis in the relations between the countries. In honour of Israel's 75th Independence Day (night of 25 April 2023), government buildings in Warsaw were illuminated in blue and white colours, and state authorities announced that an agreement was found to resume high schools' journeys to Poland, based on a renewed, yet controversial, programme.

what was foul in Zionism and why Zionism was destined to fail, and later why
the state of Israel was an illegitimate and unjust construct that had to be
resisted. [...] The 'new historians' of Israel have not exactly pioneered fresh
critical approaches in Israeli historiography. [...] Already in the 1970s, scholars
had begun to develop new and sophisticated views of Jewish-British relations
under the Mandate, of Zionism's relation to the Arab problem, of the rise of
the Arab national movement, of the nature of Zionism as the national liberation movement of the Jewish people. There was a tense and constant dialogue
between collective memory and historical scholarship, as the new approaches
slowly penetrated into the educational system and public consciousness. Since
the advent of the 'new historians', however, a new polarization has set in. For
the 'new historians' dismissed all previous historiography as apologetic.
Whoever dares to oppose or to criticize the pronouncements of these self-
styled iconoclasts is savagely maligned. [...] When reality comes more closely
to approximate our moral ideals, moralism will become redundant [...]".[24]

Yet, Shapira's stand was only partially true. Both Nakba and Holocaust
history-writing could benefit from state archives made available to
researchers in the mid-1980s. Topical issues around the Jewish Yishuv, its
inner debates, policies and actions could be transformed pieces of information into historiographical knowledge, and eventually into sociopolitical public debates. Prior to "new historians", most facts had been based
either upon biographical memoirs or on party-led publications. The scientific study of these events reached greater scholarly maturation in Israeli
academe. That said, the "new history" dispute may be simply summarized
as a war of ideas, facts and interests in interpreting the Holocaust, not in
terms of national collectivization but in those of liberal privatization that
allowed the individual to frame his/her self-critique in relation to a nation-
state whose survival had already been secured. Perhaps even more important was the punctual contribution of "new history" to Israeli scholarship
in terms of professional habitus.

The intellectual "provocations", pushed forward by "new historians",
crystalized the internationalization of research methods and critical theories.
Not only did the latter facilitate comparison and generalization of aspects
related to Israeli society and history with other cases (beyond the particularistic view of Jewish democratic statehood), but the scientific trend engendered greater interdisciplinarity. Debates over the 1948 War and the Shoah
involved historians, sociologists, psychologists etc., who fashioned a more

[24] For the whole text, see Shapira, A. (1999). "The Failure of Israel's 'New Historians' to
Explain War and Peace. The Past Is Not a Foreign Country", *The New Republic*, 29
November 1999, pp. 26–36 (translated by William Templer).

pluralistic academic universe (Ben-Gurion University, e.g., incorporated the Faculty of Humanities and that of social sciences in light of intellectual interconnections as well as for budgetary constraints). By engaging in this kind of debates, "new historians" received legitimacy, as a novel historiographical generation. Though, they were not unable to create an autonomous unified "school" (due to their low number and the mutual accusations exchanged between main key figures such as Morris and Pappé), they formalized an alternative perspective to traditional historiography. Any rhetoric around "new historians'" perpetual status of "outsiders" would be self-contradicting in light to the fact that most of them work within the Israeli academic establishment and were co-opted by it and attained tenure-track positions (with the exception of Ilan Pappé). Moreover, in addition to public universities, many "new historians" hold positions at the Jerusalem-based Van Leer Institute, which is a semi-governmental institution (founded in 1959), known for its critical views expressed on its interdisciplinary journal *Teoria u'Bikorert* (lit. "Theory and Criticism").[25]

Notwithstanding, some scars within the Israeli historiographical field keep bleeding. Gelber (2007a, b, 9–10), a historian identified with the positivist traditional perception of history, commented:

---

[25] The biannual journal was founded in 1991 and published jointly by the Van Leer Institute and the Ha-Kibbutz Ha-Meuhad Publishing House (the publishing house was founded in 1939 by the Socialist Zionist movement): both highly prestigious in the local intellectual field. The inaugural issue presented critical intellectuals such as Adi Ophir (modern continental philosophy), Hannan Hever (comparative literature), Yehuda Elkana (history and philosophy of science) and others, soon followed by various academic and public figures, namely Arab public intellectual (later politician) Azmi Bishara, Avigdor Feldman (civil and human rights lawyer) followed by Ariella Azoulay (art curator and filmmaker), Yoav Peled (political scientist and social activist [Peace Now]), Amnon Raz-Krakotzkin (Jewish history) etc. Israeli sociologist, Uri Ram, pointed out that the review served as the main stage for post-modernism and post-Zionism in Israeli academia during the 1990s, since its content was inspired by the stances of notable intellectuals, such as Michel Foucault, Jacques Derrida, Jacques Lacan (Ram, U. (2006). *The Time of the Post: Nationalism and Politics of Knowledge in Israel*, Tel-Aviv, Resling [in Hebrew]). Amongst the seventeen special issues of *Teoria u'Bikoret* (with a thematic scope), there is the 1996 issue (n. 8) dedicated to the "New Historians", edited by prof Adi Ophir (born 22 September 1951), an Israeli philosopher who teaches at the Cohn Institute for the History and Philosophy of Science and Ideas at Tel-Aviv University, fellow of the Van Leer Institute, editor-in-chief of the journal from its foundation to 2000 (then replaced by sociologist Yehouda Shenhav [born in 1952] known for his contributions in the fields of bureaucracy, management, capitalism as well as for his research on ethnicity in Israel, editor: 2000–2010). See the journal's website: http://theory-and-criticism.vanleer.org.il (in Hebrew).

[T]o undermine the historical studies in Israeli academia at the time in the name of winds blowing in the 'western world' and make those trends to new orthodoxy dictating historians' conscience and methodology. One of the expressions of this undermining is the attack on the department of Israeli Studies arguing it is 'ideological' and bends research findings in favour of the 'Zionist narrative'. [...] It appears, anyhow, that in the western world almost nothing has been left of the historical discipline, which has lost its monopoly on the past. [...] One of the questions [...] indeed is whether historiography is an endangered species, or is it still possible to stop the process and influence the trend.[26]

The risk has remained the one indicated by Gutwein (2001), namely a spiral of "research denial" which means the decrease in historiographical value, once academic quarrels are transformed into overt ideological disputes. He writes: "[T]he relativization that informs the attack of the new historiography transforms historical research from a scholarly discipline into a kind of consumer commodity, modeled to suit changing taste of the prevailing fashion and its clients" (Gutwein 2001, 38). Hence, implications such as the weakening the discipline, its vulgarization, the lack of trust in scientific production and accusations of lack of professionalism have all echoed throughout the clashes between post-Zionist historians and their more established colleagues. Until today, historical perspectives strive for unconfutable factuality (the so-called historical truth), while "old" historians and "new" ones contend each other. Yet, it is difficult to assert there is no mutual academization of the social or socialization of the academic, meaning that political views are inevitably inherent to any scholarly work. Historians, as all social researchers, are product of their own socialization and personal preferences.

Criticism on "old historiography" did not only come from the ranks of "new historians". Some critique arrived from scholars whose professional training was not anchored to the specific fields of Jewish history, Israeli history or Middle Eastern studies. Some distinguished "general" historians expressed their intellectual discomfort. One of them was Zeev Sternhell (1935–2020), Hebrew University political scholar (specialized in fascism and revolutionary rights movements in France and Italy), who published in 1995 his only book on Israeli history: *The Founding Myths of Israel.*

---

[26] Gelber, Y. (2007b). *History, Memory and Propaganda: The Historical Discipline at the Beginning of the 21st Century*, Tel-Aviv, Am Oved Publishers Ltd. [in Hebrew]: English edition [revised]: "*Nation and History: Israeli Historiography Between Zionism and Post-Zionism*", Valentine & Mitchell, London: Portland [OR: USA], 2011.

Nationalism, Socialism and the Making of the Jewish State (French edition published by Fayard, 1996; English edition published by University Press, 1998). Sternhell was awarded the 2008 Israel Prize for political science.

Another example was Shlomo Sand (1946), a historian of intellectuals from Tel-Aviv University, who gained popularity abroad but has been heavily criticized by fellow historians for his books: *The Invention of the Jewish People*, London, Verso, 2009 (2008 Hebrew edition, 2009 English with numerous translations in French, German, Arabic, Italian, Russian, Japanese, Hungarian, Swedish, Slovene, Spanish, Chinese, Brazilian, Polish, Turkish, Bulgarian, Croat, Portuguese, Greek, Czech, and Korean), followed by Sand (ed.) *"Ernest Renan: On the Nation and the 'Jewish People'"*, London, Verso, 2010 (Hebrew edition, 2009); and *The Invention of the Land of Israel*, London, Verso, 2012 (Hebrew edition in the same year followed by various translations), and *How I Stopped Being a Jew*, London, Verso, 2014 (2013 Hebrew edition as well as in French, German, Arabic, Italian, Russian, Spanish, Brazilian, Polish etc.). Both Sternhell and Sand triggered criticism from colleagues specialized in Jewish and *Eretz Israel* history (e.g., Shapira, Bartal, Gelber, Shavit), especially on the cultural pages of Israeli daily *Haaretz*. However, their work achieved international acclaim and demonstrated rapid reception, revealing how much post-modern theories, applied to the Jewish Israeli case, enjoyed transversal readership.

OVERCOMING POST-ZIONISM: A THIRD WAY FOR ISRAELI HISTORIANS?

As one can imagine, the "new history" state of mind stabilized its position in Israeli academe, since its "eruption" in the late 1980s. The two historiographical visions coexisted in a sort of intellectual truce. The period that followed Rabin's assassination brought about a democratic malaise which spread throughout Israeli politics and society. The civic certainties of the civilizing Mamlakhtiyut, which had established the interdependency between state and citizenry (the Jewish one), fell into crisis in front of the political assassination, a transgression of Israel's democracy and its myth of exceptionality, namely being equally democratic as Jewish. The *mamlakhti* "hold" was challenged. Though the structure did not disintegrate, the undisputable primacy of the national habitus weakened. In light of parallel developments that have produced similar results, two different states of mind took form. On the one hand, the "revolutionary" post-modernist and post-Zionist state of mind was vocal, yet it soon went back to its original form, as an intellectual alternative to scholarly production and not to political action. Any formal political recognition of the Palestinians, framed in the Oslo peace process, aroused doubts regarding feasibility and future outcomes. On the other hand, the rather novel and still marginal phenomenon of Jewish messianism, much identified with Rabin's assassination and its perpertrator, became a taboo within public discourse. However, messianic Judaism, successfully scattered its seeds amongst the settlers residing in the Occupied Territories. The settlers' movement gradually regained political legitimacy, as no Israeli government advanced negotiations with the Palestinian authority. The 2005 disengagement plan, carried out by Sharon's government, and the 2007 takeover by Hamas of the Gaza Strip clearly showed the disintegration of the Oslo Accords.

Paradoxically, the central issue of new historiography, namely the expulsion and dispossession of Palestinians, identified with the radical left, encountered the extreme right that, after the post-1995 "disappearance" and the orange protest against the unilateral withdrawal from Gaza, wished to restore the "Promised Land" to its lawful owners through the messianic neo-conservative project of "Greater Israel". Both political projects seemed to dismantle the Zionist *mamlakhti* national habitus via two institutional reforms: the first, the universalization of democracy and, consequently, the dissolution of any Jewish feature of statehood; the second, the complete theocratization of Israeli society as ethnically Jewish. Despite these abysmally different interpretations, the two extremes presented Zionism as an ideological monolith, based on the use of force. While no side succeeded in the political conquest, the Israeli polity remained in its problematic twofold position: an "ethno-democratic" survival unit.[27] A process of democratic back-sliding towards autocratization (Cassani and

---

[27] The term "ethnic democracy", already used by Juan Linz in 1975, was introduced and developed in Israel by sociologist Sammy Smooha (University of Haifa), recipient of the Israel Prize (2008), in a two-volume book (*Arabs and Jews in Israel*. Vol. 1: "Conflicting and Shared Attitudes in a Divided Society". Boulder: London, Westview Press. 1989; *Arabs and Jews in Israel*. Vol. 2: "Change and Continuity in Mutual Intolerance", Boulder: London, Westview Press. 1992) and in many articles, for instance, "Minority Status in an Ethnic Democracy: The Status of the Arab Minority in Israel" in *Ethnic and Racial Studies* 13, 3 (July 1990), p. 389–413; "Ethnic Democracy: Israel as an Archetype", Israel, 1997, p. 198–241 (published in Hebrew in *"Zionut: Pulmus Ben Zmanenu"* [Zionism Controversy], *Iyunim Bitkumat Israel*, 1990, pp. 277–311); "The Model of Ethnic Democracy: Israel as a Jewish and Democratic State", *Nations and Nationalism*, Vol. 8 (N. 4), 2002, pp. 475–503.

Tomini 2019[28]) had begun, given Israel's discriminatory policies vis-à-vis the Palestinian minority within the state's international borders, qualifying as "ethnic democracy"[1] or "ethnocracy" (Smooha 2002; Yiftachel and Ghanem 2004; Yiftachel 2006[29]). The flattening of the republican component and the decrease in the institutional identification with Mamlakhtiyut gradually weakened the resilient dispositional edifice of the Jewish and democratic state, as ratified in the 1948 Declaration of Independence, and by consequence, initiated the demolition of Israel's values and norms.

The sociopolitical, perhaps even intellectual and educational, weakening of the Israeli national habitus uncovers the contemporary banalization of Zionism, as a wide-range ideology (with inner, vibrant, conflictual currents), which has been a factor in the decline of Israeliness, ever since (Kimmerling 2001). The endemic crisis of the Israeli habitus in its rupture of continuity with the Jewish past vis-à-vis the geopolitical circumstances of the present. Following the "flood" of new historians, the dichotomy between Jewish Zionist national particularism vis-à-vis another national particularism found minor interest in historiographical research (yet, new archival materials kept being scrutinized from different angles by both "old" historians and "new" ones).[30] Neither the history of the victors nor that of the dispossessed (paraphrasing Walter Benjamin's 1940 essay "On the Concept of History") inspired a new generation of Israeli historians. The latter sought to overcome the dichotomic historiographical inheritance of the 1990s. The grand geopolitical structural aspects of the Israeli survival unit were left aside. In the by then polychromatic historiographical landscape, some have spoken of post-post Zionist historiography (Likhovski 2010).

---

[28] Cassani, A., Tomini, L. (2019). "What Autocratization Is". *Autocratization in post-Cold War Political Regimes*. Berlin, Palgrave Macmillan: Springer International Publishing.

[29] Yiftachel, O. & Ghanem, A. (2004). "Towards a theory of ethnocratic regimes: learning from the Judaization of Israel/Palestine". In Kaufmann, E. P. (ed.). *Rethinking ethnicity: Majority groups and dominant minorities*. Routledge, 179–197; Yiftachel O. (2006). *Ethnocracy: Land and identity politics in Israel/Palestine*, Philadelphia, University of Pennsylvania Press.

[30] Recent publications regarding the 1967 War exemplify this point: Oren, M.B. (2002): "*Six Days of War. June 1967 and the Making of the Modern Middle East*", Oxford, Oxford University Press (translated into Hebrew in 2004); Segev, T. (2007): "*1967. Israel, the War, and the Year that Transformed the Middle East*", New York, Metropolitan Books (translated from the 2005 Hebrew edition). Even more recent is the interest in the War of Attrition (1967–1970), Gelber, Y. (2017): "*Hatasha: HaMilchama Shenishkechah*" (lit. "Attrition: The Forgotten War"), Or Yehuda, Dvir Publishing (in Hebrew), and ibid., (2018): "*The Time of the Palestinians: Israel, Jordan and the Palestinians, 1967–1970*", Or Yehuda, Kinneret Zmora-Bitan Dvir (in Hebrew).

This ideological and historiographical state of mind has emerged in recent years as a trend and fashion reflecting contemporary society. Accordingly, a new generation of Israeli historians begins to occupy the academic field. Unlike the previous generations who were interested in the ideological strands and strains in Zionism (Labor/Herut, Haganah/ IZL/Lehi), or of the movement's central figures (Ben-Gurion, Jabotinsky, Katznelson, Begin etc.), the new cohort of scholars approaches Israeli history via innovative forms of urban and cultural history (Anat Hellman and Orit Rozin), gender history (Devorah Bernstein, Ofer Nur and Rina Peled), intellectual history (Etan Bloom, Adi Gordon, Yotam Hotam, Nitzan Lebovic, Amos Morris-Reich, Boaz Neumann, Dimitri Shumsky and Yfaat Weiss) and others, while seeking to re-contextualize Zionist history through the mundane routinized practices of Jewish daily lives in Palestine/Israel. Their works, therefore, present the *Artziyut* of contemporary Israel. By researching micro-themes, which had been ignored by *mamlakhti* old and new historians, these scholars have placed Israeli historiography in line with global trends in the profession.

As in the case of "new historians", some of the scholars are trained in social sciences, rather than in history. "The third wave in Israeli historiography", whose research is collocated in "the post-revisionist phase" entail a new kind of reflexivity through the careful examination of Jewish history, while eschewing any "immanent causality" (Myers 2009a, b).[31] While prioritizing social aspects such as mentalities, rituals and emotions, food consumption and trends and attitudes in health, these Israeli historians have produced works that much differ from those of their trainers. In addition, these scholars are less dependent on state archives but on the more local (and private) archival documentation of smaller communities (urban or agrarian centres etc.).

In this sense, the post-post Zionist generation of scholars embodies the individualization process in Israeli society, originated in Begin's socioeconomic and sociopolitical legacy. The once state-centred historiography has been abandoned for the sake of more practical micro-research. The private sphere has gained room over the public one, inasmuch as the latter engenders conflicts and unrest. Their studies, therefore, tend to be less ideologically motivated and more individualistic and culture-oriented. The approach aims to de-politicize what has been

---

[31] Myers, D.N. (2009a). "Is there still a 'Jerusalem School?' Reflections on the state of Jewish historical scholarship in Israel", *Jewish History* (2009) 23: p. 389–406. See also Myers, D.N. (2009b). "Between Israel and the Nations: Reflections on the State of Jewish Historical Scholarship in Israel", *Zion*, 74 (2008/09) 339–52, especially p. 345 [in Hebrew].

politicized by previous historiographical generations. One can hypothesize that the shift from a solid sociopolitical monomorphism to a structurally polymorphic social and political fabric, though uncertain, set in motion this post-post Zionist cohort as one of the formers' positive reactions, namely a creativity linked to necessity to overcome the high degree of conflict in Israeli society and academe alike. This requires the generational renewal of the survival unit through self-critique, its actualization, while assuming, of course, that there is no blind fortification by dominant positions. The general phase of *Artziyut*, as national banalization, makes this scholarly generation an inbetweener experience, since the national habitus has not formally changed but has already faced several states of mind which contributed to its stratification, for better or worse.

Yet post-post Zionist historians profess an attitude towards Zionism that is often more empathic than that of "new historians". Perhaps because this last generation of Israeli historians had been chiselled neither by the eventful 1948 nor by the political divisive consequences of the 1967–1973 period. The trivialization of the Israeli occupation of Palestinian territories and the cyclic occurrences of violence have become social and cultural normalcy, if not an element, changeably dormant, of the Israeli national habitus. The latter further justifies the "post-post-Zionist" label, since it suggests the acceptance of things as they stand with scarce possibility to promote radical changes. One might accuse this generation of escapism or passivity. Nonetheless, Zionism as a national project is neither praised nor taken for granted. These scholars, according to Kaplan (2013, 151), "desire to rediscover some of the early tenets of Zionist thought: the idea that political self-reliance is the best political and social option in uncertain times".[32] This body of scholarship, already institutionalized within Israeli universities, critically appreciates Zionist Israeli history (having interiorized the lessons of "new historiography") and examines the sociopolitical fabric the nation-state has woven over the decades, hence the habitus, without denigrating the existent. That said, their conscience and awareness concern, as for each and every group, generational differences.

Another element to be reckoned with is that the national habitus is resilient, which means it possesses the intrinsic "ability to face and overcome changes through an equilibrium of adaptation and self-preservation" (Helled and Pala 2024, p. 93). Hence, the Zionist national habitus which

---

[32] Kaplan, E. (2013). "Post-Post-Zionism: A Paradigm Shift in Israel Studies?", *Israel Studies Review*, Volume 28, Issue 1, Summer 2013, p. 142–155. The article is a review essay which focuses on Likhovski's abovementioned article (2010).

is the anchor of Israeli socialization has been capable of overcoming the conflictual disputes originated by post-modernist thought, the "new historians" and the escapist attempts by post-post Zionist scholars. This makes the Israeli Zionist habitus an almost "hysteresis-proof", since it manages to remain intact despite rather volatile circumstances. What Bourdieu referred to as "hysteresis", that is, a state in which structural transformations challenge the habitus' interiorized dispositions, as it clashes with external environment and changing objective conditions, has not engendered, so far, dislocation and disruption of societal regularities ("hysteresis effects"; Bourdieu 1977, 2000). As the chronicles of recent Israeli historiography reveal, the resilience of the Zionist habitus and the structural incisiveness of the national Jewish survival unit have been successful in integrating and adaptationally englobing the abovementioned ideological challenges into multi-level polymorphous academic discussions, and consequently allow the re-stabilization of power relations, in spite of the mismatch between norms (namely Zionist adherence) and possibilities (the post-Zionist and post-post Zionist variations).

Moreover, the fact that people did not live through the same sociopolitical set of experiences and were shaped differently and with sometimes divergent sensibilities makes this last generation of Israeli historians more pluralistic in the capacity to contain divergences without the need to engage in overt contrast, as did their professional predecessors. Furthermore, their works are much more integrated in the international academic context, where American universities having Israeli studies curricula have become partners of continuous exchange. One example for this internationalization is the Association for Israel Studies (AIS), founded in the USA in 1985, which is devoted to the interdisciplinary academic and professional study of modern Israel and gathers more than 500 researchers from all over the world[33] (less significant than the AIS is the equally interdisciplinary European Association of Israel Studies).

[33] AIS President for the 2021–2023 period is professor Arieh Saposnik (Ben-Gurion University) and the society's vice-president is professor Raphael Cohen-Almagor (Hull University): both are Israeli-born. The organization's executive director is Dr Asaf Shamis (University of Haifa) and its treasurer is Dr Ilan Ben Ami (The Open University of Israel). Former presidents include: Prof Myron (Mike) Aronoff, Prof Robert Freedman, Prof Ian Lustick, Prof Pnina Lahav, Prof Ilan Peleg, Prof Hanna Herzog, Prof Alan Dowty, Prof Joel Migdal, Prof Rachel Brenner, Prof Ilan Troen, Prof Aviva Halamish, Prof Gad Barzilai, Prof Menachem Hofnung, Prof Donna Robinson Divine and Prof Yael Aronoff. The association's journal is *Israel Studies Review* (ISR).

In addition, post-post Zionist historians, contrary to new historians, remain identified with their Israeliness within these scholarly associations. They may diverge from the *mamlakhti* scholars who keep defending their position or collaborate with them once necessary (such as in the recent case of the "Historians' letter" against the Netanyahu-Gantz government, published on 20 October 2020, as well as their participative support to the AIS statement regarding the planned judicial reform proposed by Netanyahu's current government, conveyed on 17 January 2023). Consequently, unlike the antagonistic relations that characterized the "big-bang" of "New Historiography", this stream in Israeli scholarship maintains greater freedom in its approach to the study of Israeli history as well as in the expression of sociopolitical criticism. Yet, Israeli history remains written by the victors of Zionism, and whose halo, painted around their heads, would still open long intellectual discussions with some crucial questions to be answered.

To conclude, the contradictory perceptions of Israeli history and the banalization of the Israeli national habitus, that is, the trivialization of national identity, symbolic automatisms and daily practices which are seemingly taken for granted, demonstrate the cohabitation of different states of mind. Neither has this process engendered a structural transformation of the content of the collective habitus nor has the antagonistic concurrence between Zionism and post-Zionism threatened the integrity of the Israeli survival unit as both Jewish and democratic. The integrational and disintegrational aspects, as expressed in Israel's last generations of history-writing, have, indeed, sharpened the edges of Israeliness but did not erode or invert the dominance of the institutionalized Mamlakhtiyut. Critical and accusatory as historiographical factions may be, they still indicate somewhat nostalgic and "confessional" features in professing hard love to the homeland, or at least testify the simple understanding there is "*no country other*".

References

Almog, O. (2000). *The Sabra: The Creation of the New Jew*, Berkeley [California], University of California Press.

Aronson, S. (2000). "Historia Meduma Le'Umat Historia Re'huya le'Shema ("Faked History in comparison to well-deserved history"), Iyunim Bitkumat Israel, Vol. 10, 2000, pp. 678–687 (in Hebrew)

Bauer, Y., Friling, T. (1993). "No Tom, No Segev: Joel Brand's Mission and the 'Seventh Million'", *Iton 77*, N. 160–161, May–June, pp. 24–28 [in Hebrew].

Ben-Amos, A. [ed.] (2002). *History, Identity and Memory: Images of the Past in Israeli Education*, Tel-Aviv, University of Tel-Aviv: Ramot Publishing House (in Hebrew).

Ben-Artzi, Y. (2011). "Out of (Academic) Focus: On Ilan Pappé, Out of the Frame: The Struggle for Academic Freedom in Israel", *Israel Studies*, Vol. 16, No. 2 (Summer 2011), pp. 165–183.

Billig, M. (1995). *Banal Nationalism*, London: Thousand Oaks: New Delhi, Sage Publications.

Bourdieu, P. (1977). *Outline of a Theory of Practice*. Cambridge: Cambridge University Press.

Bourdieu, P. (2000). *Pascalian Meditations*. Stanford, CA: Stanford University Press.

Brown, W. (2010). *Walled States, Waning Sovereignty*, New York, Zone Books.

Cassani, A., Tomini, L. (2019). *Autocratization in post-Cold War Political Regimes*. Berlin, Palgrave Macmillan: Springer International Publishing.

Cohen, H. (2013). *Year Zero of the Arab-Israeli Conflict 1929*, Jerusalem, Keter (in Hebrew).

Del Sarto, R. A. (2017). *Israel under siege: the politics of insecurity and the rise of the Israeli neo-revisionist right*, Washington: Georgetown University Press.

De Swaan, A. (2015). *The Killing Compartments: The Mentality of Mass Murder*, New Haven: London, Yale University Press.

Douglas, M. (1995). "Forgotten Knowledge" in Marilyn Strathern (series editor) *"Shifting Contexts: Transformations in Anthropological Knowledge"*, London: New York, Routledge, 1995 [first edition].

Elias, N., Scotson, J.L. (2008). *The Established and the Outsiders. A Sociological Enquiry into Community Problems*, Dublin, University College Dublin Press.

Frilling, T. (1992). "The Seventh Million as the March of Folly and Evil of the Zionist Movement", *Iyunim Bitkumat Israel*, Ben-Gurion Research Institute for the Study of Israel and Zionism: Ben-Gurion University of the Negev, Sede-Boker), N. 2, 1992, pp. 317–367.

Friling, T. (2009). "A Blatant Oversight? The Right-Wing in Israeli Holocaust Historiography", *Israel Studies*, Vol. 14, No. 1, "Israelis and the Holocaust: Scars Cry out for Healing" (Spring 2009), p. 123–169.

Friling, T. (2012). "Do not worry Chloe, Not everything is lost-At Least not for the Time Being", *Israel*, N. 20, 2012, p. 209–218.

Friling, T. (2014). "Remember? Forget? What to Remember? What to Forget?", *Israel Studies*, Vol. 19, N. 2 (Summer 2014), pp. 51–69.

Gelber, Y. (2005). "Why did the Palestinians Run Away in 1948?", "History News Network", 8 August 2005, www.hnn.us.

Gelber, Y. (2007a). "The History of Zionist Historiography. From Apologetics to Denial", in Morris, B. (2007). *Making Israel*, Ann Arbor, University of Michigan Press.

Gelber, Y. (2007b). *History, Memory and Propaganda: The Historical Discipline at the Beginning of the 21ˢᵗ Century*, Tel-Aviv, Am Oved Publishers Ltd. (in Hebrew).

Gelber, Y. (2008). *The New Post-Zionist Historians*, New York, American Jewish Committee.

Gelber, Y. (2011). *Nation and History. Israeli Historiography between Zionism and Post-Zionism*, London, Vallentine Mitchell.

Gorny, Y. (1996). "From Post-Zionism to the Renewal of Zionism" in "Zionut: Pulmus Ben Zmanenu" [Zionism Controversy], *Iyunim Bitkumat Israel*, 1996 (thematic issue edited by Bareli and Ginossar), pp. 514–530.

Gutwein, D. (2001). "Left and right post-Zionism and the Privatization of Israeli Collective Memory", *Journal of Israeli History*, 20:2–3, pp. 9–42.

Gutwein, D (2009). "The Privatization of the Holocaust: Memory, Historiography, and Politics", *Israel Studies*, Vol. 14, No. 1, "Israelis and the Holocaust: Scars Cry out for Healing" (Spring, 2009), pp. 36–64.

Helled, A., & Pala, C. (2024). When Nations Adapt: National Resilience between State(s) and Identity(ies). *Political Studies Review*, 22 (1), 93–107.

Kaplan, E. (2013). "Post-Post-Zionism: A Paradigm Shift in Israel Studies?", *Israel Studies Review*, Volume 28, Issue 1, Summer 2013, pp. 142–155.

Karsh, E. (1996). "Rewriting Israel's History", *Middle East Quarterly* Vol. 3: N. 2, June 1996, pp. 19–29.

Karsh, E. (1997). *Fabricating Israeli the 'new historians'*, Ilford: Essex, Frank Cass.

Karsh, E. (2002). "The Unbearable Lightness of My Critics", *Middle East Quarterly*, IX (2002), N. 3, p. 63–73.

Kimmerling, B. (2001). *The Invention and Decline of Israeliness: State, Culture and Military in Israel*, Los Angeles and Berkeley: University of California Press.

Kumarswamy, P.R. (2017). "How Fortunes Of Israeli Revisionist History Came To Be Reversed", *Swarajya Magazine*, special issue: *Passage To Israel*, June 2017.

Leibowitz, Y. (1954). *The People, the Religion and the State* [in Hebrew: "Ha'Ham, Ha'Dat ve Ha'Medina"], Deot, Vol. A, republished in the book: *Judaism, Jewish People and the State of Israel* [in Hebrew], 1975, Tel-Aviv, Schocken Books.

Leibowitz, Y. (1971). "State and Religion" [in Hebrew: "Dat u'Medina"], *Hadereh*, N. 4 (May), published in the book: *Judaism, Jewish People and the State of Israel* [in Hebrew], 1975, Tel Aviv, Schocken Books.

Likhovski, A, (2010). "Post-Post-Zionist Historiography", *Israel Studies*, July 2010, Vol. 15(2), pp. 1–23.

Lindblom, C.E. (1982). "Another State of Mind", *The American Political Science Review*, 76(1), pp. 9–21.

148   A. HELLED

Lissak, M. (1996). "'Critical' Sociologists and 'Institutional' Sociologists in the
Israeli academic Community: Ideological Struggles or An Academic Matter-of-
Fact Discussion", *"Tzionut: Pulmus Ben Zmanenu"*, *Iyunim Bitkumat Israel*,
1996, pp. 60–98.

Morgan, R. (2000). "A European 'Society of States'-but only States of Mind?",
International Affairs,76(3), p. 559–574.

Morris, B. (1988). "The New Historiography: Israel Confronts it's Past", *Tikkun*
3/6 (1988), pp. 19–23.

Morris, B. (1996). "Undeserving of a Reply", *Middle East Quarterly*, September
1996, Vol. 3, N. 3. pp. 51.

Morris, B. (1998). "Refabricating 1948", *Journal of Palestine Studies*, XXVII
(1998), n. 2, pp. 81–95.

Morris, B. (2000). "Segev is negligent in diagnosing the facts", Israel, N. 1, 2000,
p. 143–148 (in Hebrew).

Myers, D.N. (2009a). "Is there still a "Jerusalem School?" Reflections on the state
of Jewish historical scholarship in Israel", *Jewish History* (2009) 23, pp. 389–406.

Myers, D.N. (2009b). "Between Israel and the Nations: Reflections on the State
of Jewish Historical Scholarship in Israel", *Zion*, 74 (2008/09), pp. 339–352.

Oz, A. (2018). *Dear Zealots: Letters from a Divided Land*, Boston: New York,
Houghton Mifflin Harcourt.

Pappé, I. (1996). "My Non-Zionist Narrative", *Middle East Quarterly*, Vol. III,
1996, N. 3, pp. 51–52.

Pappé, I. (2001). "The Tantura Case in Israel: the Katz research and the Trial",
Journal of Palestine Studies, XXX (2001), n. 3, pp. 19–39.

Podeh, E. (2002). *The Arab-Israeli Conflict in Israeli History Textbooks, 1948–2000*,
Westport [CT]: London, Bergin and Garvey, Greenwood Publishing Group.

Porath, Y. (2000). "The Dubious Mandate of Tom Segev", Azure (Tchelet), N. 9,
pp. 158–166.

Ram, U. (1993). "Society and Social Science: Institutional Sociology and Critical
Sociology in Israel" in Ram, U. [ed.], *Israeli Society: Critical Aspects* [in
Hebrew]), pp. 7–39.

Ram, U. (1995). *The Changing Agenda of Israeli Sociology: Theory, Ideology, and
Identity*, Albany [NY], State University of New York Press.

Ram, U. (1999). "The State of the Nation: Contemporary Challenges to Zionism
in Israel", *Constellations*, Vol. 6, No. 3, Blackwell Publishers Ltd, p. 325–338.

Ram, U. (2001). "Historiographical Foundations of the Historical Strife in Israel",
Journal of Israeli History, Vol. 20: 2–3, pp. 43–61.

Ram, U. (2006). *The Time of the Post: Nationalism and Politics of Knowledge in
Israel*, Tel-Aviv, Resling (in Hebrew).

Ram, U. (2009). "Ways of Forgetting: Israel and the Obliterated Memory of the
Palestinian Nakba", *Journal of Historical Sociology*, Vol. 22 No. 3 September
2009, pp. 366–395.

Renan, E. (1992). *What is a Nation*, Paris, Presses-Pocket (English translation of the original 1882 "Qu'est-ce qu'une nation?

Rielly, J.E. (1987). "America's State of Mind", *Foreign Policy*, (66), pp. 39–56.

Rose, J. (2005). *The Question of Zion*, Princeton, NJ and Oxford, Princeton University Press.

Shapira, A. (1999). "The Failure of Israel's "New Historians" to Explain War and Peace. The Past Is Not a Foreign Country", *The New Republic*, 29 November 1999, pp. 26–36 (translated by William Templer).

Shlaim, A. (1996). "A Totalitarian Concept of History", *Middle East Quarterly*, Vol. III, 1996, N. 3, pp. 52–55.

Skey, M., Antonsich, M. [eds.] (2017). *Everyday Nationhood Theorising Culture, Identity and Belonging after Banal Nationalism*, London, Palgrave Macmillan.

Smooha, S. (1989). *Arabs and Jews in Israel*. Vol. 1: "Conflicting and Shared Attitudes in a Divided Society". Boulder and London: Westview Press.

Smooha, S. (1990). "Minority Status in an Ethnic Democracy: The Status of the Arab Minority in Israel", *Ethnic and Racial Studies*, 13, 3 (July 1990), pp. 389–413.

Smooha, S. (1992). *Arabs and Jews in Israel*. Vol. 2: "Change and Continuity in Mutual Intolerance". Boulder and London: Westview Press.

Smooha, S. (1997). "Ethnic Democracy: Israel as an Archetype", *Israel*, 1997, pp. 198–241.

Smooha, S. (2002). The model of ethnic democracy: Israel as a Jewish and democratic state. *Nations and Nationalism* 8(4), pp. 475–503.

Yablonka, H. (1999). *Survivors of the Holocaust*, Basingstoke: London, Macmillan Press.

Yiftachel, O. & Ghanem, A. (2004). "Towards a theory of ethnocratic regimes: learning from the Judaization of Israel/Palestine". In Kaufmann, E. P. (ed.). *Rethinking ethnicity: Majority groups and dominant minorities*. Routledge, 179–197.

Yiftachel O. (2006). *Ethnocracy: Land and identity politics in Israel/Palestine*, Philadelphia, University of Pennsylvania Press.

Walgrave, S., Lefevere, J., Tresch, A. (2012). "The Associative Dimension of Issue Ownership", *Public Opinion Quarterly*, Vol. 76, No. 4, Winter 2012, pp. 771–782.

Zerubavel, Y. (1995). *Recovered Roots: Collective Memory and the Making of Israeli National Tradition*, Chicago: London, University of Chicago Press.

Zerubavel, Y. (2002). "The "Mythological Sabra" and Jewish Past: Trauma, Memory, and Contested Identities", *Israel Studies*, Vol. 7, No. 2, *Memory and Identity in Israel: New Directions* (Summer, 2002), pp. 115–144.

PART IV

At the End of the Road

Conclusions: *Historiographical Generations and National Habitus: Final Remarks*

The book pursued the different phases of Israel's national habitus through the institutionalization and autonomization of the local historiographical field or, better said, the subfield of Jewish, Zionist and Israeli historical studies vis-à-vis other fields, intercrossing intellectual, political and social changes. It aimed at tracing the major actors, structural conditions and objective relations in Israeli national history-writing from its pre-state sociogenesis to recent decades. The enquiry focused upon the Jewish Zionist historians, as a privileged group of scholars who are both producers and products of their national identity. In order to shed light on the interdependencies between personal individual agency, social dispositions and structures, the enquiry delineated the significant interactions of both biographical and social elements. Hence, it collectivized the former and contextualized the historiographic profession into the latter. Furthermore, the analysis dwelled on the multitude of fields and struggles that Israeli historians have intercrossed between the academic field (the immediate professional surroundings), Israeli society and the omnipresent role played by the state in building the Israeli national survival unit: an Eliasian concept which permits the construction of a dynamic figurational structure that shapes and contains the identification of socialized individuals with the societal order, as they experience it.

Tensions, interconnections and sometimes even contradictions exemplify how ideology, national identity and individual stories are so intimately

A. Helled, *Israel's National Historiography*, Palgrave Studies on Norbert Elias, https://doi.org/10.1007/978-3-031-62795-8_6

intertwined. They reveal generational specificities and processual tendencies in habitus-stratification, therefore, the codes and norms interiorized
by a determined collectivity via socialization, and that bear an intrinsic
appropriateness though which each and every generation can be inter-
relationally integrated into a socio-psychic "identikit" in a progressive (or
regressive) societal process.

In the specific case of Israeli historians, objective, yet dialectical, interrelations concerning different positions produce and reproduce not only
the professional dispositions in the academic role but in the active participation of individual historians in studying and depicting the national history to which they belong. Two sorts of habitus interact and uncover their
constitutive features. Through the attentive contextualization and examination of Jewish Zionist historiography and its producers, the enquiry
demonstrated the twofold generations of historians and historiography.
The analysis provided three indicative generations whose habitus present
interesting sociological properties in relation to continuity and change.
Not only do these generational cohorts characterize the historians themselves, and consequentially the historiographical discipline tout court, but
the Jewish Israeli society in its entirety as well. By adopting an approach,
inspired by and based on the sociological teachings of Norbert Elias and
Pierre Bourdieu—though not exclusively—the analysis mirrored constan-
cies and shifts with intellectual and sociopolitical relevance. Variations in
scientific paradigms, ideology and social positions thus unfolded.

Our itinerary commenced with tackling the interconnections between
national identity and scholarship which then accompanied Israeli historiography as a case-study. The first part of the book introduced the scope of
the research and discussed the existent literature from which the research
question took inspiration. It also presented the salience of the enquiry and
placed it as an interdisciplinary and multi-level analysis (state, academia,
generations). Additionally, it covered the research itinerary on which the
book is based. Aims, scientific approach and methods were presented and
discussed to show their empirical profitability.[1]

---

[1] This book might have seemed too historical for a sociologist to write or too sociological for
a historian to read. However, the author is an intellectual product of both disciplines, which
shaped the scientific sensibility that accompanied the research process throughout its different
stages. Hopefully, the immersion into history through sociological theories was also pleasant
and enriching for the reader. The need to combine two different scholarly "mentalities" derives
also from the inherent complexity of the Israeli case. Israeli society and politics often internationally echo regarding either domestic transformations or regional and global geopolitics. This
twofold character of the Jewish democratic state, as implemented in the Middle East by
European-born Zionism, is to be considered the sociogenetic feature of this complexity.

The second part of the book was dedicated to historiography, identity and state-building through the vantage point of habitus and generational-based analysis. This conceptual "geography" was introduced to the reader before approaching the empirical case of Israeli historians. The conceptual map, namely "habitus", "field", "survival unit" and "generation", provided analytical instruments through which processual mechanisms of socialization become empirically traceable beyond the intellectual *milieu* of Israeli historians and their specific profession. In other words, the conceptualization enabled the combination of overlapping micro and macro social phenomena which would belong to different fields, but which are interrelated and interdependent once systematized with the tools of historical sociology. This facilitated the unfolding of long-term dynamics in Israeli societal processes that the reader encountered throughout the reading of book. This part also discussed the history-writing as a profession that has been instrumental for collective identity to achieve structural relevance. Therefore, the historical interpretation of facts was discussed and emphasized in relation to the question of means, context and knowledge at the disposal of the historiographical endeavour (namely, linguistic and cognitive elements, ideological basis, fashions and so forth). Observations about identity, nationalism and factuality were made. The discussion stressed on the construction of historical congruence and the aim of historians to enable nationalization and collectivization of the sociopolitical community of Jews in Palestine under the aegis of Zionism. The latter exemplified the multiple crossovers between sociopolitical and intellectual fields.

After the abovementioned theoretical and conceptual framework, we dived into the very core of the empirical analysis of the three generations of Jewish Zionist history in Israel. Chapter 3, "*Komemyiut*: Pre-statehood and Historiographical Enterprising", discussed the first attempts of historical writing and academic sociogenesis in the years before Israeli independence. As such it unpacked the primal motivations and structuring actions of Jewish historians in pre-1948 Palestine. The influential interiorized dispositions present in the local historiographical field were thus applied to the pre-state period (namely, the early 1920s), starting from the sociogenesis of the discipline and its autonomization within the nascent Hebrew University of Jerusalem. The reconstruction of the cultural and structural conditions of the time, the biographies of most relevant actors as well as the trajectories of their careers revealed a plurality of voices and sensibilities going much beyond the simplistic intuitive hypothesis that assumed an automatic commitment to the national cause amongst Hebrew University's exclusively male professorship. Nonetheless, despite the low numbers and the still precarious conditions, one cannot minimize the contingent long-term influence of the so-called Jerusalem School. Prominent founders consisted of Jewish immigrants from Central and Eastern Europe, who had been trained in the Berlin-based *Hochschule für die Wissenschaft des Judentums* and in some other German universities. As for any social phenomenon the roots of that historiographical generation developed and transformed into something new.

Known for the positivistic and philological historiography of Jewish chronicles, showing tensions between Palestinocentric and Diasporic approaches, this pioneering generation of local historiography was significantly orchestrated by the exceptional persona of Ben-Zion Dinur who, at the juncture of the nation-building-process and its aftermath, succeeded in finalizing ideological creed and personal ambitions. He set an exemplary trajectory of intellectual engagement in politics. His legacy, and to a lesser extent than of his peers, institutionalized, codified and handed down the prevalence of the Zionist ideology through the appropriation of Jewish history resulting in modelling it into a particular autonomous field. The latter meant a radical shift from envisioning the Jewish past in religious terms (*historia sacra*), adjusting it to secular modern terms (*historia profana*), while bridging the millennial existence of Jews in Diaspora with Zionism. Though national revival placed active engagement and involvement in determining the Jewish fate as the utmost priority, the interdependency between the historiographical perspective and the ideological one was neither monochromatic nor immutable. Hebrew University historians shared much of their method; however, followers and successors within the "Jerusalem School" also showed noticeable divergent scholarly sensibilities. Nonetheless, different interpretations did not refute the existence of a common habitus. The generational habitus of *Komemyiut* consisted in the corrective rebellion against Jewish precariousness in Diaspora and espoused the modern national cause in light of full cultural emancipation which gradually became sociopolitical. The synthesis between the European disciplinary roots of local historiography and the events in situ sets the foundations on which all flowing generations had to come to terms with.

Once the Jewish nation-state was founded, the political domain established the ground rules of the Israeli national habitus, as discussed in Chap. 4: "*Mamlakhtiyut*: The Silver Platter and Consolidation of Israel's

National Habitus". This chapter focused on the development of the Jewish nation-state and academia in the period between 1948 and 1977, showing the weight of the first "Israeli" historians and the autonomization of the discipline in relation to Jewish studies. Under the aegis of labour Zionism, headed by David Ben-Gurion, the foundations of *Mamlakhtiyut* were laid down. The sociopolitical creed moulded a nonpartisan civic-consociational res publica in which the sovereign nation-state assumed its role as the sole stakeholder of the societal order, an undisputable protagonist whose presentability, solemnity and honourability were to guide nascent citizenry vis-à-vis the complexities and challenges of the Israeli "melting pot". This ideological approach shaped the entire public system, including the expanding academic system. With the inauguration of new universities, during the 1950s, the *mamlakhti* principle found its way into the formers' institutionalization. The primogeniture, which had been the fortune of the "Jerusalem School", remained, despite the fact that the first generation of historians was gradually replaced by another one. New historians, though academically socialized and professionalized by the first generation, expressed novel sociocultural attitudes and interest in Jewish history. They endeavoured in exploring the geopolitical and ideological processes of state-building, as championed by Zionism itself. A process with which they identified themselves, either as Sabras or as new-born children who had left post-WWII Europe.

By establishing historiographical journals, which were soon to become inter-/multidisciplinary, they formalized a local historiography that sought to better understand the dawn of Zionism and the eventful recent past of the Jewish settlement in Palestine. The autonomization of this historiographical took root, especially at Tel-Aviv University. The latter inaugurated the Chaim Weizmann Institute for the Study of Zionism and Israel. It attracted young scholars and became a hub for the study of Zionist history in the 1970s. Despite an apparent generational homogeneity that espoused Zionism, the stratification of the new historiographical field meant neither automatism nor intellectual one-sidedness, not to say, a once-and-for-all stability. Transformations in the Israeli societal fabric had already been present in the 1960s, while the symbiotic relationship between the academic and political fields seemed most harmonious. Yet, the occurrences of the 1973 Yom Kippur War and the 1977 political upheaval announced the decline of Israeli *Mamlakhtiyut*. The civic republican nation-state, its structures and habitus did not succeed in guaranteeing a unified citizenry. Inner partitions, sectorialization and individualization

deepened existent cleavages. These became an easy target for politicization, while the original voluntaristic fervour of Zionism was waning away.
Historiography reflected these ongoing transformations, inasmuch as it
had to reckon with the decline of the national *mamlakhti* habitus. Second-
generation historians, who considered the nation-state the only possible
survival unit for the Jewish people, began to face calls for historical
revision.

Chapter 5, "*Artziyut*: No Country Other and the Double-Edged
Banalization of Israeli National Habitus in Israeli Historiography", discussed the trends in contemporary Israeli historiography and society. The
passionate debate, which encompassed novel fashions, namely post-
modernist paradigms, espoused post-Zionist and other critical stands in
relation to Israeli politics. Originally new criticism was advocated by sociologists and historians who proclaimed "new historiography", while
attempting to crack the old system by offering alternative paradigms.
Moreover, the new demand combined professionalism and political activism. It thus echoed throughout the academic field and even beyond. Yet,
that was also the reason for the dispersion of positions and the inability
which completely replaced the *mamlakhti*-based historiography.

Most of the so-called new historians were eventually absorbed by the
preexistent academic system, especially in the case of Ben-Gurion
University. The critical historiographical generation, however, attested the
relativizing interpretation of the national habitus vis-à-vis contemporaneity, including that of national banalization. Consequently, they embodied
the phase of *Artziyut* which has consisted in the double-edged banalization of the Jewish nation-state. On the one hand, the Zionist national
habitus has maintained apical centrality in Israeli society. On the other, the
intellectual debate has accepted, and eventually even embraced, different
perceptions, methods and interpretations. In fact, the post-Zionist historians have been succeeded by post-post Zionist historiographical awareness.

The non-militant scholarship learned the lessons by both Zionist and
post-Zionist historians and, therefore, harbingered the current post-
revisionist phase in local historiography. Whereas Zionist historiography
concentrated upon the origins of Zionist pioneering and the post-Zionist
prioritized the geopolitical effects of the 1948 War and Holocaust on the
Israeli-Palestinian-Arab conflict, the post-post Zionist historians have chosen to engage in more social and cultural topics of research. The latter
focus on the private and individual spheres of Israeli history. Not only has
the current situation overcome the Zionist versus post-Zionist dichotomy,

but it has also corresponded to the general phase of *Artziyut* conceptualized as an institutionally less ideological constellation of the Jewish and democratic nation-state.

However, that is not to say Israeli society has become any less complicated. Radical and extreme stands have been manifested in politics and have thus occupied space in all fields of society. Nonetheless, following the fervent debates of the 1980s and 1990s, the academic field now tends to de-politicize content in order to offer less judgemental and more observational, not to say self-reflective, insights regarding Zionism and its political accomplishments. This scholarly mode seems to have contributed creativity and unfolded new perspectives which capture the multifaceted history of Israel. The positivistic or militant historiographies of the past generations made room for an almost anthropological and literary approach to history. Historiographical polyphony now enriches local Jewish history. One may even say that the political equidistance characterizing the current situation is fruit of the lack of the eventful constituent moments in Jewish and Israeli history. No Holocaust, no 1948 War, no 1973 War etc. divide the perception of that emerging fourth generation of Israeli historians. Nevertheless, it may be also a sort of escapism attempting some kind of normalcy in the permanent unresolved geopolitical situation in which Israel finds itself, that is, the occupation and the democratic unrest, not to say regression, which has characterized the last few years of local politics (reference to the five electoral rounds in the period 2019–2022, as well as to the mass protest against the judicial reform by Israel's thirty-seventh government, which had been put on hold de facto, even prior to 7 October 2023[2]).

At any rate, none of the abovementioned post-*mamlakhti* historiographies demonstrate a monolithic field. Neither intellectual, nor sociocultural, nor sociopolitical counter-actions seem to have institutionally

---

[2] Noteworthy is the fact that on 9 August 2023, hundreds of Israeli and American academics published a statement claiming that the ultimate purpose of the judicial reform was to "annex more land, and ethnically cleanse all territories under Israeli rule of their Palestinian population". The statement invoked clear "apartheid" further drift in under the Israeli-occupied territories in the West Bank and Gaza. The initial 800 signatories included Jewish American academics, Israelis, Palestinians, religious leaders and lawyers. Amongst prominent Israeli signatories one must mention the two precursors of Israeli "new history", that is, Ilan Pappé and Benny Morris, as well as former speaker of the Knesset Avraham Burg. See Ishaan Tharoor's column: "Leading Israel scholars invoke 'apartheid' in critique of status quo", published on *The Washington Post*, 11 August 2023.

adverse to the change of paradigms. The academic structure did not limit them. Though not separately institutionalized, as in the case of Israeli history which remained under Jewish history, the renewal of local historiography appears to be largely contained. The academic boundaries of critique and debate, mainly concerning the method and interpretative sensibilities, may consist in strong antagonisms and competition. Nonetheless, the interaction, ardent as it can ever be, remains one of the ground rules of academic field. Led by what are universally viewed as ideals of scientific fairness, integrity and transparency, the presumable "old-school" Israeli historiography, whose core orbited around the positivistic objectivity of historical truth, finds no followers, inasmuch as most active historians are aware of the benefits of interdisciplinarity (mostly expressed through methodological contamination of written and oral materials).

Hence, the professional habitus of Israeli historians, as it has been engendered, conserved and reproduced by their predecessors, is a result of struggles for autonomization and recognition as well as transformations in terms of societal development and generational differences shaping the Israeli survival unit. The field of Israeli historians, defined as scholars dedicated to the history of their own nation-state-based survival unit, is indeed an interiorized meta-structure of inter-subjective relations, interests and challenges. However, it contains no definitive cohorts. On the contrary, it consists in a cacophony of voices, often in disagreement, which are hardly collectivized into conspicuous categories. The sophistries and casuistries that have been intrinsic to the discipline never enabled a thoroughly "wrapping up" of the profession by top-down nationalization. Consequently, the evident conviction regarding Zionism and the sympathies it generated in local historiography did not reach a blind Zionization of the entire field, irrespective of the methods and fashions practiced by individual historians. These historians who have dedicated their careers to national history continuously dialogue with general, universal, history as well as with other academic disciplines. Israeli historiography is a microcosmos which has witnessed forms of convergence and dispute, integration and disaggregation.

The plurality of interests and methods emerged and diversified the discipline which developed and enriched its scope. This may explain the scarce tendency towards "public intellectual" status amongst this hermeneutic community. Israeli historians, unlike the exemplary case of Ben-Zion Dinur (a socio-intellectual model which continuously crossed over between academe and politics), prefer to keep rather low profiles. They do participate in ministerial committees and governmental foundations, yet remain somewhat on the margins of the Israeli public sphere. They enjoy acknowledgement when attributed. Large-scale accolades are rare (the only case is the Israel Prize) and usually do not reach massive public exposure. Their achievements are professional, confined within the epistemic community of expertise which has gradually become multidisciplinary and international in order to better defend itself in relation to scholarly changes and challenges. These historians cannot be identified with a single monochromatic label, neither intellectually nor in relation to their career trajectories. The core of their profession, namely a document-based analysis of the past, gathers them into a specific academic field which entails practical ground rules. Seldom are they in a position to directly provide contribution to greater society. The confrontation between "old" and "new" histories seemed to be a unique period. An exception that confirms the rule, rather than a dominant habitus-shaper disposition.

The fragmentary and nonlinear context of Israeli society has additionally brought about a decline in their professional status. This last point is easily generalized to the contradictory stances about the Israeli habitus and its container, namely the nation-state as the only possible survival unit for the Jewish people, the glue of republican democratic citizenry. The trivialization of national identity, symbolic automatisms as well as daily practices, which have been taken for granted for many decades, reflects a societal order oscillating between disintegration and integration, as witnessed by many Westernized societies which have experienced the good and bad globalization has had to offer (not only economic but also ideological, intellectual and cultural).

Critical and accusatory factions are still present. Nonetheless, Israeli historians find themselves as many Israelis in an individualistic society where state-based collectivizing habitus remains formal and codified yet far from being transversally omnipresent as in the sociogenetic phase of nation-state building. Experiences and sensibilities diverge from one another with regard to ideological and political choices in both past and present. A common thread moving between nostalgia and ideology delineates continuity and change, evident transformations, while doubts indicate intergenerational tensions professing hard love to the homeland, as they testify disappointment and hope alike. In other words, the situation Israeli historians depict is very far from any modern Jewish *republica literaria*, inspired by the values of *Haskalah* and cultural Zionism (which had been the guiding principles of Zionist intelligentsia). In conclusion, the current Israeli *Artziyut* sees Israeli historians place themselves in a more critical position vis-à-vis the Israeli academic system, the state and society without breaking any bonds. A sort of sliding doors between personal perspectives and ideological stands receives the deserved attention, as generational self-awareness in the historiographical profession now seems to have appropriated. Yet, no clear path has been fully traced. National history has reached dispersion, while still being practiced and produced. In Eliasian terms, the socio-psychical dispositions and the interdependencies that foster Israeli historiography remain valid. However, their strength, once anchored to a certain verticality between state and academe, has somewhat declined. No field is an island, and therefore, the academic profession cannot be detached from the larger trends in society.

Following the description and analysis offered by the enquiry further questions arose *in itinere*. A topical issue such as gender surely deserves deeper analysis with regard to career trajectories not only by established professors but perhaps mainly in relation to the future generation of historians, junior and senior lecturers. In addition, the operation itself of "generational labelling" could be further refined by also including MA students and PhD candidates, and thus integrate nascent generational perspectives before they complete any formal maturation and structural recognition. Such future enquiries might shed further light upon professional socialization, the place of national identity and the state in the lives of younger academics, whose interests and sensibilities have been shaped in a sort of post-*mamlakhti* Israel. The latter can also be compared with historians and scholars affiliated to neighbouring disciplines such as social and political sciences. This analytical possibility may even follow an intradisciplinary comparison of history studies tout court. It would mean to take into account and consequently juxtapose general, Jewish and Middle Eastern historians and thus widen the field to the empirically traced trajectories of careers and topics amongst the three interconnected parallel and supplementary historiographical specificities. Not only is there room to compare the characteristics of those scholars, but also to focus on the thematic comparison between the mentioned periodicals and equivalent journals in general and Middle Eastern history.

A further point inviting additional research are the differences and similarities between Israeli historians working on Zionist and Israeli history in Israeli academia compared to Israeli-born historians working on the same issues abroad, namely in foreign universities, hence meaning, "academic diaspora" or "cosmopolitan intellectuals". This could be done by tracing the main international reviews on Israeli, Jewish and Middle Eastern histories, which would enable content-based analysis. Yet, the conceptual framework of national habitus and survival unit would have to be revised and interpreted differently. An additional enquiry could be conducted with regard to historiography produced in academic colleges, which, although not considered research institutions but teaching ones, still provide tenure-track positions as job opportunities. Moreover, the case of the public "Ariel University", located in the West Bank but belonging to the Israeli academic landscape, would be an interesting case-study per se. Of course, all these question marks require further resources: time, enthusiasm and intellectual curiosity to begin with.

I thus invite and call for this topical reading of the historiographical, academic, intellectual field to be implemented, slowly but surely, in order to nurture a more ample examination of the sociopolitical and sociocultural features of different processes regarding habitus-building in relation to nationalism and collective identification between professions and citizenry vis-à-vis contemporary forms of statehood. The inevitable combination between personal and professional "selves", as they reflect greater trends in the national collective habitus of a complex, fragmented and contradictory sense of belonging.

Certainly, the abovementioned goes much beyond the Israeli case, especially in relation to the political contexts encountered worldwide. Phenomena identified as waves of populism, nationalism and neofascism seem to bring about radicalization of identity politics within societies which experience either domestic or international conflicts. The latter present challenges to any sort of definition of national identity and national habitus in mature, somewhat fatigued, democracies. Since the solidity of the nation-state depends on civilizational shifts attesting greater or lesser degree of interdependency, the historical narratives and memories, which politics shapes, formalizes and engraves in the public conscience, deserve the meticulous examination of the role of intellectuals, the stratification of national identity (as espoused by the former), alongside the public policies and mechanisms that enable their interrelations. One may find the routinized banalization of national identity as well as its potential explosiveness.

This is, of course, one side of the story. The other may well be, the attempts, though seemingly limited, to overcome the nation-state and the nationally historico-centric common sense it engenders. Globalization and international political entities (such as the European Union) might succeed, one day, in producing a supranational collective habitus (the hope of

Norbert Elias himself). Hence, there is room for research seeking equivalent double-edged banalization of national identity, while considering both centripetal and centrifugal civilizing and decivilizing processes. As historiography indicates different phases in the existence of a collectivized "national self", it is a valuable domain to critically and empirically investigate such transformations in other contexts. Any analysis starting from similar assumptions would satisfy the constant need to bridge, at least partially, the realm of ideas and the realm of politics. Inasmuch as such efforts delineate crossovers between fields and the plurality of struggles, change and continuity would reveal themselves and enrich our understanding. As this study did its best to follow and respect the standards of fairness, verifiability and transparency, it hopes the story/history it uncovered adds some knowledgeable insight to readers, while it clearly invites others to tell other good (hi)stories.

A CONTEXTUAL WISHFUL AFTERWORD

This book originates in my own doctoral experience (2014–2019), though it increasingly matured in the last year or so and thus met the challenge of Israel's own pains, tensions and conflicts. The topicality of the manuscript has been evaluated positively in general but circumstances pushed its publication forward in an accelerated manner whose logics combine opportunity and personal sense of intellectual and personal responsibility.

The events of 7 October 2023 already mark a crossroad, an inescapable watershed line in the history of Israel. The entire democratic habitus-led has clashed with political responsibility by government towards citizens and the principles of state sovereignty have been grossly offended by an atrocious attack engendering a reaction which by itself shows the precariousness of holding together two distinctive intuitively contradictory values of identification: Jewishness and democracy. The eventful tragedy for two peoples, two collective habitus, shows how the Israeli-Palestinian conflict is pinned, not to say conditioned and manipulated, by highly politicized national claims. The abovementioned assertion that "No Holocaust, no 1948 War, no 1973 War etc. divide the perception of that emerging fourth generation of Israeli historians" will be clearly put into question.

The contradiction of 7 October, during which not only Jews were killed but also Bedouins and Israeli Palestinians by unprecedented terrorist attacks, attests the complexity of the Israeli polity. Problematic are of course the disproportions of current warfare and the heartbreaking images and stories from Israel, Gaza and the West Bank. Peace seems so far away, especially as the Israeli Knesset plenum voted 99 to 11 against any unilateral recognition of a future Palestinian state (21 February 2024). One asks whether any hypothetic peace could ever be unilateral to begin with, or whether the Israeli democratic parliamentary system could one day reset the seemingly transversal refusal of enacting peace-seeking legislation in favour of a lasting solution between the two peoples and reach reconciliation between them. Equal participation and universal civil rights are the only structural way to overcome barriers and dissolve the violent relations of reciprocal otherness of Jewish and non-Jewish citizens in Israel and in Palestine.

In one of her recent opinion articles, professor Emerita Dina Porat wrote:

> The work of remembering and preserving the horrors of the event in the future, in Israel and in the world, began immediately, but alongside it, as always, began the anti-memory work, which is the attempt to erase the memory of the event. *For every crime that is committed, there is immediately someone who denies it and tries to prevent it from being embedded in the mind.* The first book that denied the Holocaust was published as early as 1945. The denial and prevention efforts continue from the first moment for years, and do not stop—this is also the case with regard to the massacre of the Armenians, the killing of millions of Chinese by Japan, the murder of the Tutsis in Rwanda, and more. And it is *needless to say that the attempt to erase from memory also prevents, or at least reduces, the possibility of imposing an adequate punishment on the perpetrators*" (my translation and italics).[3]

In Porat's words the inherent complexity of the Israeli case-study bleeds its sorrow and traumatic truths. Memory, denial, perpetrators and victims are instinctive labels to use and cultivate in a collectivity facing such dramatic circumstances, while seeking to keep some tangible evidence to facilitate commemoration; therefore, handing down symbolic pain to future generations. Nonetheless, instincts are no long-term rationale and they are not always productive in condemning perpetrators, on the one hand, and in cherishing the memory for the sake of innocent victims. Given the savage potential to further increase a compartmentalist historical and historiographical siege over this period in the land's chronicles,

---

[3] An article titled *"בכל יישוב, בכל קיבוץ—להשאיר בית אחד שרוף"* ("in every town, in every kibbutz-To Leave One House Burnt Down"), published contemporaneously on the Israeli daily *Yedioth Ahronoth* and its website: Ynet (https://www.ynet.co.il/news/article/yokra13661583).

even beyond any Zionist or post-Zionist perspective, one has to labour for a solution. As beautifully hoped and theorized by Elias, a self-considered civilized society has to foster interdependencies and integrational habitus that will eventually bring down walls and deactivate weapons. Not a mutilated society too frail to resist decivilization but a safe and confident society which is able to unite different particularisms into respectful pluralism, even when tragic scars are still visible to the naked eye. In this sense, inspiration can be found in the history of Europe, since WWII, rather than reproducing the dynamics that had preceded it. Elias knew much about it, too.

INDEX[1]

---

[1] Note: Page numbers followed by 'n' refer to notes.

© The Author(s), under exclusive license to Springer Nature Switzerland AG 2024
A. Helled, *Israel's National Historiography*, Palgrave Studies on Norbert Elias, https://doi.org/10.1007/978-3-031-62795-8